The Archaeology Coursebook

The Archaeology Coursebook is an unrivalled guide to students studying archaeology for the first time. Comprehensive and user-friendly, it will interest pre-university students and teachers as well as undergraduates and enthusiasts. Written by experienced archaeologists and teachers it makes sense of the major themes and issues in archaeology and also gives students the necessary skills to prepare for their examinations in the subject. Chapters include:

• Presenting the past • Religion and ritual • Settlement • Material culture and economics • Social archaeology • Project work • Examinations • Where next?

Specially designed to assist learning, *The Archaeology Coursebook*:

■ *introduces* the most commonly examined archaeological methods, concepts and themes, and provides the skills necessary to understand these step by step

■ *explains* how to interpret the material students may meet in examinations and how to succeed with different types of assignments and exam questions

■ *supports* study with case studies, key sites, key terms, tasks and skills development

■ *illustrates* concepts and commentary with over 200 photographs and drawings of excavation sites, methodology and processes, and tools and equipment

■ *links* from its own site to other key websites in archaeology.

Jim Grant is a Principal Examiner in A level Archaeology and Head of Humanities at Cirencester College. **Sam Gorin** is a Principal Examiner in A level Archaeology and Head of the School of General Studies at Newark and Sherwood College. **Neil Fleming** is a Chief Examiner in A level Archaeology and upper-sixth House Master at Christ's Hospital, Horsham.

The Archaeology Coursebook

an **introduction** to study skills, topics and methods

Jim Grant, Sam Gorin and **Neil Fleming**

London and New York

First published 2002 by Routledge
11 New Fetter Lane, London EC4P 4EE

Simultaneously published in the USA and Canada
by Routledge
29 West 35th Street, New York, NY 10001

Reprinted 2002 (twice), 2003

Routledge is an imprint of the Taylor & Francis Group

© 2002 Jim Grant, Sam Gorin and Neil Fleming

Typeset in Garamond by Florence Production Ltd, Stoodleigh, Devon
Printed and bound in Great Britain by St Edmundsbury Press,
Bury St Edmunds, Suffolk

British Library Cataloguing in Publication Data
A catalogue record for this book is available from the British Library

Library of Congress Cataloging in Publication Data
Grant, Jim, 1958–
    The archaeology coursebook : an introduction to study skills, topics,
and methods / Jim Grant, Sam Gorin, Neil Fleming.
        p. cm.
    Includes bibliographical references (p.) and index.
    1. Archaeology—Study and teaching (Higher) 2. Archaeology—
    Methodology.   3. Archaeology—Examinations—Study Guides.
    I. Gorin, Sam, 1946-   II. Fleming, Neil, 1955–   III. Title.
    CC83 .G7 2001
    930.1′0711—dc21   2001019758

ISBN 0–415–23638–X (hbk)

ISBN 0–415–23639–8 (pbk)

Brief Contents

Contents

Figures

Index of Skills

Throughout *The Archaeology Coursebook* we have linked skills to content. However, as you may want to focus on the suggestions for skill development outside this sequence, we have listed them separately. These are generic skills which should apply to most parts of your course.

Acknowledgements

Thanks are due to the many people who provided both moral and practical help with this book. Sam's colleagues in the East Midlands supplied advice on current archaeological practice, in particular Mick Jones, City of Lincoln archaeologist, and James Megoran who both read the proofs and whose thoughtful suggestions for improvement were extremely valuable. Neil's colleagues in Barcelona – Toni, Christina, Paloma and Javier – provided inspiration and constructive criticism and he received much practical help from Christ's Hospital School. I was provided with ideas and sources by Royston Clark, Sarah Cole, Don Henson, Richard Reece, Nick Trustram-Eve and Robin Wichard. In addition there were many people who responded to my requests for information and pictures, particularly on the Britarch news group.

Our students at Cirencester College, Christ's Hospital School and Newark and Sherwood College have been guinea pigs for much of the material and their feedback has been valuable in fine-tuning the text. Thanks are also due to those who kindled our own interest in archaeology, particularly Pat Carter and John Alexander at Cambridge, Malcolm Todd at Nottingham and Richard Bradley at Reading. No one forgets a good teacher! Finally, this book would never have happened had Vicky Peters at Routledge not believed in it and Moira Taylor and her team not shown me how to put it together.

Writing a textbook on top of teaching and examining always means that those close to you make sacrifices. This book is therefore dedicated with love and thanks to our families for their considerable support and tolerance. To Marlene (who also helped with typing) and Russell Fleming. To Sally Gorin who has uncomplainingly shared in excavations and site visits and provided help with research. To Dawn, Zack (sorry there are no dinosaurs) and Marnie for giving me the time to write it.

Jim Grant
February 2001

Illustration Acknowledgements

We are very grateful to those below for supplying illustrations and permission to use them.

Ginny Baddiley, Nottinghamshire SMR (1.4)
Mary Baxter (8.9)
Paul Brooker (1.9 and icon)
Royston Clarke (8.20, 9.6, 10.4)
Sarah Cole (7.1)
Controller of Her Majesty's Stationery Office (1.15)
Empingham Archive (2.4, 3.12, 5.2, 6.7, 8.12)
Martin Green (2.6)
Gwilym Hughes (2.20)
Mick Jones, Lincoln Unit (2.19)
David Knight (2.31, 2.32)
Peter Masters (1.10)
Harold Mytum (2.2 and 5.9)
Norfolk Archaeology and Environment Division (2.24)
Joshua Pollard, Negotiating Avebury Project (2.1)
Francesca Radcliffe (1.13 and 9.7)
Jim Russell (7.4)
Roger Thomas (12.7)
Jane Timby (2.3)
Nick Trustram-Eve (1.7, 1.8, 9.15, 9.16, 12.2, 12.4, 12.9, 12.10, 12.11)
University of Cambridge Air Photos (1.17 and 1.18)
Robin Wichard (2.12, 2.26, 2.27, 3.5, 3.6, 7.9, 8.19, 9.12)
Brian Williams (11.10)
Kate Walton (3.8, 3.10, 3.13, 3.14, 8.2, 8.8, 8.11, 10.22, 11.8, 11.9
12.6 (after Lake))
Colin Jarvis (12.8)

Introduction

The Archaeology Coursebook is a guide for students studying archaeology for the first time. It is not another introduction to archaeology, neither is it a specialist guide to archaeological methods. There are a fantastic array of books and websites already available which fulfil these functions. The aim of this book is to get you started and help you succeed in your academic study. It does this by:

■ providing brief introductions to the most commonly examined archaeological methods, concepts and themes. Whole books have been written on the meanings of particular terms and there may not be consensus on their use. We will concentrate on providing you with working definitions and examples rather than debating meaning
■ explaining how to interpret the sort of archaeological material you may meet in examinations
■ showing you how to succeed with different types of assignments and examination questions
■ providing brief, relevant case studies which you can use in your own work
■ providing links to easily accessible sources including internet sites.

As authors we are all teachers and examiners of archaeology with long experience of successfully preparing students for GCSE, A Level, Access and HE programmes. We were advised at all stages of the developing project on what was needed by many teachers, lecturers and students from schools, colleges and universities.

This book is designed as a handbook. That is, it will be of use to you at every stage of your course, from getting to grips with terminology to producing your major study. The structure of the book loosely follows the AS and A2 Level Archaeology courses studied by students in England and Wales. However, it is intended to be relevant and useful for all students studying the subject from GCSE up to first-year undergraduate level. If it equips you to produce pass-level essays and to understand what is being discussed in lectures and seminars it will have done its job. You will, of course, need other sources too. At A level and first year undergraduate level you will need case studies and to look at examples of fieldwork reports. From year 2 undergraduate level you will need greater depth of material. However, by then you will know everything that is in this book!

We have organised the book into three broad sections:

■ *Part I Understanding archaeological resources* is an introduction to how archaeologists work, how they find sites, excavate them and analyse and interpret the material they recover. It also looks at how archaeological knowledge is presented and the role of archaeology today.

■ *Part II Studying themes in archaeology* covers some of the broad themes of archaeology: religion and ritual, settlement, economics and material culture and society. Whether your course follows a period based or thematic approach, these topics will be relevant to you. We have concentrated on defining key terms and highlighting the sources and methods used to explore these themes.

■ *Part III Examination success and beyond* guides you through how to produce a successful archaeological project and helps you find ways of preparing to pass your exams. It also provides some models for you to follow. The final chapter is a guide to some additional sources of information and further study opportunities.

The study skills you will need to succeed are introduced gradually throughout the book rather than in a separate section. Each chapter has learning goals which include developing your skills as well as your understanding. In the early chapters key skills boxes show you how to find information and use it to tackle short tasks. Later in the book, they guide you through evaluative tasks and ways to approach extended pieces of academic writing. However, to enable you to rapidly find this advice we have included a skills list as well as a contents list. Most chapters include one or more key task boxes. Some of these are closely linked to examination success, others are activities to reinforce your understanding and to stimulate your ability to make connections between content and methods.

To succeed in your courses you need to develop in three broad areas: general skills, higher level skills and archaeological understanding. In this book we explain the basic archaeological knowledge you need to understand your course and also incorporate

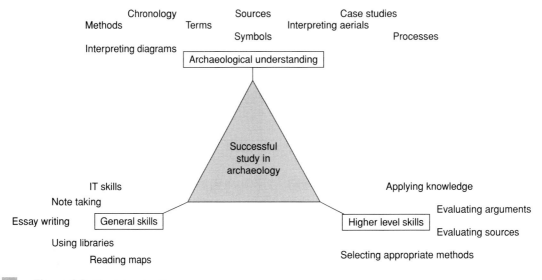

Figure 0.1 *The triangle of success*

KEY SKILL

What you have to learn to be successful

This will probably be the first time you have studied archaeology. As with all subjects, there are a range of things you must know and understand in order to succeed.

You need to:	In order to:	Examples:	By:
Learn definitions	Understand questions and explanations	Mortuary, excarnation	Memorising and testing
Understand concepts	Understand explanations and argue	Characterisation, relative dating	Testing and using
Understand processes	Assess the limits of evidence	Danebury, Sutton Hoo	Using diagrams, explaining
Know case studies	Support your answers	Taphonomy, organic preservation	Using mind maps, noting
Link methods, themes and examples	Maximise the use of your material	Boxgrove–usewear–hunting-tools	Practice
Apply understanding	Interpret sources	Aerial photos, plans	Practice

Figure 0.2

exercises to help you develop higher level skills. However, to be studying at this level you already have many general academic skills. We have therefore made suggestions on how to improve these rather than showing you how to do them.

HOW TO USE THIS TEXT

There are so many different ways in which lecturers can structure courses that it is unlikely you will follow the exact order of our contents sequence in your own study. We have taken this into account by providing a full index and full contents list which includes all the main sub-headings. We have also used a system of cross-referencing throughout the

book from one topic to related topics. Content, skills and resources are all linked. Look out for the following signposts which all provide links from the text immediately preceding them.

► (arrowhead) guides you to related material on another page

(bone) indicates a key website or other resource

(trowel) indicates a key text

Examples are given for most of the points we make and a range of case studies is provided to deepen your understanding of the ideas and methods discussed. Where they are relevant to your course, you should use them as content to support your written work. They are about the right length and detail for essays up to year 2 at university. We have introduced and defined key terms as they have arisen in the text. The glossary on p. 307 contains a working definition of all the words printed in **bold** in the text. You should look there first whenever anything new arises. You may find it helpful to find an example from your own course for each relevant word or phrase in the glossary.

Where you need specific content for your course you should be getting it from your lessons and the detailed books in your library. You should also keep a file of newspaper cuttings on recent archaeological discoveries. We have also assumed that you have access to the internet. A key feature of this book is that it is designed to be used alongside your PC. It provides explanations and gives you a range of websites to look at for examples and illustration. Archaeology is such a visual subject and so well served by many excellent sources on the Net that it is foolish not to use it. We hope to supplement *The Archaeology Coursebook* in the future with a companion website to provide you with updated links.

Part One
Understanding Archaeological Resources

Archaeological Reconnaissance

Archaeologists use a wide range of reconnaissance techniques to locate archaeological sites and to investigate sites without excavating them. Some archaeologists predict that future advances in these non-invasive, and non-destructive, methods may see them emerge as an alternative to excavation. Reconnaissance techniques are also used to

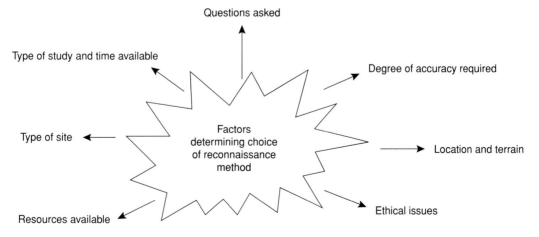

Figure 1.1 *Factors influencing the choice of reconnaissance method*

✎ KEY SKILL

Successful note-taking

Right from the first day of your archaeology course you should be taking and filing notes on what you have learnt. You have probably already developed your own style of note-taking but it is worth considering alternative forms of note-taking depending on what is required of you and the purpose of the information you are recording. For example, the type of information you need to record as the raw material for a major essay is likely to be very different from what is required to remind you of the meaning of a concept. It is as easy to accumulate too many notes as too few. The acid test is whether they are useful for their purpose. As Figure 1.2 makes clear, different styles of notes are appropriate to different situations.

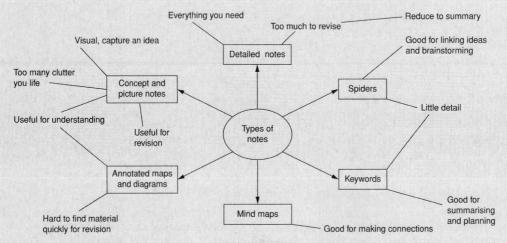

Figure 1.2 *The strengths and weaknesses of different types of notes*

Detailed written notes may be necessary when you are working from library texts on a major project. If you take notes from texts you always have access to, such as *The Archaeology Coursebook*, then you are wasting your time. What you want instead are brief notes which remind you of key points and direct you to places in your texts where the detail is. Try to experiment with a range of notes when preparing for discussion, revising and planning. Many people learn better from visual notes than they do from dense written passages. You may be one of them. We have used these types of notes throughout the text. You can find examples on the following pages:

▶ Spider diagram   pp. xxvi, 4   ▶ Force field diagram   p. 210
▶ Mind map   pp. 182, 237   ▶ Picture or concept notes pp. 106, 199
▶ Flow diagram   p.59   ▶ Keyword notes   p. 287
▶ Target diagram   p. 197   ▶ Grids   p. 67

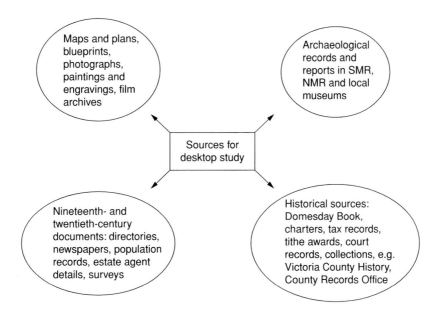

Figure 1.3 *Sources commonly used for desktop study*

map evidence of human activity in the landscape. The appropriate methods in each case will relate to the time and resources available as well as the particular case being investigated.

Every year hundreds of new sites are located. Some are spotted from the air or even from satellites in space, others through the discovery of artefacts by metal detectorists. Quarrying, dredging and peat cutting all regularly produce unexpected finds while some of the most important have come about completely by chance.

The discoveries of the body of Otzi the Ice Man by skiers and of the Altamira cave art by children are classic examples. So too was the discovery of the Neolithic tomb at Crantit in Orkney, which was found when a digger fell through the roof!

Equally, some sites were never 'lost' to begin with. Stonehenge and the Pyramids were well known before the development of archaeology and many of the buildings of the last 200 years are still in use. Other named sites were documented by historians and located by using written sources. Schliemann's discovery of Troy is the classic example but many historic battle-fields also fall into this category. In addition, a considerable number of new discoveries are made during the exploration of known sites.

Where archaeologists are actively trying to locate or explore sites through research or ahead of development there are four broad and complementary categories of methods that they use:

■ desktop study
■ surface survey
■ geophysical or geochemical survey
■ aerial survey

In addition there are a range of newer techniques, most of which can be labelled **remote sensing**.

DESKTOP STUDY

As its name suggests, this is an office-based investigation using existing records. Some archaeologists, usually concerned with shipwrecks, aircraft or the investigation of historical individuals, continue to use written sources to track down or identify particular sites. More generally, most excavations and all research in Britain today begins with a search of information that has already been recorded. The majority of these investigations are part of the planning process and their purpose is to determine whether there are likely to be archaeological remains which might be threatened by development (▶see p. 111).

Desktop study involves researching maps and historical or archaeological documents including aerial photographs about the area under investigation. If they are not in private hands, these are most likely to be held in planning departments, county records offices, local **Sites and Monuments Record (SMRs)** or the **National Monuments Record (NMR)** offices.

 http://www.english-heritage.org.uk

Historical documents

A diverse assortment of documents may be of value to the archaeologist. These will vary by county, area and period. In most parts of the country known documents are archived or recorded in the County Records Office. In many areas, useful sources have also been catalogued in a volume of the Victoria County History (VCR) which is often the first resource researchers turn to. Only a fraction of early records have survived and those that have need translation and interpretation. Amongst the potential range available, the following categories are important.

Legal documents. Records of ownership such as Anglo-Saxon charters or court records of disputes often included physical description of boundaries and occasionally land use. Wills and inventories which can be linked to particular buildings can provide lists of contents which provide clues to function.

Tax records. These are particularly valuable in helping to identify landowning units and their economic uses. The Domesday Book is the best known but later tax surveys and tithe awards are often of more direct use.

Economic records. Order and sales books are invaluable to industrial archaeologists while nineteenth-century directories are useful in exploring functions of buildings. Estate agents' bills are increasingly being preserved to record changes in important buildings.

Pictorial records. Paintings, engravings and photographs can be of value both in identification and in tracing changes. They are particularly valuable when studying standing buildings. Archives of aerial photographs (APs) such as the RAF surveys of Britain in the 1940s are key documents in tracing landscape change in the last sixty years and are often the only record of many sites.

Written accounts. Descriptions of places in books, diaries and travelogues are of use in identifying the function, construction methods and identity of many sites. The work of early antiquarians such as Stukeley is particularly valuable for descriptions of monuments as they were before the modern period.

Archaeological records. There are three main sources here. If there are previous excavation or survey results they can often be accessed through libraries or local museums. Local

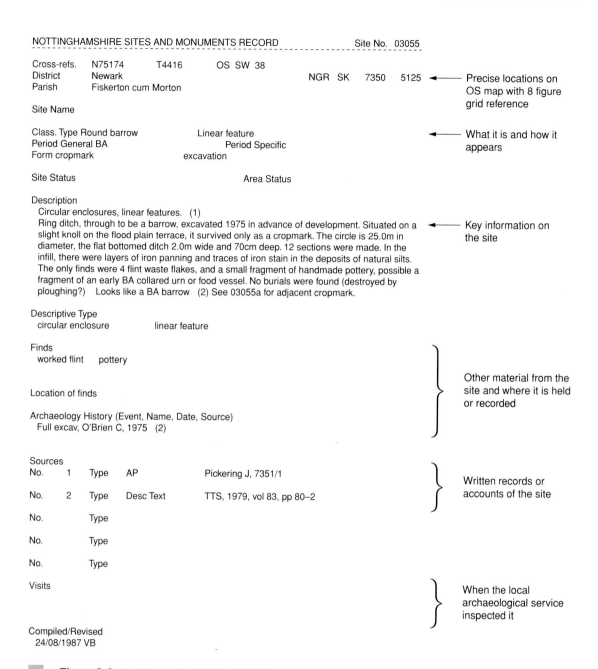

NOTTINGHAMSHIRE SITES AND MONUMENTS RECORD   Site No. 03055

Cross-refs.   N75174   T4416   OS SW 38
District   Newark   NGR SK   7350   5125   ◄──── Precise locations on
Parish   Fiskerton cum Morton   OS map with 8 figure
Site Name   grid reference

Class. Type Round barrow   Linear feature   ◄──── What it is and how it
Period General BA   Period Specific   appears
Form cropmark   excavation

Site Status   Area Status

Description
    Circular enclosures, linear features. (1)
    Ring ditch, through to be a barrow, excavated 1975 in advance of development. Situated on a   ◄──── Key information on
    slight knoll on the flood plain terrace, it survived only as a cropmark. The circle is 25.0m in   the site
    diameter, the flat bottomed ditch 2.0m wide and 70cm deep. 12 sections were made. In the
    infill, there were layers of iron panning and traces of iron stain in the deposits of natural silts.
    The only finds were 4 flint waste flakes, and a small fragment of handmade pottery, possible a
    fragment of an early BA collared urn or food vessel. No burials were found (destroyed by
    ploughing?)   Looks like a BA barrow (2) See 03055a for adjacent cropmark.

Descriptive Type
    circular enclosure   linear feature

Finds
    worked flint   pottery
                                                                              ⎫
                                                                              ⎬ Other material from the
Location of finds   ⎮ site and where it is held
                                                                              ⎮ or recorded
Archaeology History (Event, Name, Date, Source)   ⎮
    Full excav, O'Brien C, 1975 (2)   ⎭

Sources
No.   1   Type   AP   Pickering J, 7351/1   ⎫
                                                                              ⎬ Written records or
No.   2   Type   Desc Text   TTS, 1979, vol 83, pp 80–2   ⎮ accounts of the site
                                                                              ⎮
No.   Type   ⎭

No.   Type

No.   Type

Visits   ⎫
                                                                              ⎬ When the local
                                                                              ⎮ archaeological service
                                                                              ⎭ inspected it

Compiled/Revised
24/08/1987 VB

Figure 1.4 *How to read an SMR printout*

collections of finds and reports will also be held in local museums. Details of previous archaeological work and stray finds for much of Britain are held in local SMRs. These records are increasingly computerised and a national version is being built up at the various NMR offices. Printouts which include lists of earlier research can be made by inputting grid references.

Oral accounts. While living people may provide clues to the use and location of recent buildings, farmers and others who work on the land or the built environment may have valuable knowledge for archaeologists. Farmers, for example, may be able to identify areas where building rubble has been ploughed up or where dressed stones have been removed. Sometimes estate management records may hold this information for earlier periods.

Maps

Maps are amongst the most basic tools and sources used by archaeologists. They are used to locate and explore sites and to answer questions about previous use of the landscape. They are of particular value in tracking changes through time (settlement shape and location, boundaries, land units, fields and hedges). They can also be used to relate sites to geology and topography. Medieval archaeologists are often able to produce their own maps for periods before mapping began. They do this by working back from the oldest available map and cross-referencing historical sources and fieldnames. This technique is known as **regression**.

A wide variety of maps are used by archaeologists, including the following.

Early maps

Maps from the sixteenth century tend to show properties. They are not always to scale but may provide visual aspects such as illustrations of specific buildings. From the seventeenth century there are also route maps such as Ogilvy's Road Book, which is a series of linear strips. Maps were also produced to show the proposed routes of turnpikes, canals and railways in order to gain permission from parliament for building to take place.

Changes in rural landownership from the eighteenth century onwards were recorded on enclosure award maps, while taxes paid to the church by landowners were sometimes written on tithe award maps. Occasionally these can be cross-referenced and both can provide information about fieldnames, routes and boundaries, which are vital for landscape archaeology. Other maps show landscaped gardens, battlefields or provide plans of factories and mines.

These early maps are often held in county record offices. Some may be in private hands or belong to churches.

Ordnance Survey (OS) maps

During the early nineteenth century the OS mapped each county at 1 inch to 1 mile. From the 1880s OS 6 inch to 1 mile maps provided more detail of individual buildings and even hedge species. OS maps established a new standard in accuracy and a comprehensive system of coding and keys for features. A grid system was used which covered the whole country and enabled precise references to be given. By examining a succession of maps for any area, changes in land use and the built environment can be easily seen.

 www.ordsvy.gov.uk

Maps used by archaeologists

The OS 1:25000 Pathfinder or Leisure series show the location of some archaeological sites but planning maps that use the same grid system are needed for investigations. 1:10000 (old 6 inch) maps are sometimes the most detailed available for mountainous and some rural areas but 1:2500 (old 25 inch 1 mile) rural or 1:1250 urban planning maps are normally used. For field walking 1:10000 or 1:2500 is used and for excavation the 1:2500 or 1:1250 provides a base. A 1:2500 map allows you to identify individual metre squares with a 10-figure grid reference. These maps can be seen in county or district planning offices.

Other maps sometimes used include geological maps, street maps, factory plans, vegetation and climatic maps, land use and classification, soil surveys and specialist archaeological maps.

Increasingly archaeologists are using computerised mapping systems based around Geographical Information Systems (**GIS**).

As an archaeology student you need some basic map skills including the ability to:

- identify and interpret common archaeological features from maps
- 'read' contours and hachures
- use scales and at least 6-figure grid references
- produce basic cross-sectional sketches from maps
- interpret simple archaeological plans and diagrams
- use other evidence such as photographs and written accounts to interpret maps and plans.

KEY TERM

Geographic Information Systems (GIS)

This refers to powerful databases which can store vast amounts of data against individual map grid references. This can include details of topography, geology and vegetation as well as archaeological data. It can integrate data from satellites with field recordings. It can produce topographic maps and site plans in three dimensions and perform complex statistical analysis. It is revolutionising the presentation and interrogation of archaeological data. On models such as that developed for Gloucester a vast range of underlying data can be accessed by pointing and clicking on the map.

KEY TASK

Sourcing information

Take each of the following examples and list the types of source you might find useful in investigating it.

Next take a real example of one of them and find out what actual sources exist. You may be surprised.

A round barrow or cairn

A roman villa or Saxon church

A deserted medieval village or abbey

An eighteenth-century farm or canal

A nineteenth-century railway line or factory

A twentieth-century pillbox or airfield

SURFACE SURVEYS

This term can be used to encompass **fieldwalking**, **surveying** and even planned aerial photography. We will use it to describe non-destructive visual surveys at ground level. These can range from slow, painstaking searches on foot to quite rapid examinations of a landscape by Landrover, looking for upstanding earthworks. Since most sites lack visible features, the former is more common. This technique is largely concerned with finding traces of unrecorded sites. Scatters of building rubble or artefacts or slight undulations in the surface might reveal where there are buried walls or house platforms. Differences in soil or vegetation may also be indicative of past human activity. For studies of the **Mesolithic** and **Neolithic** in Britain, scatters of flint and animal bone are often the only traces of human activity visible in the landscape. To study the activities of these mobile populations, careful identification and plotting of these scatters is essential. A variation on this is the study of hedges and woodlands for traces of past economic activities and to help locate settlement areas (▶see p. 175). Surface surveys can cover large areas such as Webster and Sanders' work in the Copan Valley of Mexico and the Thetford Forest project in East Anglia.

 http://www.wkac.ac.uk/quantocks/

 http://www.harnser.fsnet.co.uk/frames.htm

 http://www.nottingham.ac.uk/archaeology/research/huancaco/

For major research studies, the design of **sampling** procedures are vital.

Surface investigations of known sites include **micro-contour surveys** of the topography. These involve detailed and precise use of surveying tools to build up a picture of variations in height and levels. Data is increasingly being entered on databases to enable computer enhancement of the landscape. These surveys can often reveal hidden features that could not be detected with the naked eye.

Recording standing buildings

One specialised area of archaeological surveying focuses on the built environment and links archaeology to architectural science. Detailed studies of the material and construction techniques of structures are made both to enhance knowledge of the development of buildings and to provide a record against future destruction or decay. Records will range between a written description and CAD (computer-aided design) based recording of every brick or stone. Most recording of buildings occurs as part of the planning process (▶see p. 111) or during conservation work. A recent variation on this is the current Defence of Britain project, which is seeking to collect records on defensive monuments of the Second World War.
{ah}

 http://www.britarch.ac.uk/projects/dob/index.html

Fieldwalking

Fieldwalking, or **surface collection** as it is known in the USA, involves systematic collection of artefacts from the ploughsoil which might be indicative of human settlement. Ceramics and worked stone are the most commonly gathered but metal, bone and burnt stone are often also collected. The method is

KEY TERM

Sampling

Whatever is deposited is a fragment of past material culture. Dependent upon the material, a variable portion of these deposits will survive. Archaeologists will recover a sample of these. Not every site can be fieldwalked, let alone excavated. Choices have to be made. If these choices are arbitrary (non-probabilistic) they could lead to bias in the **archaeological record** with certain types of evidence being neglected and others over-represented. For example, if archaeologists chose only to study hill forts from the Iron Age or, as often happens, if development only permitted excavation in one part of a town, it might create an unrepresentative picture of life in the past.

When archaeologists design research strategies they use some form of probabalistic sampling to reduce bias in recovery. This means that the chance of anything being recovered is known. Rigorous sampling is used in most aspects of archaeological reconnaissance and excavation. It is probably enough to understand four basic models. For each of them, the plan of the total area to be surveyed or the site in question (the sample universe) is divided up by a grid into numbered units. The units will vary in size according to the work to be done, for example, 1 × 1 metres for test pitting to large units for surface survey. In some cases a specified number of transects or samples of soil will be made in each square.

A simple *random sample* works like a lottery. The numbered units are selected by computer or number table. This is fair as each unit has

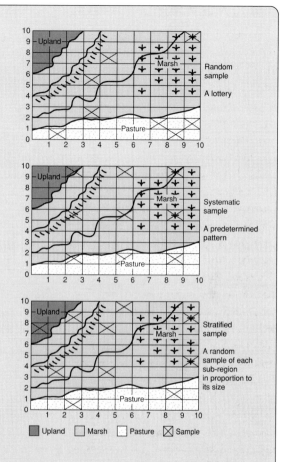

Figure 1.5 *Models of different approaches to sampling*

an equal chance of being selected, but it can also lead to clustering and thus miss features.

Stratified sampling overcomes clustering bias by first dividing the sample universe into sections. For example, if the site has natural zones such as hills, valley and plain then numbers are selected randomly for each zone in proportion to its area.

Systematic sampling overcomes clustering by selecting at evenly spaced intervals, for example every third grid or every 10 metres.

KEY TERM *cont.*

Sampling

This ensures a more even selection although it could miss things that are regularly distributed. It usually requires a higher number of samples.

Stratified systematic sampling combines the last two methods and could be used to take more samples in particular zones than others.

 http://archnet.asu.edu/archnet/unconn_extras/theory/sampling/sampling.html

destructive in that archaeological material is removed, but as it has been disturbed by ploughing, it is not in its original context anyway.

Decisions about sampling have to be made when planning fieldwalking. Not everything will be collected, particularly when building rubble is involved. For instance, will all ceramics be collected or just diagnostic pieces? Decisions also have to be taken about the width of traverses or size of grids and the space between them.

Fieldwalkers proceed along a measured section of a traverse (called a stint) or around a grid collecting material they see lying on the surface before them. This is usually soon after ploughing and ideally when rain has cleared dust from the surface. These finds are bagged and tagged with the number of the grid or stint for processing and analysis.

Figure 1.6
A Level students fieldwalking

KEY TERMS

Grids and transects and traverses

These are areas marked out on archaeological sites or areas being surveyed. They are 'anchored' to identifiable points which link into the national ordnance survey grid, enabling evidence to be precisely located. They are set up using surveying equipment and carefully checked for accuracy. Global positioning systems (**GPS**) and GIS are increasingly important in this work. Typically grids and transects are marked out with pegs, canes or flags. The same process is involved in preparation for fieldwalking, geophysics and excavation.

Once washed and identified, finds are counted for each grid or transect. This can then be plotted on a distribution map to show patterns and concentrations. There are several ways of displaying this information. Phase maps or a series of clear plastic overlays for each period or type of find are commonly used. Computer displays using GIS have an edge here since several types of data can be linked to any point and comparisons easily made.

Fieldwalking is a well established method because it has many strengths. It is a relatively cheap way of surveying large areas since volunteer labour can be used to collect and wash finds. It can help establish the function and period of a site without excavation and provide insights into location and exchange.

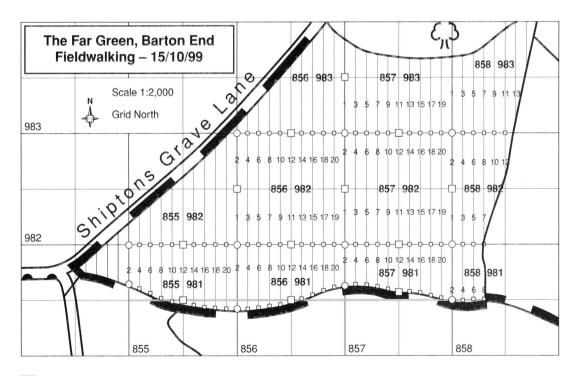

Figure 1.7 *A planned fieldwalk which has been linked to the national grid reference system*

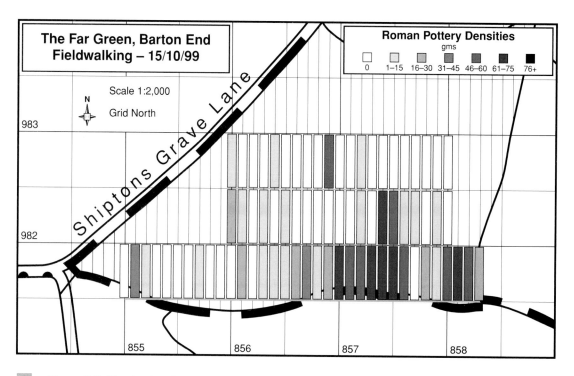

**The Far Green, Barton End
Fieldwalking – 15/10/99**

Roman Pottery Densities
gms

0	1–15	16–30	31–45	46–60	61–75	76+

Scale 1:2,000

N
Grid North

Shiptons Grave Lane

983

982

855   856   857   858

Figure 1.8 *The density of one category of finds plotted in relation to each fieldwalker's stint*

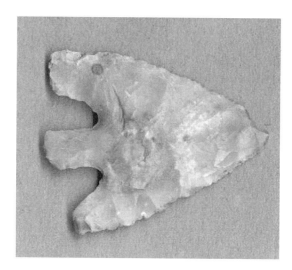

Figure 1.9 *An excellent example of a flint arrowhead recovered during fieldwalking at Thetford*

Fieldwalking can indicate the spread and foci of evidence. It does, however, have important limitations too. It is only really useful on arable land where access has been granted and then only at certain times in the agricultural cycle. In addition, its results cannot be taken at face value. For example, medieval manuring practices transferred much domestic refuse to the ploughsoil, creating a doughnut shape pattern of pottery distribution. Chris Gerrard's work on the Shapwick Project has explored two other major limitations.

Different materials behave differently in the same soil. In Shapwick, rewalking the same fields and monitoring ceramics in them showed that some material migrates further than others. Patterns for pottery from different periods were also very different. It was not always a good indication of settlement. A second

KEY STUDY

The Shapwick Project

This long-running investigation of the development of a village on an estate owned by Glastonbury Abbey has combined a full range of reconnaissance techniques and pioneered new methods including shovel pit testing and geochemical survey. Several generations of students from Bristol University and King Alfred College, Winchester, and members of the public have contributed. The research has been notable for the way maps, botany, invertebrate studies and historical records have been combined to produce regression maps for the village. It has also made a major contribution to our understanding of fieldwalking.

 http://www.wkac.ac.uk/shapwick/index.html

variable was the differential collection by different fieldwalkers. Analysis of their finds showed that some were good at recognising and collecting one type of material but poor with another. This applied to experienced walkers as well as novices. Their performance varied according to weather and slope. Taken together it means that what is recovered is a sample of what was in the topsoil and the topsoil holds a sample of what lies below. In both cases the sample varies for each type of find. Fieldwalking results therefore need to be cross-checked with other data before conclusions can be drawn.

There are a number of other prospection methods which provide alternatives to fieldwalking although all are more destructive. **Shovel pit testing** involves taking a regular number of buckets from 30 litre topsoil samples from test pits and sieving to retrieve finds. This can take place in woods, pasture and gardens where fieldwalking is impossible. It may be a more reliable guide to settlement location if the area has not been ploughed in modern times.

Coring and **augering** are also used to sample the subsoil. A device such as a bucket auger is driven into the ground and it extracts a sample of the subsoil in the same way as an apple corer. This can provide a snapshot of the stratigraphy and the sample can be examined for artefactual or environmental evidence. **Probing**, which involves driving a rod into the ground, is more useful for tracing shallow buried features such as walls on known sites.

GEOCHEMICAL PROSPECTION

These relatively new methods and expensive techniques attempt to locate areas of past human activity by detecting differences in the chemical properties of the soil. **Phosphate analysis** is the best known of these but analysis of heavy metals such as lead and cadmium and lipids (fats) in the topsoil also has the potential to be useful. These techniques can also be applied to intra-site analysis including buildings. Variations in the combinations of heavy metals in different rooms may reflect different activities.

GEOPHYSICAL SURVEYS

This term covers techniques that detect features through their physical differences with the surrounding soil. The most common techniques detect magnetic and electrical anomalies and require considerable skill to interpret. With the increasing involvement of archaeology in planning development and a shift in emphasis amongst archaeologists in favour of preservation rather than excavation, these techniques are now commonplace. The manufacture of increasingly reliable instruments for archaeology has seen magneto-metry become a standard technique.

 http://www.geoscan-research.co.uk

Resistivity survey

There are differences in the ability of different soils to conduct electricity. This can be detected by passing an electric current through the ground and comparing readings. Electricity is conducted through the soil by mineral salts contained in water. The more moisture there is the better the conductivity of the soil. A buried ditch will generally retain water better than the surrounding soil. A buried wall will conduct poorly and therefore resist the current more

 Figure 1.10 *Students using a resistivity meter*

than the surrounding soil. Electrical current flows close to the surface so it can be measured using shallow probes. The method works better with some soils than others. Clay retains moisture well, so differences in resistance between the soil and buried ditches or pits may be impossible to detect. Plants, rocks and variations in the depths of soils can also create misleading readings.

 http://www.eng-h.gov.uk/reports/ beckhampton/

http://www.brad.ac.uk/acad/archsci/ field_proj/amarsh/project.html

Early **resistivity** methods involved placing lines of spikes and wires along the ground, which made them slow. Today there are mobile units that look a little like Zimmer frames and have onboard computers to log readings. While these are relatively easy to use they are still not fast and are best suited to detailed exploration of a small area such as a site, rather than for prospecting. Resistivity can also be used to create pseudo sections of buried features. This involves taking a series of readings from a line of probes placed across a buried feature such as a ditch. Wider spacing produces data on deeper parts of the feature than narrowly spaced probes.

The depth to which this technology penetrates the soil is limited and readings require consid-erable interpretation, as the sensitivity of the meters is not great. At Hindwell in Wales, a 4-metre wide ditch identified by resistivity turned out after excavation to be a series of massive postholes with construction ramps.

Magnetometer surveying

The earth's magnetic field is generally uniform in any one place. However, local magnetic

RESISTIVITY

The resistivity meter works by detecting anomalies (differences) in the ability of subsurface remains to conduct electricity compared with the surrounding soil.

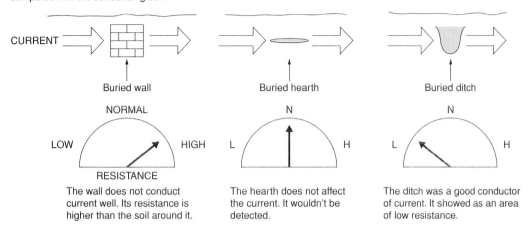

CURRENT

Buried wall

Buried hearth

Buried ditch

NORMAL

LOW — HIGH

RESISTANCE

The wall does not conduct current well. Its resistance is higher than the soil around it.

The hearth does not affect the current. It wouldn't be detected.

The ditch was a good conductor of current. It showed as an area of low resistance.

Figure 1.11 *A simplified diagram illustrating the principles of resistivity*

Figure 1.12 *A hand-held magnetometer. Note how much easier it is to move than the resistivity meter*

distortions can be caused by past human activity. Topsoil contains haematite (Fe_2O_3), a form of iron (Fe). In some forms its crystals are magnetic. A pit dug into the earth will fill up with topsoil, which will contain concentrations of magnetic material. The fill will therefore be different magnetically from the subsoil. A second type of local magnetic distortion occurs where there have been kilns or hearths in the past. Heating alters the magnetic properties of the underlying soil. A magnetometer is a sensitive instrument which can detect such minor anomalies in the local magnetic field.

The earliest magnetometers were cumbersome and slow to use. The development of hand-held fluxgate gradiometers has enabled the technique to be used to rapidly scan quite large areas to highlight anomalies. Magnetometers are also used in detailed site investigations where they can detect small features up to 1 metre down and provide images of some buried features. In Germany caesium magnetometers have been developed which are incredibly sensitive. One was brought over recently for work at Stanton Drew where it detected faint traces of hundreds of concentric postholes. However these handcart-mounted machines are very expensive.

 http://www.ebg-h.gov.uk/archaeometry/ StantonDrew/

To be able to detect anomalies, the magnetic background of the soil has to be measured and magnetometers calibrated against it. The measuring of this **magnetic susceptibility** of the topsoil can also be used as a crude survey technique in its own right. Magnetic hotspots suggest areas of past settlement or industrial activity, which could be surveyed using other methods.

 http://ds.dial.pipex.com/town/terrace/ ld36/magsus.htm

Sensitive magnetic instruments are easily disturbed by iron, including nails, pipes and wire fences as well as the zips and piercings of the archaeologist. A further limitation can be background interference from magnetic bedrock or where a long period of occupation has left a magnetic layer over a wide area. Sandy and clay soils often do not provide sufficient contrast. Fluctuations in the earth's magnetic field also have to be taken into account. It requires considerable skill and experience to interpret the results.

 KEY TASK

Test your understanding of geophysics

Which of the two main geophysical methods would normally be effective in detecting these buried features? Answers on p. 305.

1	Hearths	6	Large pits
2	Cobbled floors	7	Stakeholes
3	Stone walls	8	Building platforms
4	Graves	9	Small pits
5	Kilns	10	Ditches

Other methods

Metal detectors are useful for metal objects down to about 15 cm. These may provide clues about underlying sites, particularly burials and therefore could be used as part of wider surveys. Inexperienced detectorists will waste time by detecting slag or modern agricultural debris. Similarly, detectors can be used to sweep areas in advance of geophysics so that concentrations of metal can be plotted and taken into account.

Ground penetrating radar (GPR) which was developed for defence and engineering is starting to be used in archaeology. Aerial versions can highlight buried landscapes and rivers. Ground versions are useful for detecting voids and GPR has been particularly effective in revealing the internal structures of buildings. It is the only effective geophysics technique in city centres where it can even penetrate tarmac. However, it remains expensive and is only useful where burial deposits are close to the surface. Its value is in addressing specific questions rather than for general survey.

KEY SKILL

Comparing methods

Construct your own table for geophysics and geochemical methods to summarise and compare strengths and weaknesses as shown below. Research and add an additional example to each.

Method	Strengths	Limitations	Example
Resistivity			

Although usually classed as geophysics, *dowsing* and *bosing* are two more traditional methods that are occasionally used. Skilled dowsers use wooden sticks to locate water and some features under water. Bosing involves hitting the ground with a solid object such as a mallet and listening for variations in resonant sounds. These might indicate buried ditches or walls.

All of these geophysical techniques are used in conjunction with grids to map patterns of finds and variations. All of them are limited in the type of work they can do and they should therefore be seen as complementary. None of them are particularly useful on waterlogged sites. Their value is often in pinpointing or exploring features rather than finding new sites.

AERIAL PHOTOGRAPHY

The first aerial photographs (APs) were taken from balloons and they are sometimes still used. Today, most photographs are taken from light aircraft although even kites have been used on occasions. APs are used for mapping, finding new sites rapidly over large areas and illustrating and exploring known sites. Substantial archives of aerial photographs are available publicly and commercially so new pictures may not always be needed.

 http://rs6000.univie.ac.at/AARG/

 http://www.aerial.cam.ac.uk/

http://www.airphotoservices.co.uk/

Verticals and obliques

Aerial photographs used for mapping are taken with the camera pointing straight down at the ground (*verticals*) with the aircraft flying along grid lines. Often these are taken from high altitude. This is the case with the RAF archives dating from the 1940s which are now housed at the NMR. Overlapping vertical photographs can be viewed through a stereoscope to see the landscape in 3D. Their main value is in planning and illustrating sites. Where some dimensions in the photograph are known, reasonably accurate plans can be drawn of sites, including their contours. This is known as photogrammetric mapping.

Oblique photographs are the most widely used in archaeology to locate sites and illustrate features. These are taken from low-flying aircraft with the picture taken at an angle to the ground. Aerial reconaissance usually precedes field survey. While is is fast and gives good coverage, it can be expensive and can miss features if their **signatures** are not visible from the air. Equally, there may be features which

are invisible at ground level and this provides the only means of recording them. There are three main ways in which archaeological sites show up from the air.

Shadow sites

In low light, either at the start or end of the day, shadows are at their longest and even quite minor variations in ground level cast shadows, for instance ploughed out barrows or the remains of early field systems.

APs taken from a low-flying aircraft and recorded with a camera pointed into the sun have a distorted perspective which best picks up shadows. The technique is best used for

Figure 1.13 An excellent view of the deserted medieval village (DMV) of Bingham's Melcombe, which shows up because of shadows cast by low sunlight. Traces of houses, enclosures and trackways are all visible

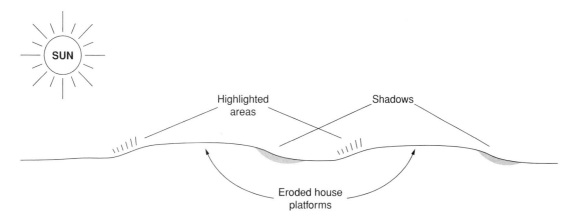

Figure 1.14 *Why slight earthworks are visible as 'shadow sites'*

illustrating existing sites and locating details within them, for example evidence of features inside a hill fort. However, shadows are also created where crops are at different heights (see below) and occasionally new sites can be detected. Winter is the best season for photography as the sun is low and vegetation which might mask sites has often died down. Snowfall and flooding can accentuate the appearance of hollows and earthworks and create some of the most dramatic images of **shadow sites**.

Cropmarks

The ripening and growth rate of crops is related to the amount of moisture their root systems can access. Plants with better access to moisture will often grow taller and turn a different tone or colour than those plants around them. If there are buried archaeological features under a field this can result in patterns showing in the crop. A buried ditch with its infill of humus and topsoil will often hold moisture, creating a dark green line in the crop above. This 'positive' **cropmark** is visible from the air. The opposite occurs in plants over a

buried wall. They are likely to be stunted and produce a yellowish, 'negative' cropmark. 'Parch marks' show on grass for the same reason.

Cropmarks sometimes only show for a few days a year. Repeatedly flying over areas over time can pick up new and different features. Some only show up in drought conditions when crops with access to moisture have the greatest advantage and colour contrast is exaggerated. The technique works best on quick draining soils such as river gravels but is less good on clay or areas of deeper topsoil, where the soil retains moisture well. Cropmarks show up best in cereal crops such as wheat and particularly barley. They do not show up in many crops, for example peas and beans, and the effect of differential moisture can be overcome or masked by irrigation or fertiliser. Care has to be taken with interpretation, as geological features such as periglacial cracks and modern field drainage and underground pipelines also create cropmarks. Trial excavation is often the only way to firmly identify many sites. Cropmarks are the most prolific source of new sites, particularly for the

Figure 1.15 *An Iron Age 'banjo' enclosure on Cranborne Chase showing as a dark cropmark. The crops growing over the ditches of the feature are darker because their roots have better access to moisture than the surrounding crops. Crown Copyright 1955 & 1959/MOD*

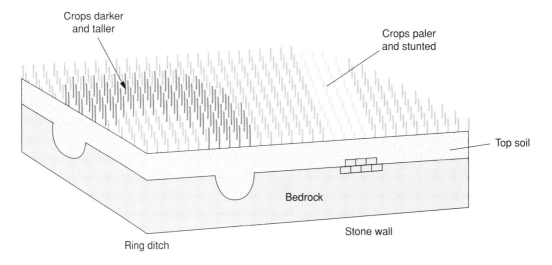

Figure 1.16 *Three-dimensional cross-section of cropmarks*

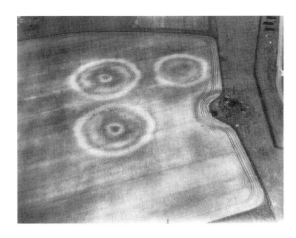

Figure 1.17 *Winterbourne Stoke round barrow cemetery showing as a soil mark. The difference in tone between the top soil and the material used for the barrow provides a clear contrast. The monuments would not be easily detected on the ground*

late Neolithic to early medieval periods, and are also used to investigate existing sites such as the extent of the harbour at Fishbourne Palace.

Soil marks

On soils where there is a marked contrast between the colour of the topsoil and subsoil, evidence of ploughed-out monuments can occur as **soil marks**. On chalk, the dark brown of ditch infill will contrast with the chalk rubble of a bank and the lighter brown of the plough soil.

Remote sensing

This can be a rather confusing term. Usually it is used to distinguish between the imaging techniques used from planes and satellites and those of ground based prospection. Sometimes it is used to describe all techniques that don't remove material. When you come across it, be sure to check which sense it is being used in. We are using it in the first sense. The results of all these techniques need to be checked at ground level.

http://www.arcl.ed.ac.uk/arch/remotesense/

Radar has been used to find sites both on land and at sea. Its ability to penetrate both clouds and dense jungle has made it particularly useful in Mesoamerica. At sea, side-scanning **sonar** has successfully located and provided images of objects on the seabed. Echo sounders or magnetometers complement it in wider and more localised searches respectively.

A variety of airborne and satellite techniques, including thermal imaging and infrared photography, are able to record temperature, dew and frost dispersal variations invisible to light-sensitive film. They all work on the principle that anomalies such as disturbed earth or buried walls will absorb and retain heat or moisture at different rates to the surrounding ground. Commercial equipment is really only suitable for large features although military developments to increase sensitivity will no doubt filter through to archaeology. Currently such equipment is too expensive for most archaeological surveys.

KEY SKILL

Short questions test

This exercise is in the format of AS Level Archaeology paper 1.

Examine the aerial photograph below.

1a Describe the markings you can see in the field.   *2 mks*

1b Why do these marks show up?   *5 mks*

1c What non-invasive investigation could archaeologists undertake to help identify these features?   *7 mks*

A suggested markscheme is on ▶p. 305.

Figure 1.18 *Aerial photo of Wyke Down*

Excavation

To many people, archaeology simply means excavation. Often their interest in archaeology stems from witnessing an excavation or viewing one on television or through other media. Excavation is often the public face of archaeology. It is only when people 'dig' deeper into the subject that they are able to recognise the role that excavation plays in the wider nature of the discipline. It has its own methodology, which constantly changes to reflect current thinking and improving technologies. There can never be one set of rules for excavation although there is general agreement on key elements of the process. This chapter will try to reflect that current consensus.

WHY EXCAVATE?

Any removal of the accumulated evidence of the past is a finite act. Once disturbed, trowelled, shovelled and bucketed away that material cannot be replaced as it was before the excavator removed it. Hence it has been frequently said that 'all excavation is destruction'. Today no one condones excavation as it took place in the nineteenth century: for the pleasure of the excavators and to establish collections of artefacts. In all but those extreme circumstances, where chance discovery of remains demands a prompt response, there should be controlled planning. This should establish the rationale for excavation and formulate a series of questions, which it is hoped, the excavation might answer.

Often the record of a site can be remarkably full if a wide range of reconnaissance methods has been applied and there are sufficient clues about hidden features or structures. In many cases, once the record of such survey activities is carefully housed in an appropriate archive, for example the local SMR, archaeologists leave the physical remains untouched. If, however, a decision is made to excavate, it should be viewed as a most serious step in the archaeological process. While most scientific experiments can be repeated over and over again in the laboratory, archaeological excavation, although scientific in its approach, does not, by its very nature, allow a second chance. Some excavation procedures, somewhat confusingly referred to as sampling strategies, have been developed to try and ensure that not all the evidence is removed in the primary investigation of a feature or deposit. Nevertheless, in essence, excavation means destruction. However, that 'destruction' is minimised if the archaeologist pays appropriate care and attention to the way the excavation is conducted and particularly to the quality of the records kept. This is sometimes referred to as 'preservation by record' (▶see p. 114).

There are other considerations. A balance must be struck between the desire to protect archaeological remains for future generations and the need to develop the discipline and advance our knowledge through excavation. It is also important that archaeology is kept sufficiently in the public eye to receive the support it needs in the wider political forum.

Today, excavators are expected to:

- provide justifications for digging a site
- use survey techniques to plan excavation strategies
- be able to cope with subsequent changes on site
- ensure that a complete recording system is in place
- select and maintain appropriate samples for analysis
- have facilities for all aspects of post-excavation work
- interpret a site from a limited excavation or sample
- 'publish' the results of the work so that they are available to other interested parties
- maintain professional standards while working under time and economic constraints.

If this is done then excavation can move beyond the possible results of survey and get to the real core of archaeology – the hard evidence left by previous people of their existence.

TYPES OF EXCAVATION

Excavations today usually fall into one of three broad categories depending on the main reason for them: research, rescue or salvage.

Research excavations

These are excavations on sites where there is no immediate threat of destruction. The site is selected by archaeologists for its suitability to answer the questions they wish to answer. It can be excavated according to archaeological needs rather than prompted by the threat of development. Research excavation is only undertaken when the perceived benefits to

KEY SITE

Avebury

Recent research has revealed much new detail of this famous archaeological landscape. The eastern lines of stones running to Avebury from the Sanctuary, known as the West Kennet Avenue, are well known but the possible avenue to the west, the Beckhampton Avenue, has been surrounded in mystery. William Stukeley recorded it in the eighteenth century but only two visible stones survive. Investigation of this key element of the world heritage site of Avebury began with investigation of a cropmark of what appeared to be an oval enclosure lying adjacent to the suspected line of the avenue.

Fieldwork and excavation to evaluate the evidence involved three universities assisted by English Heritage (EH) and the Ancient Monuments Laboratory (AML). The enclosure proved to have features similar to causewayed enclosures of the early Neolithic. Geophysics surveys on the line of the avenue revealed three pits left where stones had been removed and broken up and three still containing buried sarsen stones. These had been deliberately tipped over to remove surface trace of them.

This research answered some questions on the enclosure and the stones of the Avenue but posed others. Further research is planned.

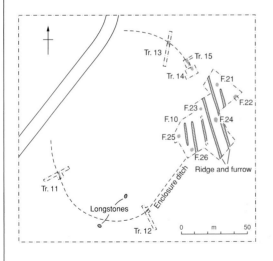

http://www.stonehenge-avebury.net/avelatest.html

Current Archaeology 167

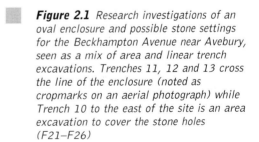

Figure 2.1 *Research investigations of an oval enclosure and possible stone settings for the Beckhampton Avenue near Avebury, seen as a mix of area and linear trench excavations. Trenches 11, 12 and 13 cross the line of the enclosure (noted as cropmarks on an aerial photograph) while Trench 10 to the east of the site is an area excavation to cover the stone holes (F21–F26)*

KEY SITE

Castell Henllys

This small Iron Age hill fort in South West Wales was bought in 1980 by the co-founder of the London Dungeon, who worked to develop it as a tourist attraction with reconstructed Iron Age houses. Subsequently it has been taken over by the Pembrokeshire Coast National Park, which has established a visitors' centre on the site.

It was necessary to excavate the site and recover the evidence on which to base the reconstructions. Students and paying volunteers have helped in the excavations each summer. Over twenty seasons, archaeologists have studied the defensive circuit, the complex phases of the gateway, and almost the whole of the interior of the fort. Reconstructions of four major roundhouses and smaller constructions have been completed.

This research has provided a much fuller understanding of the archaeology of this period and provided a link via its marketing style between archaeologists and the general public.

 http://archaeology.lamp. ac.uk/CastellH/chenter.html

 Current Archaeology 161

Figure 2.2
An area excavation to reveal the 'chevaux de frise' an Iron Age 'tank trap' protecting the entrance to Castell Henllys, West Wales. Compare with interpretation on p. 103

archaeological understanding outweigh the loss of the original site, or part of it, to future generations.

There is little public or commercial funding of research excavation so archaeologists have to finance themselves by alternative means. For instance, universities that run 'training excavations' for their undergraduates may also accept paying 'volunteers'. Applied research agencies, for example the British Academy, provide some support for this type of long-term research.

Rescue excavations

The term 'rescue excavations' was coined in the 1960s when so much development was in progress that the earlier pattern of amateur and university summer excavations could no long cope with the volume of archaeological sites being threatened and destroyed. Rescue, a charitable trust, dramatised the threat to Britain's archaeology by using as its logo an image of Stonehenge being scooped up in a bulldozer's bucket. However, this conjures up a rather more violent image than is truly the picture. In fact what was recognised was that the scale and pace of development meant that much valuable evidence was in danger of being lost if it could not be excavated and recorded. Excavation teams were needed all year round.

http//www.rescue-archaeology. freeserve.co.uk/

Some teams were centrally based within government agencies while others were formed locally to combat specific threats. The M5 Rescue Committee is a good example of a group founded with a clear but essentially time-constrained focus. From these late 1960s/early 1970s teams most of today's

archaeological **units** have developed. Many have urban bases, but demand for large urban excavation has fallen considerably since the introduction of PPG 16 (▶see p. 111).

see p. 111

Originally, rescue teams identified potential threats to archaeological sites from planned developments such as road building, gravel extraction or pipelines, and submitted bids for public funding to excavate before development began. Today planning authorities, guided by PPG 16, often require developers to prepare impact assessments and may also demand a formal site evaluation. Depending on the findings there may be excavation in advance of development and/or a watching brief during construction. On the principle of 'the polluter pays' the cost is increasingly passed on to developers. However, for most sites, full excavation with its heavy costs and delays in construction is not usually necessary. Where excavation does occur, decisions are made on whether all of a site should be excavated or just a sample. Often work will be concentrated on areas felt to be of greatest importance. Excavation takes place within a time limit but is carefully planned and involves co-operation between archaeologists, planners and contractors. Archaeologists can usually carry out their work according to correct archaeo-logical procedures. Rescue does not generally mean working under the jaws of mechanical diggers in an uncontrolled rush. If it is, this will usually be in the final days of what has previously been an ordered excavation. Non-archaeologists often find the pace of excavation slower than they would imagine and need to have the processes explained to them. The Channel Tunnel Project provides an excellent example of a considered strategy for retrieving archaeological evidence.

KEY SITE

Empingham, Rutland, Part 1

The valley of the river Gwash was of little interest to people outside Rutland until planners in the 1970s decided to build a dam across it. The area flooded would create Rutland Water – one of England's largest lakes.

Through the chance discovery of an Anglo-Saxon brooch and the process of fieldwalking two Romano-British sites were revealed which enabled archaeologists to plan rescue excavations on an Anglo-Saxon cemetery, a Romano-British farmstead and a villa respectively. All three sites lay directly under the line of the proposed dam.

Excavations over three seasons were designed and conducted with knowledge of the impending engineering development but with the normal safeguards of time for the removal and recording of features and finds. However, once the contractors arrived on site the nature of the archaeological work changed considerably . . . ▶ see p. 32.

 Cooper 2000

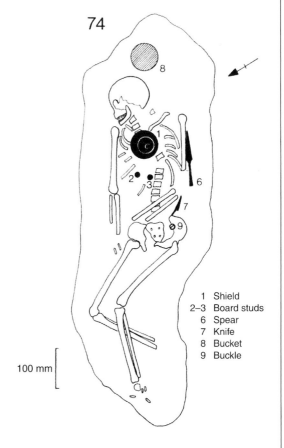

1	Shield
2–3	Board studs
6	Spear
7	Knife
8	Bucket
9	Buckle

100 mm

Figure 2.3 Burial 74 at Empingham. A plan of a skeleton in the grave to show positions of bones and grave goods. The skeleton of a male aged about 25–30 years old was accompanied by a shield boss; two board studs, a spearhead, an iron knife, a copper alloy-bound wooden bucket and an iron buckle. Preserved wood remains in the spear socket were identified as willow and poplar and in the bucket as yew. See drawing of finds in Figure 11.10 (p. 253)

KEY SITE

The Channel Tunnel rail link

The development of this new railway resulted in the largest archaeological project to date in the United Kingdom. Engineers and archaeologists worked in tandem to ensure that archaeological issues were fully considered throughout the process. Rail Link Engineering employed its own archaeologists and others involved have come from English Heritage, University College London, Kent County Council and four other units.

All forms of survey work were carried out; over 2,000 trial trenches and test pits were dug. Fieldwork informed the setting of priorities about where to excavate. Some 55 hectares of the route were identified as requiring detailed archaeological investigation. Planning of the work gave archaeologists time to 'painstakingly' record the archaeological deposits on the sites selected for detailed work. Other areas were subject to watching briefs (where archaeologists are on hand to observe work – particularly topsoil removal – so they can recognise and record features as they appear). In this particular scheme the archaeologists were empowered to stop construction work if 'features of significance' were identified. Over forty sites have been excavated with dates ranging from the **Palaeolithic** to the Second World War. The impact of the new evidence will enhance and probably alter many current perceptions of Kent's archaeology.

 Current Archaeology 168.

Salvage excavations

There are some occasions when archaeological evidence is unexpectedly revealed in circumstances where it is impossible for excavation to be pre-planned or systematic. The main decision is whether in the circumstances excavating will be a valid exercise or whether simply to note the presence of the remains is the better option. A rapid exploration is often the best that can be hoped for.

There is some overlap between these categories as the Empingham example shows. It is also the case that priorities in rescue excavations can be set to answer research questions. The bulk of excavation in Britain today is rescue work.

 KEY TASK

Identifying the nature of an excavation

Much has been written about the discovery and excavation of Seahenge (▶ p. 124)

Use the weblink to consider to what extent the excavation of this site was research, rescue or salvage. Two alternative sites are also provided.

 http://www.channel4.com/nextstep/timeteam/

 http://www.arch.soton.ac.uk/Research/Dunragit/

 http://www. suffolkcc.gov.uk/e-and-t/archaeology/eriswell/

KEY SITE

Empingham, Rutland, Part 2

A watching brief was negotiated with the developers and a series of discoveries were made as mechanical scrapers systematically stripped the landscape of its topsoil on both sides of the river for 2 kilometres back from the dam. These included:

- two burials in stone coffins

- a third major Romano-British site

- an Iron Age roundhouse

- two Anglo-Saxon grubenhauser

- a sunken Iron Age trackway

- a large Anglo-Saxon inhumation cemetery with 130 burials.

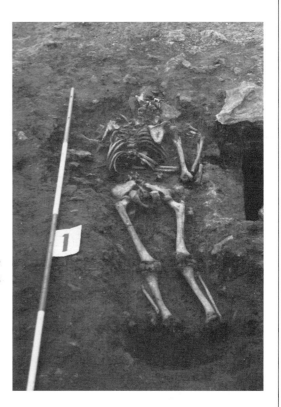

An excavation team and resources had to be gathered at short notice to deal with the situation. The Romano-British site and burials had to be excavated immediately as they lay in the path of planned engineering works, which could not be delayed. Arrangements were made for contractors to 'work around' the other sites which enabled a higher level of excavation and recording.

 Cooper 2000

Figure 2.4 *Another grave from Empingham. Note the different information provided by plan on p. 30 and photograph*

Figure 2.5 *An area excavation of the medieval burial grounds at Spitalfields in London. Note the cover over the site, both for protection of the remains and out of respect for the burials. The relatively confined space is typical of most urban excavations*

EXCAVATION STRATEGIES AND THE PROCESS OF EXCAVATION

The previous section identified reasons for excavations. In all cases there is a degree of choice available to archaeologists. Archaeologists are aware of the nature of their sites and do not dig 'blind'. While there is always the element of unpredictability, which is one of the joys of the subject, a qualified excavation director should be able to work out an appropriate strategy using prior knowledge and fieldwork results.

Defining the site in question is the first issue (▶see p. 166). In excavation terms some 'sites' are in fact a series of smaller 'sites' in themselves. For example, cropmarks may indicate a series of **features** (enclosures, pits, tracks) which can be separated out for investigation while a Roman town has a street plan and a variety of public and private buildings each capable of individual excavation. Sites are set within a landscape context and a successful excavation needs to take note of that factor too. So those planning to excavate need to determine whether it is the entirety of the site

 Figure 2.6 A Neolithic ritual site at Down Farm on Cranborne Chase top-stripped and ready for excavation. The major features show up clearly as discoloration in the soil

that is the focus of their attention or whether concentration on certain parts offers the best chance to answer the questions posed for the excavation.

 http://museums.ncl.ac.uk/raunds/index.htm

http://www.hungsteinsite.de/gibs_00/hindwell.htm

There is no set manual for archaeological field practices either in relation to where to put the holes in the ground or in how to proceed once the excavation trench is underway. This is not because archaeologists have a laissez-faire attitude to standards and procedures but because of variety in the nature of sites, evidence and questions asked. Most texts on excavation express their ideas about appropriate 'good practice' and as new methods evolve so they too appear in print. The archaeological world constantly shares its experiences and a general consensus of current good practice is evident when one looks at images of modern excavations. Practitioners learn from one another and try to keep their methods in line

with current thinking and therefore ensure that their results, when published, stand up to scrutiny and are accepted by their peers. For example, many archaeological units use the Museum of London manual.

http://www.molas.org.uk

The nature of the archaeological record in the ground is often complex. Human nature and life circumstances ensure that most sites have a developmental history, which the archaeologist needs to unravel. The people who left the evidence went about their daily business without a thought for how their activities might leave traces for future investigators. They were not simply creating 'features' much of the time, nor did they often build a structure and leave it unaltered. However, their constructional or daily activities will have created a sequence of deposits, layers or **contexts** (the words are often used interchangeably) which builds up to create the archaeological record. Contained within these deposits, which are linked to features and

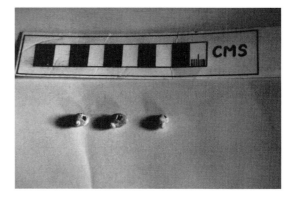

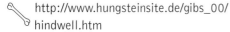 *Figure 2.7* These shells from the Palaeolithic site at Klithi in Greece were transformed from ecofacts to artefacts through modification by people. In this case they have been transformed into beads

structures, are the **artefacts** of pottery, metalwork, etc. and **ecofacts**, which provide sources for understanding the chronological, cultural and environmental nature of the site.

One further issue which excavators have to be aware of is the health and safety of their diggers. Precautions range from hardhats and reflective clothing on developer sites to ensuring that deep trenches are properly shored up or have stepped sides. Safety issues are most evident on underwater sites where air supply, currents, cold and sharks are amongst the potential hazards not faced on land.

How to dig?

The crux of the excavation methodology debate centres on the fact that all sites have two distinct but interrelated horizons. A vertical sequence of layers containing structures and finds, and the horizontal layout of an occupation area or individual structure. To record both sets of evidence is vital. Over the years methods have evolved to attempt to solve this difficult balancing trick. Unless the archaeologist can establish the correct succession of levels (▶see p. 39) an excavation and its results will have limited, if any, value. Likewise the inability to produce the plan (layout) of a building or a cemetery leaves the researcher well short of the required results. Archaeologists have therefore developed a series of methods appropriate to different types of site. The methods chosen reflect the need to achieve a full record of a site within the limits of the resources available for the excavation.

Trenches

The term 'trench' has been applied to any linear excavation and sometimes to any hole cut into the ground by archaeologists, whatever its surface shape. A stricter definition is a rectangular shaped excavation of variable width and length. Frequently the length far exceeds the width as trenches are used to investigate linear archaeological features such as defensive **earthworks** by being placed at 90° to the alignment of the feature. The trenches cut by Alcock through the defences of South Cadbury hill fort in Somerset provide a classic example. By strategically placing a series of 2-metre wide trenches around the hill he was able to study and report on the developmental sequence of the site's fortifications. This had the added bonus of disturbing a small proportion of the site in return for a volume of evidence. Most of the site was left undamaged for future archaeologists. Other linear features such as roads and boundaries can be cross-sectioned in this way. Offa's Dyke, an early medieval feature running from north to south Wales, has been the focus of a long-term study by Manchester University and over 100 trenches have been put across it to check and confirm details of its construction. Cutting across linear features on a smaller scale frequently occurs on area excavations. At Westhawk Farm, Kent (*Current Archaeology*

Figure 2.8 *A section cut across a feature to reveal its profile in section. The depth and shape of the feature can be determined as well as its fill and any stratigraphy*

168), the side ditches of the main road running through the newly discovered Roman town were identified as features when the area was extensively cleared and then excavated by the removal of sections of fill to reveal their profiles.

Those of you who have watched Time Team on Channel 4 will be familiar with the use of trial trenches to investigate possible features identified through archaeological reconnaissance. In many countries test pits, usually 1 metre square, from the surface down to bedrock, perform a similar function. They also provide an insight into the stratigraphy of the site. Trial trenches and test pits are regularly used in developer led archaeology to determine

whether excavation will be needed or whether remains can be left 'in situ'. They are less photogenic than open area excavations and less regularly seen in popular archaeological magazines.

Area excavation

This is the most common form of excavation as can be seen with reference to reports or archaeological magazines. 'Area' or 'open-stripping' occurs where the extent of the features to be uncovered determines the size of the excavation. This does not mean that whole sites are always laid bare. This can be an outcome but more frequently other factors limit the total recovery of evidence. Financial constraints may limit the amount of digging

Figure 2.9 An area excavation of the Anglo-Saxon site at West Heslerton showing that extensive features are preserved just below the surface of the ground. Attempting to interpret these features without excavation could be very misleading

while other logistical constraints could lead to a seasonal approach where parts of a site are uncovered and researched year by year. Danebury hill fort is a well-published example of such a strategy. In development areas only part of the site may be threatened or available for excavation. The depth of the archaeological deposits is important. You can excavate a greater area of a site with shallow remains than one with deeper stratification (for example urban sites) in the same time and with similar resource implications. Finally there are archaeological considerations. Only a sample of the site may be needed to address a question. It is impossible to generalise on the size of an area excavation. It is as large or as small as the demands of the archaeology dictate in the eyes of the site director.

Although destructive, area excavation has become the key approved method for several reasons.

■ Complete structures can be studied.
■ Complex relationships between features can be clarified.
■ It provides excellent recording possibilities.
■ A total understanding of horizontal relationships is possible.

When area excavation became fashionable there was criticism from those traditionalists who had used trenches. The sides of trenches have the advantage of revealing the vertical sequence of deposits (stratigraphy) and there was concern that this essential record might be lost. The depth of deposits can vary and the issue is of great significance where the stratification is deeper and more complicated. This problem can be addressed by leaving baulks (undug strips of ground) at strategic points or, increasingly, by carefully recording the horizontal picture of a site layer by layer and

feeding the data into a computer. This can be interrogated to produce sections along any chosen line. The problem is that without baulks no check is left in place if the director wishes to refer back, so the recording systems must be of the highest quality.

Box-grid or quadrant systems

These sit in an intermediate position between trenches and area excavation attempting to offer archaeologists the better aspects of each by giving access to both the horizontal view and the vertical cut simultaneously.

The box-grid system owes its origins to the work of Sir Mortimer Wheeler in the first half of the twentieth century. He would set out a grid of square 'boxes' to be excavated with baulks left in between them. This resulted in a dig resembling a patchwork quilt. An advantage was the chance to record four sections for every 'box'. Removal of spoil was also easier as baulks provided barrow runs. However, the whole layout of a site was not revealed until the baulks were finally removed. Important relationships between features or structures would not be understood while digging, which might depend on such an understanding, was progressing. The system was costly of time and manpower and its popularity short-lived though it is still possible to see some excavations where a pattern of trial trenching that clearly owes something to this earlier method is used.

The 'quadrant system' is a similar approach that is still in common usage. It is particularly relevant in the case of sites that are approximately circular in nature, such as round barrows, although a smaller scale version of this method is often employed on hearths, pits or even postholes. The feature is cut into four quarters by lines intersecting at the middle and

 Figure 2.10 *A pit which has been quartered in order to give four internal section profiles*

 Figure 2.11 *A quadrant excavation of a mound demonstrated at the Quest Project*

opposing quadrants are excavated first. It is possible after only removing half the remains to see patterns of features in plan (which if they show common elements suggest that they continue under the undug areas) and to totally record the vertical profile of the site in two directions.

KEY TASK

Simulating quadrant excavation

Students with a sweet tooth might like to enhance their understanding of excavation procedures by attempting a quadrant excavation of a gateau placed on a patterned plate. You should reveal enough of the plate to recognise patterns and see clearly the layers of sponge and cream in the excavated sections!

THE PROCESS OF EXCAVATION

Archaeologists have developed a variety of methods for removing archaeological deposits

KEY TASK

Testing the law of superposition

When you have been working at your desk for a while or after, say, half an hour of a lesson look at the way your books, papers, pencil case, sweet wrappers (or those of your fellow students) have combined in an overlapping manner. If you pick your way backwards through the evidence it should be possible to establish in reverse order the sequence of events that led to the accumulated material being in position. This will not tell you when the movement of items took place but should establish the order. The floor of your room provides an alternative site to examine.

from the ground in which they have lain to suit the varying circumstances of archaeological sites. The topsoil is removed by mechanically topstripping with a digger or by using picks, mattocks and shovels. This is either bulldozed or wheelbarrowed away to start a spoil heap. This has to be far enough away to avoid it

KEY CONCEPT

Stratigraphy

In any text about archaeological sites you will come across terms such as level, layer, deposit, stratum. They describe the make-up of the excavated ground in terms of layers. These were created either by people or nature. Archaeologists attempt to carefully record these strata – the **stratification**. By studying their relationship they can build up a sequence of events on the site. The study of the strata is known as stratigraphy.

Each layer, usually identified from those above and below it during excavation by colour, texture or content has its own spatial boundaries and relationships. Archaeologists talk and write about these relationships. If no intrusive features are present (for example a pit dug from an upper/recent layer down through lower/older layers) it would be safe to assume that layers at the bottom of any sequence are older than those at the top. Each successive layer was deposited after the one directly below it. This is sometimes refered to as 'the law of **superposition'**. But life and archaeological sites are not usually that simple. Archaeologists need to establish which layers overlie others and which cut into earlier layers or are cut by later ones. Only by posing and answering such questions then planning each layer and relating it into a vertical sequence can a picture emerge of change and development on a site.

Figure 2.12 *A picture that demonstrates how the law of superposition can tell a story. The female skeleton is lying above the mosaic at Kingscote and covered by building debris. The interpretation is that she was one of a number of 'squatters' who occupied the derelict villa building but was killed, apparently trying to escape, when it collapsed*

It is within the layers that the artefactual, environmental and dating evidence is located. They are like a time capsule. Materials in any layer are likely to be broadly contemporary and can be dated by association with dateable evidence from that layer. The layer holds the clues to the immediate context of finds and structures. Plotting the position of each layer within the site helps determine chronological patterns. Other archaeologists will use published data about the stratification to assure themselves of the authenticity of the conclusions reached about phasing on a site.

KEY CONCEPT *cont.*

The key methods of publishing information about a site's stratigraphy have long been via the medium of section drawings (▶see p. 48). While this is still quite prevalent, the Harris Matrix (invented in 1973) has revolutionised the representation of the sequence of deposits by using schematic diagrams. This recording system, which can apply equally to standing buildings or rock art as to more traditional archaeological deposits, has been widely adopted. The Harris Matrix website outlines its significance and provides a range of links. One key observation made by Harris and previously not fully developed is the idea that boundaries between elements of a section may be as significant as the layers themselves. His term for these boundaries is 'interfaces' and in the schematic drawings these can be represented as 'units of stratification'.

 http://www.harrismatrix.com

spilling over and contaminating deeper layers or burying the diggers. Although mechanical diggers are used for trial trenches, most excavation is by hand. According to the time available and the nature of the deposits, tools could range from shovels to dentistry instruments for recovering tiny fragments of material. The most familiar toolkit includes a mattock, a short pointed trowel, a dustbrush, a coalshovel and a bucket. Eventually, and very neatly, what was an archaeological resource will have been converted into a hole in the ground. The extracted evidence must be subjected to a rigorous recording process or the excavation will have destroyed the site and its potential. Recording requirements will vary for sites with less obvious collectable material or with particular distributions of evidence.

Layers of deposits in the ground are recognised, labelled and removed in sequence. On many sites such as Roman or medieval where pottery sherds and animal bones are common, their collection is linked to the contexts in which the material is found. They are collected in labelled 'finds trays' so that all the finds from each layer can be put together. They will subsequently be washed, dried and coded to their particular layer for recording.

On the same sites less common objects like metal, worked bone or stone will usually be classified as 'small finds' and a distinct and more comprehensive recording system will ensure that the precise location of each find is recorded in three dimensions by triangulation and depth measurements. They are collected in finds trays or plastic bags and given unique reference numbers. On a working floor associated with a prehistoric flint-knapper careful plotting of each flake is necessary to recreate the sequence of the earlier activity. Sometimes their position in a layer is marked by a small flag so that distribution patterns can be recorded. These finds will be kept separately and the nature and fragility of each object will determine their post-excavation scientific treatment.

Figure 2.13
Archaeologists
recording burials at
the Spitalfields site

Figure 2.14 On
Palaeolithic sites,
the position of
each flake of
stone and each
animal bone is
carefully recorded
to provide
insights into
behaviour. This
'working floor' at
Klithi has been
painstakingly
cleaned up prior
to recording

Recovery of environmental material

Not all the material to be retrieved can be recovered by trowelling. The ground contains much smaller and less obvious evidence, in particular faunal (animal) and floral (plant) evidence such as snail shells, small fish or bird bones, insect remains, seeds and pollen grains. Not all of these are visible to the naked eye. Tiny fragments of metal or worked material such as flint or glass present the same problem.

This material can be recovered on-site by using sieving or flotation or by taking strategically selected soil samples for later analysis.

Buckets of spoil from the excavation, or a sample, are tipped into a basic garden sieve and riddled over a barrow to ensure that finds not detected in the digging process are retrieved. A series of sieves with increasingly finer mesh improve collection chances and also collect different sized material in each sieve. The introduction of water to create 'wet-sieving', whether by spray or dipping into a tank, helps to remove the soil particles. Wet material is often easier to identify and locate by colour contrast.

Soil sampling

Some recovery of environmental remains occurs off-site following the collection of soil samples. These are taken from selected locations such as pits, ditches or other similar diagnostic features or layers. On peat sites, long sampling tins are hammered vertically into the sides of freshly dug sections, removed and quickly sealed in plastic to avoid contamination. They are then placed in cold storage before detailed analysis in the laboratory. The pollens and plant remains in them will be used to provide vegetation sequences and help date the site. Soil may also be sampled for chemical analysis, particularly for phosphates (▶see p. 15).

Flotation

This involves putting soil samples into water. Lighter materials such as plant remains float to the surface while the soil drops to the bottom of the container. Improvements to this basic methodology include adding oil to hold tiny particles on the surface and bubbling air from below the water to create a froth, which holds and separates lighter organic material. Water is

Figure 2.15 *Flotation bins used for separating ecofacts from soil samples*

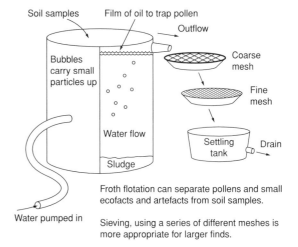

Froth flotation can separate pollens and small ecofacts and artefacts from soil samples.

Sieving, using a series of different meshes is more appropriate for larger finds.

Figure 2.16 *How a flotation bin works*

drained from the top through a sequence of increasingly finely meshed sieves.

Metal detection

On some excavations, and directly under the control of the director, it is appropriate to use metal detectors. They can be employed as part of the initial survey as a piece of geophysical equipment but they can also be used to check the spoil dump for finds. This would be applicable if the site had been stripped by machine rather than by hand or if soil removal had been by pick and shovel without subsequent sieving. Any such finds would be classed as unstratified. Metal detectors can also be used to alert diggers to potentially fragile metal objects in areas they are trowelling.

In whatever way the finds are identified and collected it is vital that the methods used allow their full potential to be exploited in post-excavation analysis and dating procedures. Individual directors of excavations have to make valid decisions about the processes they adopt in order to balance the needs of the dig to make sufficient progress with the demands of post-excavation studies.

WHAT RECORDS DO ARCHAEOLOGISTS CREATE?

Different directors will approach the task of recording, as they will the excavation itself, from slightly different standpoints. But certain common themes will feature: context sheets, plans, sections, photographs, artefact collection systems and, increasingly, the use of on-site computer technology. They also make use of a range of surveying equipment to plot the exact

Figure 2.17 *A metal detector being used to alert diggers to possible metal finds*

Figure 2.18 (right) *Close-up of a total station that combines the functions of many surveying tools in one piece of equipment*

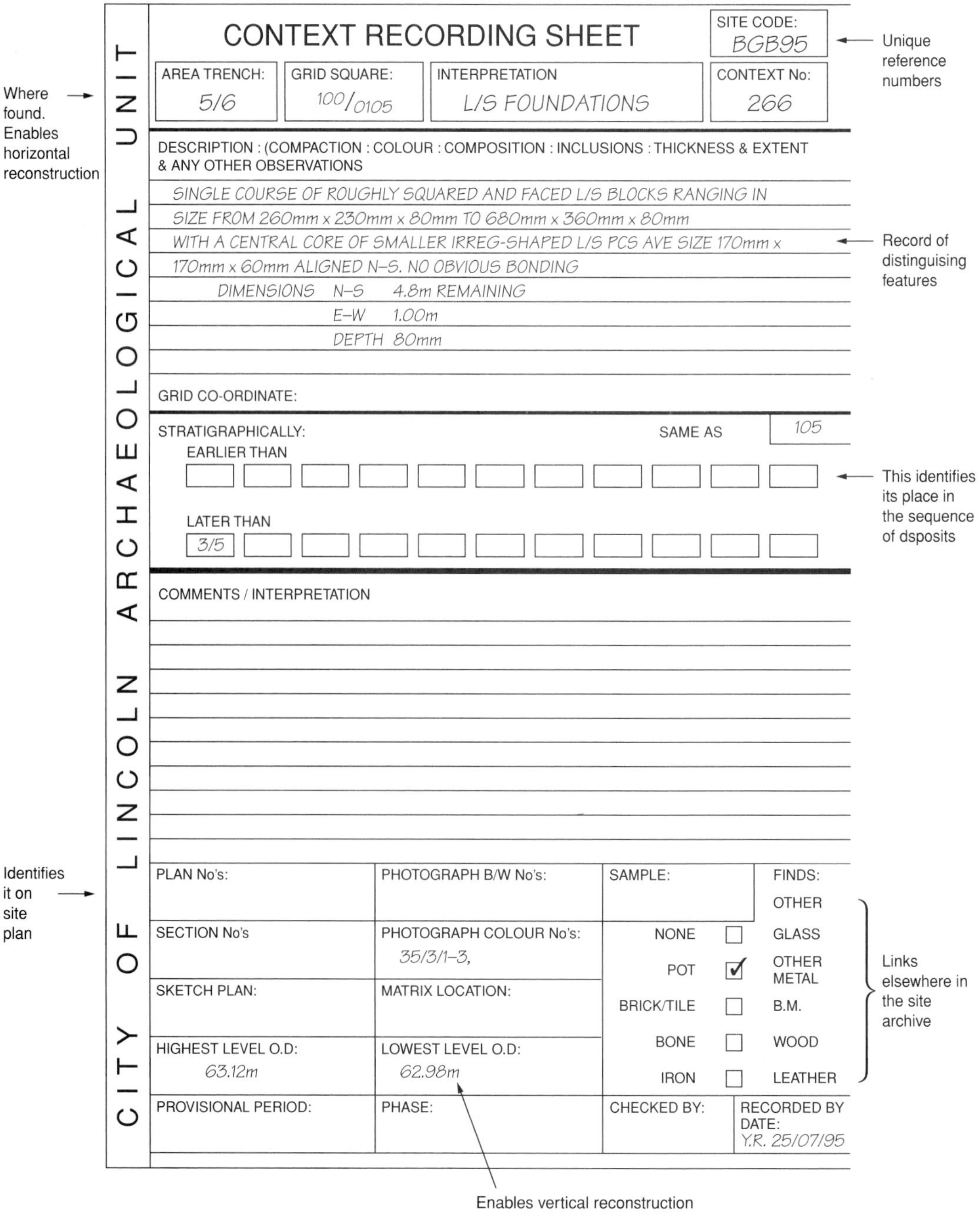

Where found. Enables horizontal reconstruction →

Identifies it on site plan →

Unique reference numbers ←

Record of distinguising features ←

This identifies its place in the sequence of dsposits ←

Links elsewhere in the site archive

CITY OF LINCOLN ARCHAEOLOGICAL UNIT

CONTEXT RECORDING SHEET

SITE CODE:
BGB95

AREA TRENCH:	GRID SQUARE:	INTERPRETATION	CONTEXT No:
5/6	100/0105	L/S FOUNDATIONS	266

DESCRIPTION : (COMPACTION : COLOUR : COMPOSITION : INCLUSIONS : THICKNESS & EXTENT & ANY OTHER OBSERVATIONS

SINGLE COURSE OF ROUGHLY SQUARED AND FACED L/S BLOCKS RANGING IN
SIZE FROM 260mm x 230mm x 80mm TO 680mm x 360mm x 80mm
WITH A CENTRAL CORE OF SMALLER IRREG-SHAPED L/S PCS AVE SIZE 170mm x
170mm x 60mm ALIGNED N–S. NO OBVIOUS BONDING
    DIMENSIONS   N–S   4.8m REMAINING
                      E–W   1.00m
                DEPTH 80mm

GRID CO-ORDINATE:

STRATIGRAPHICALLY: SAME AS   105
EARLIER THAN

LATER THAN
3/5

COMMENTS / INTERPRETATION

PLAN No's:	PHOTOGRAPH B/W No's:	SAMPLE:	FINDS:
			OTHER
SECTION No's	PHOTOGRAPH COLOUR No's: 35/3/1–3,	NONE ☐ POT ☑	GLASS / OTHER METAL
SKETCH PLAN:	MATRIX LOCATION:	BRICK/TILE ☐	B.M.
		BONE ☐	WOOD
HIGHEST LEVEL O.D: 63.12m	LOWEST LEVEL O.D: 62.98m	IRON ☐	LEATHER
PROVISIONAL PERIOD:	PHASE:	CHECKED BY:	RECORDED BY DATE: Y.R. 25/07/95

Enables vertical reconstruction

Figure 2.19 *How to interpret a context sheet*

positions of finds and features. Alidades, plane tables and theodolites are still in use alongside Electronic Distance Measures (EDMs) but increasingly **total stations** are superseding them.

Context sheets

These provide detailed records of layers and other elements of the stratigraphy of the site.

They will be used in post-excavation analysis to reconstruct the phases of use of the site and its features.

Plans

Detailed plans are used to show the location and spread of features, artefacts and structures. Large-scale plans are used to illustrate

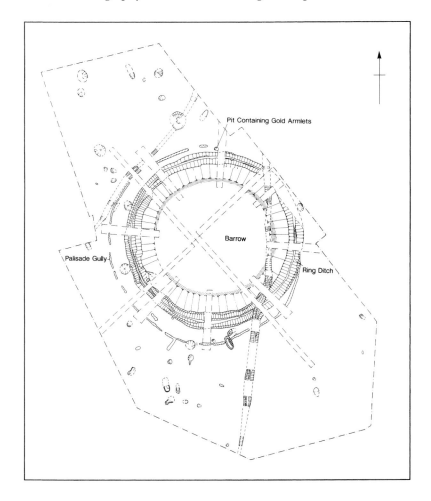

Figure 2.20 Plan of an excavated round barrow at Lockington using the quadrant method of mound removal. Circular features such as the surrounding ring ditch and palisade gully are revealed in each quadrant. Eight narrow baulks are left for extra sections. A pit containing gold armlets was located on the edge of the barrow. Although clearly important, no relationship could be established by the processes of excavation to link this pit and its contents to the barrow and the cremation burial below it

Figure 2.21 *Using a total station to rapidly plot the position of finds. At Spitalfields, so many skeletons were discovered that digital means of recording their position were used*

individual features. For example, an excavation of an Anglo-Saxon cemetery requires an overall plan to show the relationships between graves and associated features. A detailed plan drawing will be required of each individual grave to show the position of skeletal remains and the location of grave goods. The position of some of the artefacts may be better explained by a close-up drawing featuring, perhaps, the chest area of the burial.

http://www.gla.ac.uk/archaeology/staff/

All these drawings relate to the fixed recording grid on the site. Their position is plotted using surveying equipment and their dimensions carefully scaled onto paper. This usually involves placing a gridframe over the feature to assist the production of accurately measured drawings. Considerable effort after the excavation often goes into producing cleaned up versions of these plans for publication. Often finds and features will be plotted on a series of overlays related to soil and topography. Increasingly, plans are plotted onto computers because of the flexibility in presenting data they allow. GIS is revolutionising this process. Its 3D database enables the production of any section or plan and the testing of complex models.

Figure 2.22 *Planning using both old and new technologies. The traditional grid frame has been placed over the feature to assist drawing but context information is entered onto computer in the field*

Section drawings

The sides of excavation trenches, strategically placed baulks or cuts through the fill of features such as ditches, pits or postholes offer vertical slices through the constituent layers of an archaeological site.

Although methods of recording the horizontal spread and depth of each deposit have improved over recent decades it still remains true that an accurate scaled depiction of the vertical relationship of layers is commonly used to demonstrate the development of a site or

Figure 2.23 *A section across an Iron Age ditch on Twyford Down. Each layer of soil has been identified and labelled for recording by drawing. These layers are not immediately obvious in a photograph*

feature. For example, the relationship of a 'post pipe' – the evidence for the location of the post itself – within a posthole and to any packing material is best related in drawn form. As with plans, a key advantage of section drawings is that they can highlight subtle differences in the colour, texture or composition of layers. These are difficult to pick up with photographs. Before drawing it is essential that the face of the section is cleaned up and in some instances sprayed with water to improve contrast. Munsell colour charts are sometimes used to enable specific and standardised descriptions.

Where a section results from a continuous period of excavation it may be some time before it is ready for recording. Archaeologists note the presence of layers as the dig proceeds by pinning labels to the side of the excavation with context numbers to ensure that when the section is drawn it is still possible to recognise the finer points of the stratification. Such labels are frequently seen on site photographs.

Once completed, drawings are usually accompanied by an interpretation offered in textual or schematic form such as the Harris Matrix (▶see p. 40). It must be stressed that drawings are always interpretations and the quality of on-site drawings does vary according to the skill of the recorder and the conditions they are working under. Back-up photographs can provide an additional record.

Photographs

The camera is a key aid to recording although many archaeologists observe that it is less comprehensive in the detail it can show than the drawn record. Although rulers or ranging rods are usually seen in photographs to give an idea of scale, distances are distorted and film cannot be used to provide precise

Figure 2.24 *A quartered round barrow seen in profile. The picture also shows the familiar wheelbarrow runs used to remove spoil from the excavation itself*

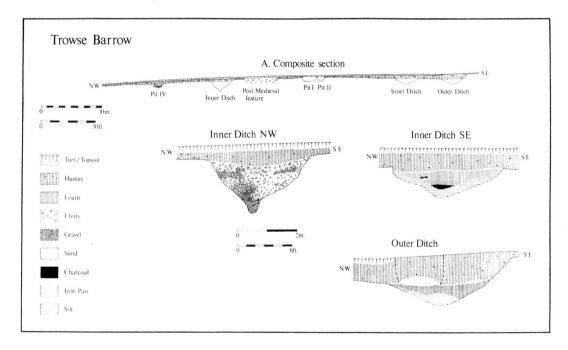

Figure 2.25 *A section drawing of Trowse Round Barrow. This barrow has two incomplete ditches surrounding it. The main composite cross-section shows the inner ditch twice, the outer ditch once and several other features. The inner and outer ditch sections are enlarged to give greater detail. A key is provided to demonstrate the soil types present. Reproduced with the permission of the copyright holder Norfolk Archaeology & Environment Division*

measurements. The camera clearly offers the chance of accurate views of features and sections whereas the draughtsperson can accentuate elements that the camera might obscure, for example similar coloured soils which have different textures. The camera also provides back up in case the drawings are poor. The two methods complement each other and both are normally used.

The essence of site photography lies in ensuring that the parts to be captured on film are clean, edges of individual structures or bones are well established, a scale is in shot, and careful spraying is used to accentuate coloration changes and contrasts. It may be appropriate to have some site/feature reference codes included in the photograph. The use of photographic towers or other means to get a camera above the excavation is common. Vertical photographs with scales can be used as an aid in the creation of plans.

Developments in digital photography are being incorporated into archaeological recording systems. Many archaeologists continue to use black and white prints for contrast while colour slides help form the basis of lectures. Increasingly, directors employ video as a support to the site diary, thus capturing details of features and colours. Digital cameras and videos enable the excavation experience to be shared online.

 http://www.brad.ac.uk/acad/archsci/ field_proj/scat/

 http://www.woodnet.org.uk/woodlandweb/ enjoy/excavat.htm

SPECIAL CASES

Most of the points in this chapter apply to all sites but there are other issues that apply to particular types of sites.

Recording standing buildings

Although the usual rules of stratigraphy may not entirely apply, one of the objectives of recording is to enable the developmental sequence of the building to be traced. Details of the fabric and construction of the building, alterations and dating evidence are gathered through drawing and photography. Buildings are often drawn stone by stone using grids as the completed drawing can often reveal patterns not obvious to the naked eye. This can be supplemented by photogrammetry. EDMs have made the task of measuring buildings much swifter while computer-aided design (CAD) enables 3D presentations of the results.

Archaeology of standing buildings

In 'traditional' archaeology interpretation of excavated evidence relies on the basic principle that the deeper the deposit, the earlier it is – the basis of relative dating by stratigraphy. Although standing buildings require a different approach to their study, the basic principles remain the same. Where a feature has been inserted into an existing one (for example a window or door inserted into a standing wall) it follows that the inserted feature is later than that into which it was inserted. Similarly, later walls may be of different construction to the original or may be butt-jointed (simply butted up against earlier walls rather than properly bonded). All of these clues help archaeologists to build up a sequence of development in the same way as on an excavation. Recording standing buildings may involve reconnaissance

▣ **Figure 2.26**
Medieval Hall in Stroud: a standing building which was properly recorded prior to redevelopment

▣ **Figure 2.27**
Plan of the ground floor at Medieval Hall, Stroud. The archaeologists have identified features of the building by date to enable the sequence of construction and alteration to be interpreted

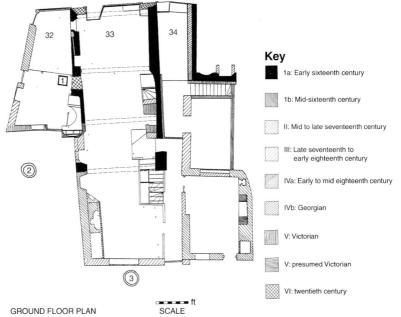

32–34 HIGH STREET, STROUD

Key

▣ 1a: Early sixteenth century

▣ 1b: Mid-sixteenth century

▣ II: Mid to late seventeenth century

▣ III: Late seventeenth to early eighteenth century

▣ IVa: Early to mid eighteenth century

▣ IVb: Georgian

▣ V: Victorian

▣ V: presumed Victorian

▣ VI: twentieth century

GROUND FLOOR PLAN   SCALE ft

techniques (▶see p. 10), dismantling, excavation or a combination of these approaches. The amount of information which may be recovered from a building will depend on many factors. Cosmetic renovation of a structure may give only a few clues (for example glimpses beneath floor boards or behind small areas of plaster) whereas a building undergoing substantial alterations or even demolition will be far more exposed to study. The aim should be to identify the earliest structural remains on the site and then, having plotted them, begin to add in later stages of development. Additions or changes to a building are never random: they will always serve a clear purpose which archaeologists try to detect, for example the extending of a room or rebuilding of a façade.

The recording of standing buildings should be every bit as rigorous as the recording of an excavation. Alongside drawings and written descriptions a full photographic record should be maintained, indicating scale and the exact point on a master plan from which the view was taken, along with any other relevant information. Sampling should include examples of different mortars and plasters. Substantial timbers may be sampled for **dendrochronology**.

Wetland archaeology

Waterlogged sites are where the natural water table has maintained a wet or damp environment since the deposition of the evidence. They have been a major factor in adding to our knowledge of past cultures. **Anaerobic** conditions, which prevent or impede normal bacterial and chemical decay processes, can result in widespread survival of organic material such as wood, leather and textiles which would normally perish. Strategies

for excavation, conservation and post-excavation analysis on wetland sites need to take into account the time and cost of dealing with additional evidence as well as the particular problems associated with waterlogged sites. In particular there are often large quantities of environmental material, especially plant remains. While the complete removal of all material for close examination is not usually a viable proposition much emphasis is put on the selection of large numbers of samples of site deposits for laboratory analysis. Once out of water, organic material will be stored in tanks of water prior to conservation

Figure 2.28 *Salvage excavation at a wetland site. Three Iron Age boats were unexpectedly uncovered at Holme Pierrepoint. The archaeologists had to rapidly excavate them before decay or mechanical diggers destroyed them*

by, for example, treatment with polyethyl-eneglycol (PEG) or freeze-drying to prevent rapid decay.

The consequence is that while the information from 'wet' sites is considered a real bonus in archaeological study, the costs of obtaining it considerably outstrip those of excavating 'dry' sites.

Unlike 'dry' sites where you can walk carefully across the site, pressure on wetland deposits can cause considerable damage. Excavators at Flag Fen erected a series of platforms on scaffolding to allow diggers to lie above the features they were excavating. Such restriction to movement makes digging, cleaning, planning and photography all the more difficult.

 http://www.crannog.co.uk/

Underwater archaeology

Although underwater sites follow the same basic rules as dry sites – the need for survey, careful excavation and recording – being below water presents additional challenges. The excavators usually require watertight diving suits, air tanks and weights. In extreme depths remotely controlled vehicles may be used. In addition to underwater hazards, cold temper-atures may make it difficult to remain stationary for long periods while poor visibility may require excavation using touch rather than sight!

To inform excavation strategy a form of sampling is often employed to gain a feel for the site. One example of this is the Tudor warship the *Mary Rose* whose position and condition was examined and investigated for several years before a full enough

understanding was derived to lead to full excavation. Where little or no wooden remains are present and finds are in a dispersed state, plans are drawn and trial trenches excavated to determine the extent of the deposits.

 http://www.arch.sotonriac.uk/Research/justin/saxon%20fisheries.html

 http://www.abc.se/~m10354/uwa/

 http://www.maryrose.org/

 http://www.culture.fr/culture/archeosm/en/archeosm.htm

Removal of spoil can employ a combination of hand movement and water dispersal but special tools are usually required. A water lance can shred sediment while a range of water vacuum cleaners can help excavate spoil and keep a site clear of sediment for recording. Objects may have suffered corrosion and created concretions that need to be broken apart. Decisions have to be made as to whether to use hammer and chisel below water or to bring the whole mass to the surface. Ordinary finds are placed in open containers, fragile finds in sealed ones and larger objects lifted by the use of inflated air bags. As with waterlogged sites, organic material is susceptible to damage if it is allowed, even briefly, to dry out during excavation. Once such material is removed from the water it must be quickly put into appropriate storage.

Plastic 2 × 2 or 4 × 4 metre recording grids are set out and the usual land-based methods of planning, context sheets and photography employed where possible. Synthetic paper enables ordinary pens to be used underwater. Photography is likely to be limited to close-up shots or carefully rigged photogrammetry rather

Key

1 Pipe sucking sediment and spoil away
2 Laminated recording sheets
3 Suspended polythene tube grids
4 Finds box
5 Ranging pole
6 Water lance and tube
7 Section (close-up below)
8 Organic materials

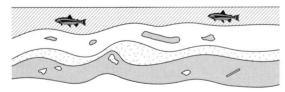

Figure 2.29 *Diagram illustrating some of the equipment used in underwater archaeology (after Thomasen in Andersen 1985)*

than general views. One advantage of underwater excavation is that the archaeologist can cross the site without treading on a trowelled surface!

Urban archaeology

While it is clear that there is a great variety in the nature of archaeological sites in rural areas, archaeologists working on urban sites face very different challenges.

In urban areas open ground is at a premium and so it is usually the clearance of a site for development that provides archaeological opportunities. The area involved is often tightly constrained by other buildings and therefore only parts of buried sites are available for study. These do not necessarily correspond to areas which archaeologists would choose if they were making the site selection on academic grounds, a good example of rescue archaeology being dictated by developer activity. Such excavations are like keyholes into the past because a full view cannot be obtained. The depth of stratification is usually much greater than on rural sites because of frequent reuse of the same site over time. It is particularly difficult to forecast the range of features, that will be encountered and the time it will take to excavate them all properly. Deep excavation also presents additional safety hazards.

Survey methods applicable to rural sites such as aerial photography and many of the geophysical procedures are ineffectual or inappropriate in preparatory work. Indeed, at a large excavation in London at Number 1, Poultry in the 1990s the evaluation consisted of a desktop survey and four shafts between 3 m and 5 m deep to reach the top of the

 KEY TASK

Comparative study of survey and excavation methods

Take either an excavation report or an article from *Current Archaeology*, *British Archaeology* or *Rescue News*. Make notes under the following headings:

- Name of site
- Reason for excavation
- Was this a research, rescue or salvage excavation?
- Source of funding
- Prior knowledge of site and survey methods employed prior to excavation
- Style and strategy of excavation
- Key finds
- Post-excavation scientific activity
- Dating methods employed

If a group of students follow this information gathering process, valuable comparative data will emerge to inform discussion on a series of key issues relating to current practice in archaeology.

Figure 2.30 *The excavation of human remains increasingly raises ethical questions for archaeologists. What ethical issues do you think are raised by the excavation and disposal of human remains from sites such as Spitalfields?*

natural geology. These gave indications of the sequences and structures which might be encountered. The excavation also produced 'wet' archaeology including about 1,500 datable (by dendrochronology) Roman timbers. This extensive urban excavation (the on-site budget exceeded £2m) continued for twelve months under the construction of the new building. Normally archaeologists have to complete their work before the building contractors arrive on site.

KEY SKILL

Tackling structured, source-based questions

These questions are found at GCSE, AS and some A Level papers. You may also have to analyse sites in a similar way at university. At GCSE you will have one source per set of questions, at AS and beyond you will usually have several sources to work with at the same time. These will be drawn from archaeological plans, sections, illustrations, tables, maps, photographs and reports. Four common areas are outlined below. Two essential pieces of equipment which you can take into the exam are a ruler and a magnifying glass. Be sure to use them.

Interpreting plans

Begin with an accurate description of the relevant sites, features and artefacts in order to build up a picture of overall function or changes. You should consider:

- size
- orientation
- spatial distribution of features
- phases of use: discuss any stratigraphic evidence for different periods of activity
- assess individual features to identify site function
- boundaries: are they defensive or just a demarcation line – a physical or a spiritual barrier or both?

When you discuss these, refer to context numbers where they are given.

Interpreting aerial photographs

Read all the questions concerned with these first. They will probably ask about method as well as interpretation and you need to match the right response to a question. For interpretation start by describing what you can see. Is it a cropmark, soil mark or shadows? What size and shape is it? Is it a boundary, structure or some other type of feature. How is it aligned? Only when you have done this, suggest specific site or period. This way you will get some marks even where you get it wrong. Questions about the method will usually require an account of why features are visible and can be recorded and why they do not show up in all areas (▶see pp. 20–3).

Appraising methods

You need to understand the basic techniques for each type of material you are likely to be tested on, for example stone, pottery, metal, and what it can tell us. Ensure you know the main principles and some of their strengths and limitations. In the case of dating and reconnaissance methods it is sensible to test yourself on their application to different types of material and sites. In all cases, one good example is useful.

KEY SKILL *cont.*

Interpreting organic remains

Questions are usually about what could be learned in a general sense from the remains. To do this you need to be familiar with common ways of presenting such data and what terms such as **MNI** mean. Before you attempt this always consider the size of the sample. Are there sufficient examples to say much at all? Also comment on their survival: why have they survived and in what ways may they have been transformed by **taphonomic** forces (▶see p. 97)?

Current Archaeology 143 and 158

http://www.museumoflondon.org.uk/ MOLsite/forum/spital0.html

http://www.molas.org.uk/

AFTER EXCAVATION

Once the digging is completed attention switches to the laboratories and the processing of finds and site records. This is dealt with in Chapters 3 and 4. The eventual outcome of the excavation used to be a full excavation report with text on the features and structures, catalogues and drawings of finds and specialists' reports. Today the emphasis is on producing a quality 'archive' which can then be adapted as appropriate into reports, more popular publications or to provide research opportunities. Increasingly records are stored digitally which offers tremendous potential for disseminating data to different audiences in different ways.

KEY TASK

Test your understanding of methods

Examine the diagrams from an excavated site at Gamston. Figure 2.31 contrasts what was seen in aerial photographs and after excavation.

1a Why would this site have shown up from the air?   *2 mks*

1b Why is there a difference between what can be seen in the two diagrams?   *6 mks*

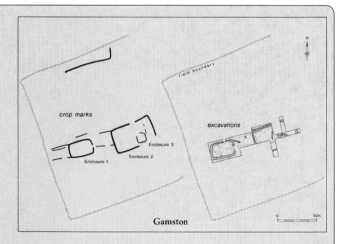

Figure 2.31 *Gamston drawing 1. Gamston was an Iron Age settlement and field system in the Trent Valley*

KEY TASK *cont.*

Test your understanding of methods

Now examine Figure 2.32

1c What information did the archaeologists need to have in order to construct these diagrams? *8 mks*

Suggested markscheme on ▶ p. 305.

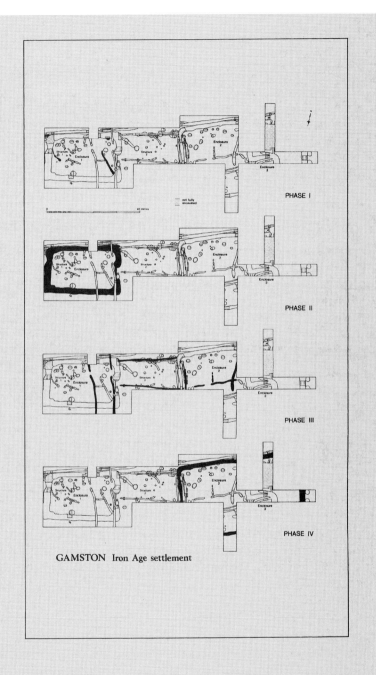

GAMSTON Iron Age settlement

Figure 2.32 *Gamston drawing 2*

Post-excavation Analysis

Analytical techniques are often the parts of archaeology courses which most students find difficult. The bulleted points above are sufficient for AS/A Level and some first year undergraduate courses and do not require detailed scientific knowledge. Most degree-level courses will at some point require a greater depth of understanding of scientific techniques and most will involve practical work. Although this will be taught, and there are many excellent texts and ILT packages available, some scientific knowledge is needed. The first half of this chapter explains general approaches and some widely used specific methods. The second half of the chapter considers issues related to particular types of material with examples selected to illustrate what analysis can achieve.

Further examples can be found in Part II of this book.

Analysis of finds and environmental data is part of the process of compiling an excavation or fieldwork archive. It takes place indoors, often in laboratories, and can involve a huge range of specialists including zoologists, palynologists (pollen) and geologists. It is the longest part of the excavation process, involving the most people, and is often the most expensive. Consequently it will usually have been planned long in advance. At the end of the process the physical remains that have been studied are put into storage and the archaeological record becomes a collection of written, graphical and electronic data and

Figure 3.1 *More time is spent on post-excavation work than digging. Much archaeological work is therefore desk based and occurs indoors. This desk is set up for identification and recording of samples*

reports. It will then need interpretation (▶see Chapter 5). The same principle of identification and classification is used with finds retrieved in other ways such as stray finds brought to museums.

Materials are treated differently according to their properties. Robust artefacts such as flint tools or pottery are cleaned in water unless analysis of residues or wear is to be undertaken. Fragile bones, metals artefacts and wood are handled with delicacy and may require conservation work before analysis can begin. For example, bone may require treatment with polyvinyl acetate (PVA) to stop it crumbling while organic samples may require mild fungicides to halt decay. The conditions they are kept in will also vary depending on their original context.

ARCHAEOMETRY

Recent scientific advances have had a major impact on archaeology with those in dating and reconnaissance being the best known. However, just as inventions such as sonar and GPS were developed for military rather than archaeological purposes, an impressive range of analytical techniques have also been adopted by archaeologists. The growth of **archaeometry**,

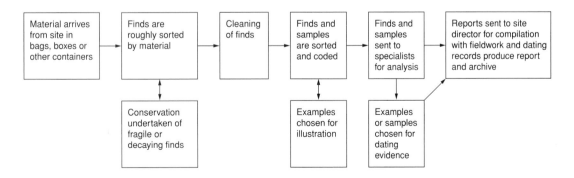

Figure 3.2 *Simplified diagram of the post excavation process*

the scientific analysis of archaeological materials, has led to the creation of a whole range of new archaeological specialisms as well as degree courses which focus on the application of science to archaeology.

Scientific analysis offers many insights into ancient objects and ecofacts including:

1   Identification of finds or specimens
2   Determining numbers of finds or specimens from particular categories
3   Identifying how materials were produced and used
4   Identifying sources of artefacts and raw materials
5   Providing data on the local environment

Scientific techniques can analyse and present data rapidly but are often very expensive. This means that scientific analysis is usually only conducted with clear questions in mind that help address the overall research questions. It also means that only selected materials are analysed.

Is archaeology a science?

The adoption of scientific techniques and the overlap between archaeology and biology in the study of human origins led some archaeologists to claim that archaeology was now a science. This would have advantages for university departments since science enjoys higher status and better funding than the humanities. However, the use of scientific techniques in itself doesn't make a subject a science. To be accepted as a science archaeology would have to demonstrate that it is following the principles of empirical methods with a view to establishing 'laws', or 'middle range theory' as it is often called. Although many research archaeologists have adopted the scientific model of generating a hypothesis and then testing, it is difficult for archaeologists to form law-like generalisations from their findings. While the relationships explored by scientists in laboratory experiments can be repeatedly tested under controlled conditions, archaeologists investigate unique events from the past and deal with material which, once removed from its context, can never be re-excavated.

Figure 3.3
Sorting pottery types according to attributes

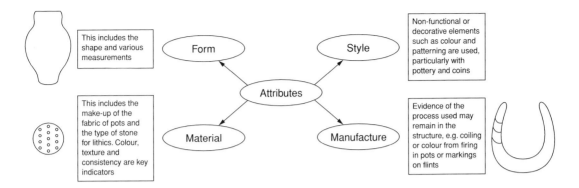

Figure 3.4 *Examples of attributes which could be used to sort material*

VISUAL EXAMINATION

The first analytical stage for most materials involves categorisation and enumeration (counting). Artefacts are sorted into types while environmental samples, once removed from soil, are identified by species. Each category can then be counted in order to say something about relative amounts in the archive and to identify on-site distribution of materials. For some materials this can be done by eye but microscopes will also be used, especially for plant and invertebrate remains (▶see p. 76). Specialists use their knowledge to categorise finds but they will also have a set of reference samples or illustrations to aid identification. These are sometimes called parallels.

Artefacts will be sorted according to physical characteristics or **attributes** into categories by material and typology. There is no right way to do this, but the end result will be classification to enable description and enumeration.

Figure 3.5 Some pottery can be identified both by its material and its decoration. This is an example of Roman Samian ware. Diagnostic sherds such as this are used by specialists to identify and catalogue future finds. Most museums will have a type series for their area

Experts will often use the feel of artefacts to assist them. Characteristics such as grittiness or greasiness are best determined by touch. Some materials, particularly metals will require further tests. Microscope examination by experts of marks on some materials can also provide clues to their use.

SCIENTIFIC ANALYSIS OF ARTEFACTS

Increasingly artefacts are investigated scientifically to determine their composition, structure and manufacturing history. The type of analysis selected in any particular case will depend on a range of factors including cost, the importance of the individual artefact and the questions the archaeologists are asking. For example, **petrology** is relatively cheap, but it is also destructive. **X-ray fluorescence** provides an alternative, which doesn't cause damage, but it can only analyse the surface of objects. An excellent range of links for scientific methods is at the University of Bradford website.

 http://www.brad.ac.uk/acad/archsci/

Characterisation studies

Scientific examination of analysis of artefacts and building material can reveal their chemical make-up. This is valuable because while stone or metal of the same type is largely composed of the same elements, their exact chemical composition varies. Each stone or metal ore was produced in a specific location under particular geological conditions. These unique circumstances mean that they contain slightly different combinations and quantities of 'impurities'. Copper, for example, may contain minute amounts of arsenic, silver and lead. These '**trace elements**' occur as a few parts per million and may have negligible effects on the material, but they provide it with a distinctive 'chemical fingerprint'. Where the geological sources of metal, clay or stone have been mapped, archaeologists may be able to identify the location from which the materials were quarried.

Petrology

This is a geological technique for locating the source of minerals. A **thin section** of a stone or ceramic artefact is cut, ground and polished till it is about 0.02 mm thick. It is then examined by microscope. The crystals of each mineral have a distinctive colour and structure. The particular combinations of key minerals enable the original source to be established with reference to geological maps. Thin sections of pottery can also be studied to provide information about manufacturing techniques.

Petrology has contributed greatly to our understanding of exchange, particularly in prehistory. The sources for the early medieval period trade in Lava quernstones throughout north-west Europe have been traced back to quarries in the Eiffel Mountains of Germany. The technique can be used for building materials including stsone and, in some cases, brick. It has been used extensively in Egypt to identify the quarries used to build the temples at Karnak and the pyramid complex at Giza. Distribution patterns based on extensive studies such as these have helped us understand the complexity of ancient trade routes, transport systems and economic organisation.

Petrology does not work in all cases. Thin sections of **obsidian** and flint look remarkably similar regardless of where they originated. Similarly, ceramics, which lack distinctive mineral tempers, require other techniques in order to source them.

Spectrometry

Spectrometry covers a range of methods that derive from physics and involve using radiation (for example X-rays) to force a small sample of material to produce light (another form of radiation) which can be measured through spectrographic analysis. In the way that sunlight can be split in a rainbow, the light emitted by different elements shows a characteristic pattern when split by a prism into its spectrum. This is projected onto a viewing screen or photographic plate, where its information can be recorded. In a compound of elements, the balance of elements is shown by the intensity of the lines in the spectrum. This is compared with control spectrums of known composition produced under the same conditions. Trace elements of a few parts per million can be recorded in this way. Spectrometry is a very accurate method for quantitative analysis and only requires small samples (less than 10 milligrams) to be taken. This makes it suitable for valuable archaeological material. It is widely employed for metal analysis but is also used for glass, faience, pottery, obsidian and occasionally flint.

X-ray fluorescence

This technique is one of the cheaper and quickest methods of analysing the surface composition of materials, particularly metals. It is also non-destructive. A beam of X-rays forces the material to re-emit X-rays. The intensity of energy given off can be measured to indicate the chemicals present and their relative abundance. Since the method does not penetrate deeply it is of little use where materials have a coating of another mineral. A more advanced method uses protons to penetrate more deeply but it is also more expensive.

Neutron activation analysis (NAA)

This is the most accurate and reliable **characterisation** technique. Tiny samples are ground down and then bombarded with neutrons in a reactor. Elements in the sample become unstable isotopes and give off distinctive patterns of radiation, which can be measured. The technique is so sensitive that elements present in a few parts per billion can be detected. The technique has been used in studies of similar ceramics in Iron Age Central Europe to establish that technology and designs were exchanged over wide areas rather than pottery. It is useful for a wide range of materials and is particularly appropriate for coins. Unfortunately it is expensive. The analysis of a single sample costs about £100.

Chemical analysis

The use of chemistry to identify elements such as phosphate in topsoil has already been mentioned. In addition, chemistry can be used for characterisation studies of stone and metal and identifying organic residues surviving in ceramics.

Isotopic analysis

Isotopes are elements with an abnormal number of electrons. Copper, lead, oxygen and carbon all have several different isotopes. By determining what isotopes are present, and in what proportions, materials can be linked to known sources with the same ratios. It was used to analyse metal artefacts from early Bronze Age Crete. These had distinctive Cretan styles but the ores of the metals are not found on Crete. Ratios for lead isotopes in the bronze and silver enabled the material to be linked to sources on the mainland. This showed that raw materials rather than finished objects were being traded. Trade in copper and marble around the Mediterranean has also been traced using isotopic analysis. In the case of marble, petrology had not been able to differentiate the stone.

Organic residue analysis

Solvents and in some cases reagents can be used to dissolve and extract chemical traces of organic materials from sherds of pottery. The resulting solution can be tested for sugars, lipids (fats) and other chemicals. The results can be matched to 'fingerprints' known from commodities such as honey, olive oil and plant resins. A team from Bradford University is currently using this technique to study the bulk import of liquids into Bronze Age Egypt through analysis of amphorae sherds. Unfortunately the process is too expensive to be widely used. Some sites produce thousands of sherds while the analysis of a single sample would cost around £10.

ANALYSIS OF PARTICULAR INORGANIC MATERIALS

Ceramic analysis

Pottery is very important to archaeology from the Neolithic onwards because it survives well in almost any environment. It provides dating evidence and can be used make inferences about exchange, economy and society. To categorise sherds, colour is described by reference to the Munsell Soil Colour Charts. There are similar charts for hardness and the grain size of **inclusions** in the **temper**. Such analysis may require the use of polarising microscopes. Manufacturing by hand, coil or wheel methods can usually be determined visually, as can form. The key indicators here are sherds from the rim, neck and base of vessels. Where possible pots are reassembled by specialists for recording. Refiring experiments

will show how the original baking was carried out.

The fabric colour and hardness provide clues to firing temperatures. Clay often contains iron, which forms a red oxide if it is heated in an oxygen rich environment or a black/grey oxide if it is oxygen poor. The colour of the molecules of clay indicates which was the case. If the clay is vitrified (where minerals have melted and fused together) it indicates that firing occurred in a kiln at temperatures in excess of 1100°C. Slips and glazes provide additional clues to origins and period.

The standard way to illustrate ceramics is to draw the whole artefact in outline but with a quarter cut away. This enables a cross-section of the vessel walls to be shown. Illustration of decoration may be limited to the particular sherds recovered.

In quantifying pottery finds there is debate amongst archaeologists over whether the number or weight of sherds is more useful. For instance there are rarely enough diagnostic sherds (for example rims) to clearly identify the number of original pots. A large urn may break into several large but heavy pieces while a small pot may shatter into many small light fragments. Depending on which measure is chosen the results can be widely different. Increasingly archaeologists measure both, but weight used in conjunction with average sherd weight can be used to reduce variability caused by different sizes of vessels.

Clay is almost entirely formed from eroded sedimentary rocks, but a tiny percentage of the material is made up of trace elements. Petrology and other characterisation techniques can be applied to pottery and bricks although 'fingerprinting' clay sources is much more

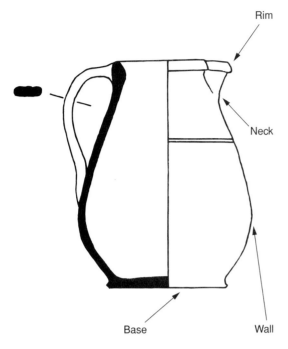

Rim

Neck

Base

Wall

Scale: 4:1

Figure 3.6 *Pottery and glass is conventionally drawn in a diagram of two halves. One half provides a cross section to show internal and external shape and dimensions, the other records the external appearance*

difficult and well developed than is the case with rocks. In many cases, experts on regional pottery will be able to suggest the origin of artefacts from the temper and inclusions in the pottery, which they identify from visual or microscopic examination.

The Ashmolean Museum website has an excellent guide to the value of pottery to archaeologists.

 http://www.ashmol.ox.ac.uk/PotWeb/

Lithic analysis

Lithics or stone tools are virtually indestructible. They have been used for all but the earliest stages of human development and for many sites and periods are the only definite sign of human activity. Examination of their surface can determine whether they were manufactured by fracturing, pecking or polishing the original stone. Reference to experimental or ethnographic examples

KEY TERM

Use wear analysis

For some artefacts, including stone tools, tiny scratches and traces are left from past activity. For example, half an hour cutting cereals will leave a polish on a flint blade. Expert analysis backed by examples from experimental archaeology (▶see p. 102) can sometimes identify the signatures of different activities. However, this may only reveal the *last* activity the tool was used for. The detection and description of wear marks can be greatly assisted by the use of a scanning electron microscope (**SEM**), which by sweeping a band of electrons over the surface of the tool being studied gives much improved depth of focus and higher magnification. This enhanced image can then be displayed on a screen. Recent work has involved the study of starch grains on stone blades in Polynesia and the analysis of blood residues on some of the equipment carried by Otzi the Ice Man. Similar ideas have been applied to the examination of cut marks on bones, for example in studies to determine whether early hominids were predators or scavengers.

(▶see Chapter 5) can help identify signs of techniques such as indirect percussion and pressure flaking. Artefacts can be sorted by type of stone, colour and **typology**. Specialists will use reference material for relative dating and suggestion of function. Manufacturing debris (**debitage**) is often recovered and sometimes can be refitted to show the sequence of manufacturing and even whether the knapper was sitting or standing, left- or right-handed. Petrology has been the most widely used means of characterisation for lithics although the other techniques are increasingly used.

Metallurgical analysis

Some metal artefacts require special treatment to remove corrosion. They may also need X-raying to see the shape of the artefact beneath a crust of oxidised material or to identify cracks or seams where several pieces of metal were joined to form complex artefacts. Metallurgists use microscopes to explore manufacturing techniques. **Metallography** includes examination of the size and shape of the grains of minerals in the material for traces of heating, working and alloying. Where they are available, SEMs are preferred. Their magnification at 1000x may be similar to the best optical microscopes but the depth of field they provide enables fine detail to be identified. This is particularly important when exploring the manufacturing techniques used in jewellery or weapons making. The manufacture of iron sword blades often involved hammering folded layers of metal. This process can be detected by examining a cross-section of the blade. Analysis of the carbon content may reveal enrichment due to roasting in charcoal in order to produce resilient weapons.

The first recorded use of metal is in the form of jewellery and ritual items. These were made from 'soft' metals (gold and copper) which would be worked by hammering. Only very simple objects could be made this way. Complex items required moulds into which molten metal could be poured. Stone, metal and clay moulds have survived together with by-products of manufacturing such as crucibles, slag and waste metal. Artefacts themselves provide evidence of casting errors, mould seams, cold working after casting and decorative techniques.

Metal objects were frequently ornamented by means of a range of engraving tools whose shapes may be identified when magnified. In the case of the Gundestrup Cauldron, Taylor was able to identify the number of punches used to decorate it suggesting the number of craftsmen involved. The style of decoration also enabled him to identify the region and ethnic identity of the makers.

Scientific American 266(3)

Taylor 1997

Greene 2000

Besides the characterisation techniques already discussed a number of other methods are used with metals. Measuring the specific gravity of artefacts and comparing with known examples often identified alloys of gold. A more precise technique is **atomic absorption spectrometry** (AAS). A small sample is dissolved in acid and then vaporised. When light of known wavelengths is passed through the gas, the amount that is absorbed indicates the minerals present. This technique has been used to trace the seventh-century debasement of coins in the Merovingian Empire. AAS is also widely used for bronze and copper. A limitation of this

KEY SKILL

Noting methods of analysis

The vast range of scientific methods used by archaeologists to analyse materials looks very daunting at first site. The key to starting to grasp them is to learn some of the more commonly used approaches and to understand them in simple terms before you tackle specialist texts. We have adopted this approach in the selection presented in this text. After reading this section, you should make some notes to clarify points in your own mind. There is little point in rewriting this chapter so a useful exercise would be to turn some key points into the table

Which analytical methods are appropriate for which material?

	Ceramics	Stone	Flint	Copper	Iron	Glass
Thin section						
Petrology						
Spectrometry						
Isotopic analysis						
Use wear analysis						
AAS						

Test yourself by copying this table and ticking approprate methods for each material. You can add to the list as you become familiar with a greater range of techniques.

technique is that where metal artefacts were made from several sources the 'fingerprint' is obscured. In the ancient world, valuable commodities such as bronze were often recycled with new artefacts made from scrap from a variety of sources.

The study of coins is a very specialised area. The analytical techniques already described provide information on the metals used. The degree of debasement in gold and silver coins can be used as an approximate form of dating although the images and inscriptions on the surface are usually more valuable. Coins have been used to explore topics as diverse as trade, territories and particular events.

ANALYSIS OF ORGANIC REMAINS

Soil

The chemistry of soil can provide clues to the type of vegetation and by extension, fauna and agriculture it could support. The early farmers in central Europe, for example, seemed to favour particular soil types for their farming settlements. Soil change can also record the impact of humans on the land. Sediments in valleys in Cyprus were used to explain the abandonment of Bronze Age sites. Deforestation or overgrazing had led to erosion of topsoil on the hillsides which had then been deposited in the valleys. Soil is also analysed for what it holds. Pollen, invertebrates and even microbes can be recovered to provide clues about environment and economy.

Faunal remains

Archaeozoology or zooarchaeology is the study of the remains of animals from archaeological contexts. Humans interact with animals in several ways including their use for human food or other resources and indirectly as the occupants of ecological niche alongside humans. Faunal (which for our purposes includes fish and birds as well as mammals) remains are vital to archaeologists in two ways: to reconstruct past environments (▶see p. 169) and to identify the contribution which animals made to the human economy (▶see p. 197).

(▶see p. 169)
(▶see p. 197)

Figure 3.7 *Animal bones after washing*

Bones survive best in arid or waterlogged conditions but alkaline soils, including well-drained sand or gravel, usually preserve some bones. Acidic soil can destroy all but burnt bone. Many sites turn up vast quantities of bone and in some cases archaeologists opt not to collect or record it. Where they do collect it, samples are often biased towards larger animals and larger bones. Bird and fish bones in particular are often omitted. This is partly through poor survival and partly because of recovery problems. Flotation can be used to recover them but large numbers of samples are needed for conclusions to be drawn.

The first element in analysis of bone **assemblages** once bones are identified is establishing how many animals of each species are present. Because it is rare for whole skeletons to be present, two calculations of numbers are made:

Number of identified specimens present – **NISP**

Minimum number of individuals – **MNI**

The raw data only shows the relative abundance of a particular species not how important it was to people and their economy. There is more meat on a cow than on a sheep, so while the MNI for sheep may be greater than for cows, they may contribute much less to the overall diet. Several additional measures have been developed to assess dietary contribution such as meat weight versus bone weight. A further complication arises when we consider the body elements that are present. Some animals may not have been slaughtered on-site and bones that are low in meat, such as the spine and feet, may have been discarded off-site. Careful examination of butchery marks can reveal the process by which animal bone reached the site of deposition.

Establishing the age and sex of the animals represented in a bone assemblage can help reconstruct the system of hunting or agriculture practised (▶see p. 198). For example, the sex ratio and age structure in herds of cattle kept for dairy products are different from those kept for meat. The sex of bones can be identified from anatomical features such as antlers (deer), large canines (pig) and penis bone (dog) in males and pelvic shape and structure in females. The dimensions of bones can also be used as males are larger in many species. The ratio between two or more measurements from one bone is used rather than a single measure (for example length) as that may be dependent on the age of the animal. Identification of changes in the skeleton, especially the fusion of bone elements, and patterns of eruption, growth and wear in teeth are used to age animals. Tooth eruption and antler shedding may establish the season of death of the animals. However, such analysis is not always reliable, as bones may not have been deposited at the time the animals were killed. Note that Star Carr was thought to be a winter site from antler evidence, but recent discoveries of stork and crane bones suggest it was used in summer.

Bones can be used to approximately date sites. For example, reindeer bones on a site might indicate a period during the last ice age. Smaller mammals such as voles, which evolve quickly, are often the most useful for this **faunal dating**. It is also possible to analyse bone collagen for dating and for environmental information from the minerals and amino acids it contains. Animals provide clues to the environment although we cannot always be certain that they occupied similar habitats to today's animals. Bones can also provide insights into human behaviour. The spread of species may be related to trade while analysis of damage to bones provides data on hunting, butchery and craft technology.

Human remains

Human remains can be divided into two major categories: hard and soft tissue. The evidence that these two types provide and the conditions in which they are preserved vary considerably.

Soft tissue

Like other organic remains, soft tissue is only usually recovered on sites with unusually good preservation. They are not likely to be a

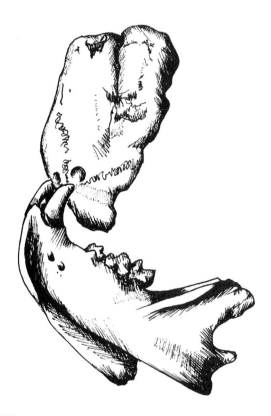

Figure 3.8 *Drawing of bone evidence from a cave site in South Africa. A leopard jaw was found whose teeth fitted exactly the marks on the skull of a young hominid. This was used to demonstrate that hominid remains in caves do not always mean that the hominid lived there*

representative sample of the wider population but are useful none the less.

Desiccated (dried) bodies such as Egyptian mummies often preserve facial features well, if a little distorted from the drying process, together with internal organs, nails and hair. Accurate sexing of the body can usually be done from the external sexual organs, or from facial hair. There are always exceptions. 'Mummy 1770', which had probably spent some time in the Nile as a result of an unfortunate encounter with a crocodile, could not be sexed at the time of mummification by the priests. He/she was therefore prepared for either eventuality in the afterlife by being given both a false penis made of a roll of bandage,

and gold nipples. In addition to providing details of clothing and **mortuary practices**, tissue samples can be rehydrated to give useful evidence about disease, for example the sand pneumoconiosis suffered by one of 'The Brothers' in Manchester Museum. Dry sites sometimes also provide copralites. Analysis of these can recover hair, bone, seed and parasites to reveal information about diet and health. Analysis of deposits from the latrines at Bearsden Roman Fort revealed little trace of cholesterol but lots of wheat bran, suggesting that the legionaries ate little meat. The Dungfile website provides all the links you might want.

http://www.ualberta.ca/~abeaudoi/stuff/ dung/human.htm

Frozen corpses like Otzi the Ice Man and the Pazyryk 'Ice Maiden' provide similar evidence to dry bodies except that stomach contents are often preserved as well. The general level of distortion and decay is often so low that these bodies can almost seem asleep not dead. The Peruvian Inca children are especially extraordinary in this respect. In one case the trauma that caused death – a blow to the head – could still be identified in a CAT scan. In another example the red-stained vomit from the symbolic 'achiote' dye that the child had been forced to ingest still marked his face and the front of his clothing. Without Otzi's preserved skin we would not have known about his tattoos, which may be the earliest evidence of medicinal acupuncture.

Figure 3.9 *A latrine at Housesteads fort. Analysis of soil at similar sites has provided valuable evidence about the diets of legionaries*

Bodies from anaerobic conditions such as the famous 'bog bodies' of northern Europe, including Lindow and Tollund Man, have been used to study diet, internal parasites and trauma. The acid nature of bogs can lead to the almost complete demineralisation of bone while tanning the skin to perfection.

 http://www.archaeology.org/online/
features/bog/index.html

 http://www.pbs.org/wgbh/nova/peru/

http://www.nationalgeographic.com/
mummy/index.html

http://www.gla.ac.uk/Acad/IBLS/DEEB/
jd/otzi.htm

http://www.bps.org/wgbh/nova/
icemummies/iceman.html

In some soil conditions, in East Anglia for example, where the soil is wet and acid, neither hard nor soft tissue survives well. The only surviving trace of the presence of a body may be a stain in the bottom of the grave that provides a silhouette of the original body. The 'sand man' in Mound 1 at Sutton Hoo may have been such a burial.

 http://www.suttonhoo.org/

Figure 3.10 *Drawing of a hominid skull from a very different species to our own. In this case, Homo erectus from around 1 million to 500,000 years ago*

Hard tissue

Bone is much more frequently recovered by archaeologists than soft tissue. Similar analysis to that used on faunal remains is carried out to determine the composition of assemblages of human remains.

Species. Many aspects of bone morphology are used to identify and classify the various species of early humans. For example Homo sapiens neanderthalensis is recognised by its long low skull, large nasal aperture and huge square teeth.

Sexing. The principal ways to establish sex from human bones are through examination of the pelvis. The space at the front of this bone is larger in women than men to allow for the passage of the baby's head during birth. Women are therefore said to possess a larger sub-pubic arch. In the blade of the pelvis, below the socket for the hipbone (femur), is the sciatic notch to which is applied a rough 'rule of thumb', in the words of the forensic anthropologist Rebecca Storey. 'You stick your thumb in and if it wiggles it's female and if it doesn't it's male!' The brow ridge is often larger and projects further in males than females but this is less reliable. Because of widespread variation amongst males and females no physical method is totally reliable and it is almost impossible to sex children. **DNA** testing is accurate, but is very expensive.

Ageing. As with animals, age is generally established by examination of bone fusion rates (epiphysial fusion) and tooth eruption. Bones fuse at different rates during an individual's life until full maturity in a person's twenties. Using wear on bones to estimate age for older individuals is notoriously unreliable. Theya Molleson made a comparative study on the collection from Spitalfields Crypt where the

Figure 3.11 *Hard tissue, such as the skull and torso of this skeleton emerging from its grave at Spitalfields, will always survive better than soft tissue*

actual ages were known from the coffin plates. In the case of Louisa Courtauld, the archaeological estimate of her age using bone was wrong by over twenty years. However, a newer technique of thin-sectioning teeth, which relies on measuring the amount of translucence in the root, provided a much closer estimate.

Health. Where a large sample of human bones is recovered one can *start* to gain some tentative insights into age structure and health of the population. Some diseases leave marks on bones. These include polio, tuberculosis and genetic disorders such as cleft palate, along with syphilis and various types of cancer. Early medical treatments such as trepanation (cutting or drilling a hole in the skull) are also fairly common.

Damage to the skeleton through accidents, activities undertaken during life, murder and warfare injuries and even childbirth can all be evidenced by physical traces left on bone. Female skeletons at Tell Abu Hureyra (▶see p. 247) were shown to have traces of arthritis

from using grindstones, while the murder of prisoners at the Battle of Towcester has recently been investigated through meticulous examination of skeletons from a pit near the battle site.

 http://www.brad.ac.uk/acad/archsci/ depart/report97/towton.htm

 http://www.bbc.co.uk/history/programmes/ meettheancestors/index.shtml

Diet. The main approach to diet relies upon studies of isotopic traces in bone. Particular diets such as one dependent on marine foods or one heavy in maize consumption will leave a signature in the bone collagen. A Homo erectus from Lake Turkana was found to have an extra scab of bone around its femur. The most likely cause was an excess of vitamin A caused by eating too much raw meat, especially liver; a reminder that the transition of our species from plant eaters to meat eaters was not without its problems. Tooth wear is also used to demonstrate gritty diets while earth from the abdominal area of buried skeletons can be analysed for pollen and seeds which may have been in the stomach.

 http://www.brad.ac.uk/acad/archsci/ depart/resgrp/palaeodiet/

Genetic links. Shared genetic differences in populations often have a visible effect on bone, which allows people with this trait to be grouped together. Much work has been done in this area in the USA in order to establish tribal affiliations for government programmes to repatriate bones from museums to their tribal homelands and also to trace the origins of diseases currently affecting native populations. Through the application of PCR (polymerise chain reaction) genetic scientists have amplified small amounts of genetic material found in archaeological contexts. This has enabled human evolution to be traced. Through the study of mitochondrial DNA, the identity of the female founder of our species, the 'African Eve', has been established.

Organic artefacts

Organic artefacts are far rarer in archaeology than those made of stone and clay. Inevitably this has distorted our view of the past because so much material culture is invisible to us. Sites where organic finds survive in large amounts are unusual and in some cases may not be 'typical' sites. However, they do provide tantalising glimpses of the skills, culture and economics of the periods in the past from which they came. A breathtaking example of surviving textiles at the Spitalfields Market site illustrates this point particularly well.

Textiles, including wool, silk and leather, only usually survive in wet contexts. Great care must be taken during the removal of such artefacts from the ground. The usual practice is

Figure 3.12 *Wet sites are of such value because of the range of organic ecofacts and artefacts that are preserved on them. Wood, such as this shoe-bottom from Empingham, rarely survives on dry sites*

 KEY SITE

Spitalfields Market

During the excavation of Spitalfields Market in the City of London, a lead coffin dating to the Roman period was found within a stone sarcophagus. Inside lay the body of a well-nourished young woman in her early twenties. Glass and jet grave goods and the elaborate nature and decoration of her coffin indicated that she was of high status. Her clothes, which were preserved in the wet sludge in the bottom of the coffin, underlined this impression, for they were of superb quality. Two distinct materials were discoverable under the microscope.

The first was a gossamer chequered weave of damask silk. This was fabricated in the workshops of Damascus in Syria from silk imported from China. It relied for its effect on the play of light on its surface creating 'interference colours', like the wings of tropical birds. It must have created a truly exotic impression in the streets of Roman London.

The second garment was woollen, probably dyed with purple. This too was a status symbol. The dyestuff was obtained from Murex shellfish in the eastern Mediterranean and was interwoven with very fine strands of gold foil, carefully twisted into gold tubes encasing the woollen threads.

 http://www.bbc.co.uk/history/ancient/ archaeology/princess_1.shtml

to isolate the artefacts, leaving them lying on a block of soil. A supporting base is then slid underneath. Such artefacts are bagged and kept wet until consolidation and conservation can take place in a laboratory.

Plants

For the archaeologist samples of plant remains divide into the microscopic and the macroscopic. Both types usually require specialised methods of conservation and analysis. Plants can tell the archaeologist about past climate, economic practices, the nature of past environment and environmental change. We can explore the exploitation of plants for food, medicinal and narcotic purposes while the study of wood leads us into construction, carpentry and woodland management.

Plant macrofossils

Plant macrofossils are specimens that are visible to the naked eye. They include seeds, leaves and twigs. They are usually preserved in the following unusual conditions:

- Waterlogged, where wet anaerobic conditions inhibit the growth of the bacteria that cause decomposition. For example, bran in Lindow Man's stomach or moss used as 'toilet paper' in Viking York.
- Carbonised, where charring has converted material to inorganic carbon which is less susceptible to the forces of decay, for example grain in the pits at Danebury.
- Mineralised, where the organic content of the specimen is replaced by minerals such as iron and manganese from groundwater in the soil.
- Frozen, usually in conditions of permafrost when the ground is permanently frozen and

organic remains within it can be perfectly preserved, for example coriander seeds in the 'Ice Maiden's' grave or the stomach contents of Siberian mammoths.
- As impressions in mudbrick, pottery or daub, for example corns cobs at Ceren and olives at Pompeii.

Wood

Dealing with wood from archaeological contexts presents huge problems, but may also offer sources of evidence unavailable elsewhere. Leaving aside its use for dating through dendrochronology, wood is valuable as physical evidence for structure and artefacts. Archaeologists cannot study carpentry practices from the past, which involved complex joinery, without part of a ship or building to show how the joint was made. The discovery of wooden structures is also important in revealing the huge range of uses to which wood was put in the past.

Shipwrecks such as the *Vasa* or *Mary Rose* are time capsules: a moment frozen in time. Inside these two warships were a bewildering array of wooden artefacts from mundane spoons and bowls to sophisticated navigational aids. ►See also the shipwrecks discussed on p. 221.

 http://dover.gov.uk/museum/boat/home.htm

Similar ranges of wooden implements have been recovered from crannogs such as Oakbank in Loch Tay and 'fennogs' like Flag Fen. In addition to domestic utensils such as wooden 'porridge' spoons, the huge numbers of wooden piles used to construct these sites speak eloquently about the ability to fell, shape and move massive tonnages of timber in prehistory. The Sweet Track on the Somerset Levels also provided evidence of Neolithic carpentry and woodland management. Three tree species had been selected for particular roles in construction and produced by **coppicing** to suit the demands of a wet environment. Huge quantities of timber were also recovered in excavations of the London waterfront. It was too expensive to conserve all of the material so selection and sampling had to take place. Some of the wharf timbers proved to be the remains of derelict buildings. This enabled the development of carpentry and construction techniques to be studied over an extended period.

All of this material derived from wet contexts. The wood, though flimsy and insubstantial, retains much of its form and details such as axe marks. Wood from dry contexts also sometimes survives but is frequently warped and distorted. Once wood is removed from a wet environment, decay sets in rapidly unless proactive measures are taken. Observations at Oakbank showed that excavated wood when freshly broken retained the colour of fresh timber, but once exposed to the air the wood turned black in about twenty seconds. In the short term wood is kept wet with biocides added to the water to prevent fungal growth. Longer term conservation may involve freeze-drying but this is only a viable option for artefacts and small timbers. Larger specimens require different techniques. Replacing the water in the cells of the wood with a soluble wax such as PEG (polyethylene glycol) treats shipwreck timbers, which have the consistency of wet cardboard and consist of 80–90 per cent water. This treatment can be very time-consuming. The *Mary Rose*, which has been treated with PEG, is still not ready for display more than ten years after she was raised.

Indirect evidence for the use of wood can also be detected. At Sutton Hoo the imprint of an Anglo-Saxon ship's timbers remained in the sand while at Garton Slack there was a stain from the varnished spokes of a chariot's wheels.

Other plant macrofossils

The quantity of plant material in natural sediments is usually low but on archaeological sites can be abnormally high, especially where activities such as deposition of food waste and human faeces (**coprolites**) or food processing and storage has have taken place. Archaeologists must also bear in mind that care must be taken in presentation of data if the sheer quantity of small seeds produced by some species is not to artificially dominate an assemblage at the expense of other species which produce fewer and larger seeds. A comparison between the size of poppy seeds and almonds makes this point.

On most sites archaeologists will want to know about the local environment and the use of plant foods including crops (▶see Chapter 10). However, biases can occur in samples for a number of reasons. Differential survival may bias the range of plants known from a particular period either because plants do not preserve well or because they grow in locations lacking suitable conditions for preservation. People may also have introduced plants into the site either deliberately through plant collecting or cultivation or by accident as in the case of Otzi the Ice Man, in the form of cereal grains adhering to his grass cape. This means that the archaeologist must study very carefully the formation processes (▶see Chapter 5) that led to the creation of the deposit that contains the plant remains under consideration.

Through the study of ethnographic parallels for the processing of plants in contemporary societies that still rely on simple technology, archaeologists have reached a good understanding of the main stages of processing. These are usually reaping, sowing, winnowing and threshing. Each stage produces a characteristic assemblage of plant macrofossils according to which parts of the plant are left by that point – at the storage stage, for example, one would expect to find an assemblage dominated by clean grains with few remnants of stalk or husk present.

Plant microfossils

Plant microfossils are remains that can usually be studied only using microscopes. Three types that are important to archaeologists are pollens, diatoms and phytoliths.

Pollen

The study of pollen is known as **palynology**. The species of individual grains of pollen are readily identifiable by palynologists through their characteristic shapes. They survive well, especially in wet acid conditions, because they possess a tough outer case. Pollen can be retrieved from most soil samples but is most useful when taken by coring or from a column of samples from a ditch or pit to show vegetation changes. Species frequency in samples can be counted and the numerical data plotted to show relative quantities. Some species produce more pollen then others, so depending on wind, animal and human action a particular assemblage of pollen may represent a very local or a more regional sample.

The relative quantities of pollens provide a record of environmental change. In well-researched areas it has been possible to define pollen zones which characterise particular periods according to the relative amounts of each species. These pollen assemblages can be used to assign relative dates to samples from

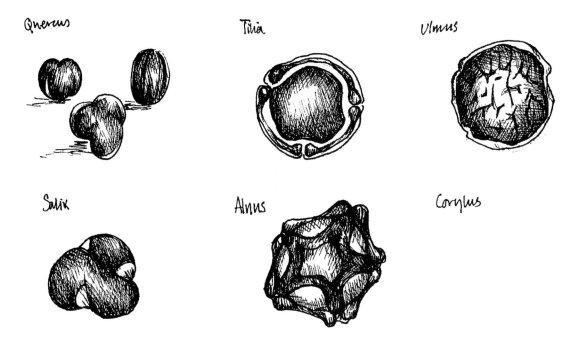

Figure 3.13 Drawings of examples of magnified pollen grains, illustrating the different shapes for each species

KEY STUDY

The decline of the Maya

Rue (1989) collected samples by coring a peat bog to produce a long thin column of sediment which encapsulated the environmental history of the Copan valley. Once processed the data revealed a surprise. The general view was that Maya society declined rapidly after AD 800 so Rue expected this would be reflected in the pollen evidence with maize being less prominent and tree pollen becoming dominant as the forest cover regenerated. In fact maize continued to be planted until at least AD 1100 and only after that did hardwoods like the mahogany, suggestive of fully established rainforest, became apparent on a large scale. Either the standard textbooks about the Maya were wrong or Rue's data were. His results were supported by Freter, who was working on obsidian hydration dating of blades found on Maya sites of this period. Her dates also suggested a long drawn out decline over several hundred years rather than a cataclysmic demise for the Maya. This provided a new 'model' to explain the end of Maya civilisation and also highlights the view of modern archaeology as a discipline made up of many subdisciplines which often provide complementary evidence and news way of looking

other sites according to where they match the established environmental sequence. This is known as **pollen dating** (▶see p. 83). The samples can also be dated using radiocarbon dating.

Diatoms

Diatoms are microscopic single-celled plants usually found in open water or in wet conditions such as bogs and waterlogged soils. They are very sensitive to changes in their local water. Their hard outer shell survives well in alkaline or anaerobic conditions. Changes caused by human action such as deforestation or pollution can be inferred from changes in the species of diatom.

Phytoliths

Phytoliths are silica from the cells of plants. They survive well enough in alkaline soils to be identified to particular groups of plants. It has been suggested that sickle gloss on flint blades from the early Neolithic in the Near East is indirect evidence of abrasive cereal phytoliths, while in Mesoamerica maize phytoliths have been used to demonstrate the spread of agriculture.

Invertebrates

The shells of many tiny living creatures are surprisingly resilient. They provide evidence of the local environment and in some cases human diet and activity, as with the layers of seashells in coastal middens. Two important categories are beetles and snails.

Beetles

Beetles (or Coleoptera) are one of the most diverse types of invertebrate and they can be found in virtually every environment. Their shell or exoskeleton is very resistant to decay and sufficiently variable to allow identification sometimes down to species level. In evolutionary terms, beetles have changed very little for tens of thousands of years, so comparison of samples with modern reference collections is relatively straightforward. The large number of types of beetle can make species lists rather unhelpful as there may be up to fifty species present in a collection of 100 specimens with only one or two in each category. A more profitable approach has been to group species together by their food or habitat preferences into classes such as 'phytophages' (plant eater) or 'obligate aquatics' (living in water). Archaeologists can then discover their local habitat and what taphonomic processes (►see p. 97) led to their decomposition in a particular deposit. The kind of archaeological information provided by the beetles can be summarised as follows:

- Reconstruction of ground surface conditions. Buckland (1976) used beetles to analyse the floors of houses at Reykholb in order to infer the use of different rooms.
- Reconstruction of vegetation and climate. The discovery of Oades gracilis in southern Britain during the Palaeolithic has been used to infer the existence of much cooler conditions during glacial periods since this species now has a largely Arctic distribution.
- Information about stored products and the utilisation of plants resources. In Roman granaries at York grain beetles have been discovered which prove the exploitation of cereals even though there is no physical evidence of the plants themselves.

Molluscs

Land snail shells are preserved in calcareous, chalky soils because their shells are made of calcium carbonate (chalk). Most snails are so small (around 2 mm) that you can't normally see them. Those larger snails you may have seen, or even eaten, are much bigger and represent only three or four varieties of the

Figure 3.14 *Laboratory examination of snails. A microscope is used to identify the different species to provide insights into local habitats*

hundreds of species of snail. Snails are especially useful to archaeologists as different species have particular vegetation habitats.

Microscopic shells are carefully sieved out of the soil (rather like seeds), identified and counted by the specialist. All snails need shade as they must not dry out, but some species are more tolerant to areas with less shade. This enables classification into three broad groups. Open country species can survive in grassland areas with little shade, unlike the woodland group. A catholic group is frequently found in both habitats, but some have quite specific preferences. Snails do not move far so although you cannot tell what any past habitat was like from just one or two shells, you can from a whole assemblage.

Figure 3.16 (right) *After excavation, finds are stored in archive boxes. This enables future researchers to access them*

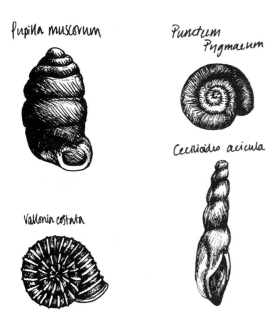

Pupilla muscorum

Punctum Pygmaeum

Cecilioides acicula

Vallonia costata

Figure 3.15 *Drawing of magnified snails to illustrate the varied shapes which enable each species to be identified*

AFTER ANALYSIS

Finally all the reports are united with the dating evidence and the fieldwork record as a complete site archive. It still needs to be interpreted. In the tradition of scientific reporting, published archaeological reports tend to be descriptive and analytical with a fairly minimal amount of assessment and interpretation. The archive is there for others to draw their conclusions from. For members of the public and many students, reports are often frustrating. What they want are the works of synthesis and interpretation that are largely produced by academic rather than field archaeologists. The examples and discussions in Part II of this book are largely drawn from these interpretative accounts.

KEY SKILL

Reinforcing class learning of methods

Learning methods can sometimes be dull, and comparing and contrasting them can be difficult. One approach is to use games. Two examples follow:

Balloon debate. Several students are each given the name of a different development in archaeology. They have to prepare in advance to answer questions on it, including providing examples. On the day of the debate the chosen students have to argue 'X has been the most important contribution to archaeology in the last 100 years.' The rest of the class have to each ask a question and will then vote for the winner. Over the course, similar debates could be used to ensure that all students have a go. The game builds up skills in argument too.

Who or what am I? Cards are dealt out with methods written on them. Without looking at it, one student sticks their card to their forehead. They then have ten questions to guess what they are. The other students can only answer yes or no.

Chapter 4

Understanding Dating in Archaeology

YOUR GOALS

You need to understand

■ the underlying principles of dating

■ the essence of how the more common techniques work

■ reasons why particular techniques are appropriate for specific situations

■ how to 'read' some of the more common types of charts and diagrams used to present dating data.

Archaeologists have used many different techniques to work out the age of artefacts and sites for which they have no historical dates and the order in which they were used. These dating techniques can be broadly subdivided into two groups:

■ **Relative dating** techniques which identify the order in which sites or artefacts were used in a sequence from earliest to latest.

■ **Absolute** (or chronometric) **dating** techniques that try to establish an exact or approximate calendar date for a site or artefact.

The techniques selected depend on the specific task and evidence as well as practical considerations such as cost. Many of the scientific techniques are expensive and require high levels of technical skill to use and to interpret. The span of human history studied by archaeologists is so vast and environments so varied that techniques suitable for one place and period may be unsuitable for another.

Historical dating

For sites less than 5,000 years old there may be written or artistic evidence which can provide precise dates as long as the original language can be decoded. For example, coins, seals, inscriptions and clay tablets were used by the civilisations of the Mediterranean and Middle East. Sometimes historical records such as dates, calendars or lists of rulers are available. These have allowed sites such as Egyptian tombs or Mayan temples to be precisely dated. When artefacts from these civilisations appear in non-literate areas they can be used to provide approximate dates in those areas. Flinders Petrie, an archaeologist working in Egypt in the 1900s, was able to use pottery from Egyptian sites that had been dated against historical records to cross-date sites in Greece where the same pottery occurred. For more recent periods the exact dates for the introduction of many artefacts from clay pipes to beer bottles are known and can be used to date sites. Where artefacts are used for dating it is critical that their precise position within the stratigraphy is accurately recorded. Such 'indirect dating' of sites provides two types of date:

- *Terminus post quem* (**TPQ**): the earliest possible date for an archaeological deposit
- *Terminus ante quem* (**TAQ**):the latest possible date for the deposit

RELATIVE DATING

Typology

In its simplest form, this involves putting a number of finds into chronological order. On a site with a clear and undisturbed stratigraphy, items from lower levels are older than those in higher levels. In the nineteenth century, observations about the types of artefact from different layers led to the creation of a time frame for prehistory known as the '3 age system', based on the introduction of tools made from stone then bronze then iron. Today many flaws are apparent in this scheme but the terms are still used to distinguish different 'periods' in the past. A more sophisticated technique was popularised by Flinders Petrie in the 1900s. He noted that the design and decoration of pottery from the Egyptian tombs he excavated changed gradually over time. He was able to place the different types into a chronological sequence. Once a good typological sequence for an area is established it can be referred to when new finds and sites are discovered and used to 'cross-date' them.

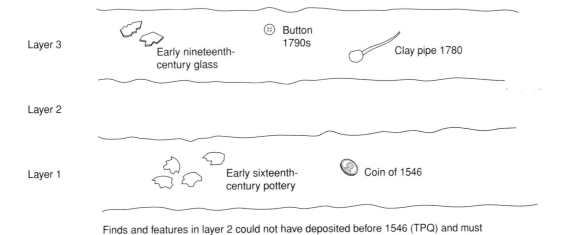

Layer 3 — Early nineteenth-century glass — Button 1790s — Clay pipe 1780

Layer 2

Layer 1 — Early sixteenth-century pottery — Coin of 1546

Finds and features in layer 2 could not have deposited before 1546 (TPQ) and must have been deposited by 1780 (TAQ)

Figure 4.1 *The use of finds to provide earliest and latest dates for a layer*

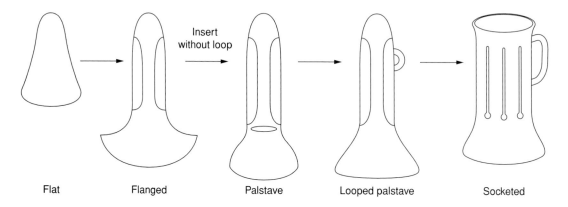

Flat   Flanged   Palstave   Looped palstave   Socketed

Figure 4.2 *An example of a typological sequence: the development of copper and bronze axes*

In addition to design, the fabric or material used to make the artefact is also analysed. If you take a piece of pottery into your local museum, typology will be used to assign your sherd to a particular period.

Successive groups of contemporary artefacts, which are commonly found together (known as assemblages), have been used to form culture sequences over wide periods. Before the advent of absolute dating techniques this technique enabled a timetable of the spread of 'cultures' across Europe in later prehistory to be constructed, based on changing combinations of grave goods.

Seriation

Most artefact styles appear rarely at first in the archaeological record, then become more common and eventually dwindle in numbers again. This pattern has enabled a sophisticated statistical technique known as seriation (ordering) to be used. The frequency with which each form of artefact appears can be plotted as bars on a timeline. Ideally this will produce a shape known as a 'battleship curve' because it looks like an aerial view of a

battleship. The changing popularity of each form will appear as a sequence of battleship curves. Other sites can be dated relative to the first site by comparing their seriation.

Problems with these techniques

■ Although they can put sites and artefacts into order, they can only be used to provide calendar dates where elements of the sequences are tied to historical data.

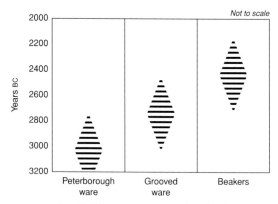

– Length of lines represent proportion of a given type at that point in time

Figure 4.3 *A simplified diagram to show how a model of seriation can be constructed. The relative proportions of pottery types at a new site would allow it to be approximately dated*

Depth of sample in centimetres
or number of sample level

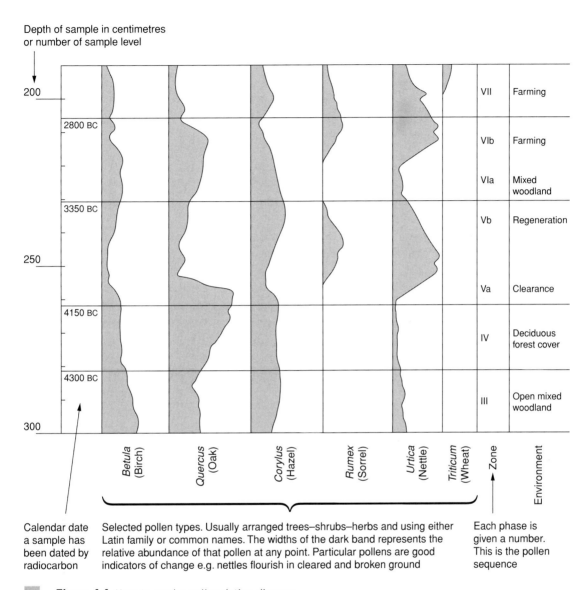

		Zone	Environment
		VII	Farming
2800 BC		VIb	Farming
		VIa	Mixed woodland
3350 BC		Vb	Regeneration
		Va	Clearance
4150 BC		IV	Deciduous forest cover
4300 BC		III	Open mixed woodland

Betula (Birch) *Quercus* (Oak) *Corylus* (Hazel) *Rumex* (Sorrel) *Urtica* (Nettle) *Triticum* (Wheat) Zone Environment

Calendar date a sample has been dated by radiocarbon

Selected pollen types. Usually arranged trees–shrubs–herbs and using either Latin family or common names. The widths of the dark band represents the relative abundance of that pollen at any point. Particular pollens are good indicators of change e.g. nettles flourish in cleared and broken ground

Each phase is given a number. This is the pollen sequence

Figure 4.4 *How to read a pollen dating diagram*

■ The introduction of radiocarbon dating showed that archaeologists had under-estimated timespans in prehistory and also constructed sequences which fitted their assumptions that all developments happened around the Mediterranean and then spread north and west to the 'less civilised' areas.

■ One type of artefact doesn't always succeed another. For many years it was thought that pointed hand axes were earlier than oval ones after they were found in lower levels on some sites. However, at Boxgrove both were found together suggesting that other influences on choice were important.

■ **Curation,** the preservation of valued artefacts, can lead to items being deposited a long time after their manufacture. Basing dates on a few isolated artefacts could lead to errors.

Geoarchaeological dating

For early periods of prehistory archaeologists have borrowed techniques from the earth sciences to reconstruct the environments of early people and also to establish a relative chronology based on environmental changes. As the climate altered, so too did the types and relative numbers of different plants and animals. Where organic preservation is good, changes can be traced by analysing pollen (palynology) contained in sediments and animal bones. To provide a pollen sequence a core through a deposit such as peat is taken and for each layer the proportions of different types of pollen are identified. Sites within these deposits can then be cross-dated to particular phases of climate history in local sequences. Analysis has to take account of many factors including the different amounts of pollen produced by each plant and the different distances the pollen travels. Similarly, sites can be relatively dated from the type of animal bones present. This is particularly useful where the sequence of the appearance or extinction of species (for example mammoths) is known. Absolute techniques are needed to date these sequences.

Obsidian hydration

Obsidian is a volcanic glass that can be worked to provide razor-sharp cutting edges. In the Middle East and Mesoamerica it performed a similar function to flint in northern Europe. As soon as a piece of obsidian is broken it begins to absorb water from the atmosphere at a known rate (in much the same way as a stick of rock which goes soft on the outside). By measuring how far water has penetrated into the obsidian (hydration) on one site a relative date can be estimated compared to other sites. In some cases, obsidian can be calibrated to provide absolute dates but that requires considerable additional data since the speed of hydration varies with local temperatures and the chemical make-up of the obsidian. This is one of the cheaper laboratory dating techniques.

✎ http://obsidian.pahma.berkeley.edu/
anth131.htm

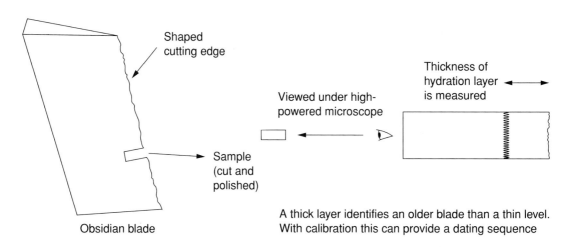

Shaped cutting edge

Sample (cut and polished)

Obsidian blade

Viewed under high-powered microscope

Thickness of hydration layer is measured

A thick layer identifies an older blade than a thin level. With calibration this can provide a dating sequence

■ *Figure 4.5* *How obsidian hydration works*

Chemical dating of bones

Buried bones absorb fluorine and uranium from water in the ground whilst their nitrogen content declines as collagen in the bones decays. These processes occur at a uniform rate so it is possible to establish the relative age of different bones by measuring the proportions of these chemicals.

ABSOLUTE OR CHRONOMETRIC DATING

Since the middle of the twentieth century new methods have been used to provide calendar dates. With the exception of dendrochronology, they all have margins of error and are expensive to use.

Dendrochronology (tree ring dating)

This is the most accurate chronometric dating method. Every year trees produce a ring of new wood under their bark. The rings are wider in good conditions than in poor ones and can provide a record of local climatic variation. Trees in the same area will have similar ring patterns which means wood from different periods can be matched in overlapping sequences. These are tied to historical dates by modern trees. Californian Bristlecone Pines, which live for 4,000 years, were used to construct sequences over 7,000 years in the USA while oaks preserved in bogs have been used in Europe to take sequences back nearly 10,000 years. The Sweet Track, a Neolithic pathway across marshland in Somerset, included wood with the bark attached.

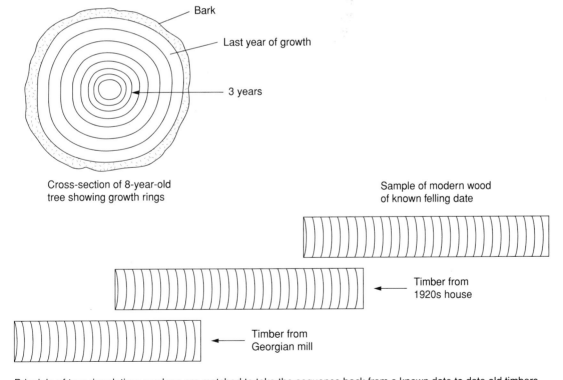

Bark

Last year of growth

3 years

Cross-section of 8-year-old tree showing growth rings

Sample of modern wood of known felling date

Timber from 1920s house

Timber from Georgian mill

Principle of tree ring dating: overlaps are matched to take the sequence back from a known date to date old timbers.

Figure 4.6 *The key principles of dendrochronology*

Dendrochronology established that the trees used to build it were felled in the winter of 3807–3806 BC. However, the method has limitations. Not all areas have sufficiently varied seasons or enough surviving timber to be able to construct sequences. To effectively date wood around fifty years of tree rings are needed. Since this represents quite a thick piece of wood, the technique is better for dating building timbers than artefacts. Its direct use is from the Neolithic onwards when buildings were used and it has been widely used on medieval ships and buildings. Dendrochronology actually dates when the tree died or was felled. Where wood has been reused, as often happened with structural timbers in the past, this method can overestimate the age of a structure. However, dendrochronology is also the key method for calibrating radiocarbon dates (see below) and therefore is indirectly used in dating a wide range of organic materials for up to 11,500 years.

 http://www.shef.ac.uk/uni/academic/ A-C/ap/dendro/dendro.html

 http://www.ltrr.arizona.edu/

Radiocarbon dating

All living things absorb several types of carbon isotope from the atmosphere in similar ratios. About 1 per cent of this carbon is an unstable isotope known as carbon 14 (C-14) which decays at a known rate. By comparing the weight of remaining C-14 with amounts of other carbon isotopes in organic samples it is possible to work out how much C-14 has decayed. This indicates how long it has been since decay began (and the creature or plant was alive). It was thought that the dates

produced by radiocarbon dating were precise until it was recognised that amounts of carbon in the atmosphere have varied over time. This had led to underestimating the age of prehistoric sites by up to 800 years. To get round this problem, radiocarbon dates are calibrated.

Radiocarbon dates are never exact. Even after calibration there is a margin of error that is calculated statistically. This usually means that there is a 68 per cent chance or 'level of confidence' (LOC) that the real date is within the range indicated and a 95 per cent LOC that it is within twice the range. C-14 is mainly used to date organic materials including bone, shell and plant remains. It does not work on cremated bone although it will work for charred bone. It is more precise with wood samples from twigs and nuts than from trees that may have lived for hundreds of years. Radiocarbon's practical use is for periods from 200 to about 10,000 years with less reliability to around 40,000 years. Until recently at least 10 grams of charcoal or 200 grams of bone were needed for results. However, development of a process known as **accelerator mass spectrometry** (AMS) has enabled much smaller samples of material to be dated, down to the one grain of cereal. Great care has to be taken with samples to avoid contamination.

 http://www.radiocarbon.org/

 http://www.c14dating.com/

C-14 dates are expressed in the following ways:

■ Lower case letters are often, but not always, used to show that dates are uncalibrated, whereas capitals should mean they have

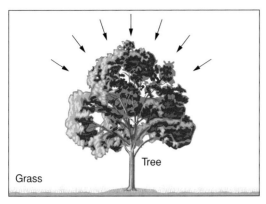

C-14 is formed by cosmic radiation in the atmosphere and absorbed by plants through photosynthesis

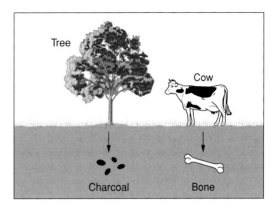

C-14 is absorbed by animals from plants. It enters the archaeological record in burnt wood (charcoal) or bones

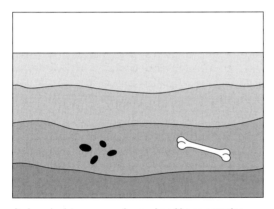

Archaeologists recover charcoal and bone samples to date a layer

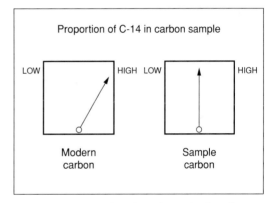

Laboratory analysis gives time since animal or plant died and C-14 decay began

Figure 4.7 *How radiocarbon is formed and reaches the archaeological record*

been calibrated. Increasingly 'Cal' is added to a calibrated date to avoid any confusion.

■ Calendar dates are expressed as ad or bc (uncalibrated) and BC, AD, Cal BC, Cal AD (calibrated)

■ Radiocarbon dates are expressed as BP or Cal BP (calibrated). **BP** means 'before present' (1950) and is often preferred for early prehistoric periods for which BC and AD are relatively meaningless.

Thermoluminescence (TL)

Radioactive decay in the quartz crystals found in clay leads to a build up of electric charge at a known rate. The electrical charge is released as light when the crystals are heated. When pottery is heated in a laboratory the energy in the flash of light is measured and used to calculate the time since it was fired. The technique can be used for materials such as glass and burnt flint or stone for periods from

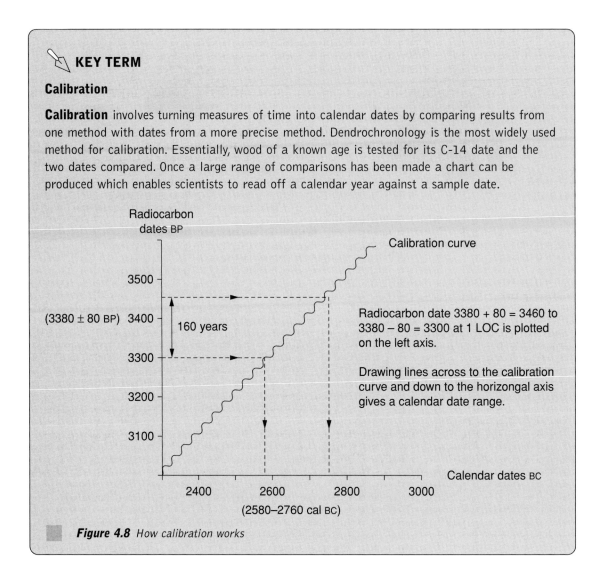

✎ **KEY TERM**

Calibration

Calibration involves turning measures of time into calendar dates by comparing results from one method with dates from a more precise method. Dendrochronology is the most widely used method for calibration. Essentially, wood of a known age is tested for its C-14 date and the two dates compared. Once a large range of comparisons has been made a chart can be produced which enables scientists to read off a calendar year against a sample date.

Radiocarbon dates BP

Calibration curve

(3380 ± 80 BP) 3400

160 years

3500

3300

3200

3100

Radiocarbon date 3380 + 80 = 3460 to 3380 − 80 = 3300 at 1 LOC is plotted on the left axis.

Drawing lines across to the calibration curve and down to the horizongal axis gives a calendar date range.

Calendar dates BC

2400   2600   2800   3000

(2580–2760 cal BC)

Figure 4.8 How calibration works

the present to around 400,000 years ago. It is less accurate than C-14 dating and can give false readings due to radiation from the soil or if the initial firing was at low temperature. However, it is useful for older periods and instances where there are no organic remains such as dating Upper Palaeolithic figurines.

 http://www.info.ox.ac.uk/departments/rlaha/

Potassium–argon dating

As potassium in rock crystals decays it produces argon gas at a known rate. Measuring the amounts and ratios in a laboratory provides a date at which the crystal was formed. It has been used in volcanic regions to date layers of rock which sandwich human remains. For instance, at Koobi Fora in East Africa early hominid remains were dated to 1.89 million years BP ±0.01 million years. The technique can

Figure 4.9 *Understanding a radiocarbon date*

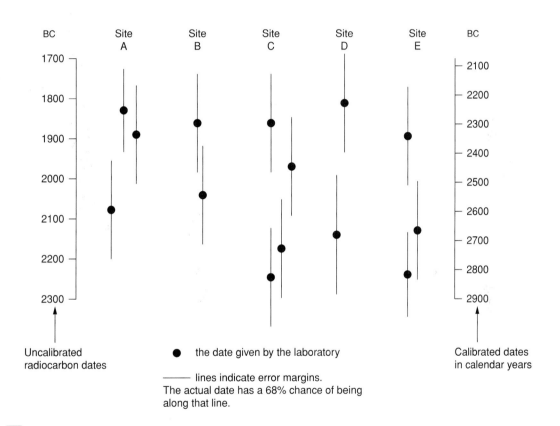

Figure 4.10 *Reading a radiocarbon table*

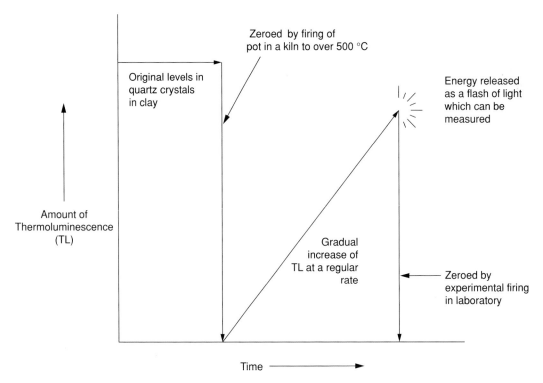

Zeroed by firing of
pot in a kiln to over 500 °C

Original levels in
quartz crystals
in clay

Energy released
as a flash of light
which can be
measured

Amount of
Thermoluminescence
(TL)

Gradual
increase of
TL at a regular
rate

Zeroed by
experimental firing
in laboratory

Time

The amount of energy released is relative to the amount of time since last
heated to over 500 °C

Figure 4.11 *How thermoluminescence works*

be used for periods from around 200,000 to several million years ago but it is limited to sites with the right geology.

Other absolute dating techniques

Figure 4.12 covers less commonly used methods, some of which are still at an experimental stage. You do not need to know them in detail although you should be aware of the situations where they might be used. Like radiocarbon dating, most of them rely on data showing known rates of chemical change or decay that can be measured in laboratories. Several of them measure the age of layers rather than the human deposits themselves and are thus limited to particular types of geology. Most methods are used in combination with cross-check dates.

	How it works	What it can be used for	What periods it is used for	Comments/limitations	Examples
Amino acid racemization	The chemical structures of the amino acids found in all living things change slowly over time at a known rate	Bones, teeth and shell	1000 to 1 million years	Must not be cooked. Needs calibrating. Varies with climate	Ostrich eggs on Paleolithic sites in Africa
Archaeomagnetism	The earth's magnetic field changes over time. When iron oxide is heated to around 600 °C and cools, it records the magnetic field at that time. Variations in the earth's field have been calculated which enables the date of initial heating to be established	Ceramics, lava, hearths and kilns that contain iron oxide	Up to 5,000 years	Local variations in magnetism. Sites must be undisturbed when measured. Needs to be calibrated, e.g. by varves. Can provide inaccurate dates where the same polarity occurred more than once	Clay ovens in south-west USA
Electron spin resonance (ESR)	Electrical charges build up at a known rate in some crystal structures. The time since the process began can be calculated by measuring the charge	Teeth enamel, shells calcite deposits in caves	50,000 to 1 million years	Works best in dry environments. Wide error margins	Palaeolithic sites in Israel and Africa
Fission track dating	Uranium decays regularly through fission (splitting) which releases energy and damages crystalline structures, leaving a 'track'. Tracks or holes are counted to estimate the time the process of decay has taken	Glass, burned obsidian, heated stones containing uranium. Sites sandwiched between volcanic layers	Mainly 100,000 to several million years although some recent glass has been dated	Difficulty in differentiating tracks from crystal defects. Over 10% error margins	Homo Habilis bones at Olduvai Gorge from around 2 million years ago
Uranium series	Uranium isotopes U235 and U238 are soluble in water and decay to produce deposits of thorium and protactinium at known rates. By measuring the ratios of the elements the date at which the deposits was laid down can be established	Analysing calcium carbonate deposits where water containing uranium has seeped into caves and been deposited (e.g. as stalactites). Teeth enamel, shells	Early human sites in Europe. 50,000 to 500,000 years	Prone to ambiguous results. Needs a high uranium content	Dentine on Neanderthal/ early human teeth in Israel
Varves	Melt-water from glaciers lays down different sediment at different times of year. This creates annual layers like tree rings. Changing climate will lead to changing deposits which can then be cross-referenced over large areas	Analysing cores taken from ancient lake beds. Where they contain pollen they can be tied to geoarchaeological sequences	Up to 20,000 years	Key dating role is by calibrating other techniques such as radiocarbon and archaeomagnetism	A sequence of 17,000 years has been established in Scandinavia and 20,000 in the USA

Figure 4.12 *Comparison of the major scientific dating methods*

KEY TASK

Test your grasp of dating methods

1 Which methods might you use to date the following? Check your answers on p. 305.

- A wooden spear tip from 200,000 years ago
- Shells from a mesolithic midden
- Seeds from a Roman well
- Burnt flint from a paleolithic hearth
- Walls made from baked mud bricks from an ancient house
- Human bones from a Saxon cemetery
- An Aztec kiln site from Mexico
- Bison bones found in cave deposits
- A terracotta figurine from a Roman temple
- Timbers from a bronze age boat

2 Construct a bar chart to show which methods are useful for which period in the past.

- List each method on the vertical axis at regularly spaced intervals.
- List the following dates (in years BP) on the horizontal axis at regularly spaced intervals: 0, 100, 500, 1,000, 5,000, 10,000, 50,000, 100,000, 500,000, 1,000,000, 5,000,000.
- Shade the period for which each method is useful in the relevant row.

Archaeological Interpretation

As humans, we use ideas and models to interpret the world around us. It is impossible to describe something or another person without likening them to something or somebody else. The same is true for archaeology. The goal of archaeology is to explain (not really reconstruct) past behaviour, but archaeologists do not dig up behaviour. They excavate material remains from the past and assume that behaviour and the ideas that motivated behaviour will be reflected in these remains. They then use theories from the present to make sense of the archaeological record. For example, you need theory to interpret a dark circular mark as a posthole or a particular burial as that of a chieftain. This way of thinking, which links material remains to their interpretation as evidence, is known as middle-range theory.

 KEY TERM

The archaeological record

This is the raw data for archaeology. The physical remains of past activities include features, artefacts and ecofacts (including human remains). The archaeological record comprises these remains in the contexts in which they come down to us.

Debates between archaeologists often stem from differences in their assumptions about how the archaeological record was created and how one should interpret it. On degree-level programmes you will encounter a variety of theories of archaeological knowledge. Below

Figure 5.1 *Excavation of this dark circle of earth can define shape, dimensions and content. Establishing what it once was will always require interpretation. This example was a lime kiln*

Figure 5.2 *This stone built feature at Empingham was identified as a corn dryer through reference to other sites, ethnographic example and experiment*

KEY CONCEPT

Archaeological theories of knowledge

There are a wealth of texts on this subject and on the debates between rival schools of thought. In recent years, as in most academic disciplines, relativist ideas have become very influential. They share a belief that there are no absolute facts since all knowledge is subjective. For example, the values and assumptions we have determine the way we think. The way we think structures what we see in such a way that it makes sense to us. When we think we are discovering patterns in archaeological data, what we are really doing is organising data so that it reflects the structures already in our minds. For example, a female skeleton in a prehistoric burial with a flint arrowhead by her neck might be automatically interpreted as a victim if you have already assumed that only men fired arrows. Archaeologists with other assumptions might *see* her as a hunter or warrior.

degree level you don't need to know about specific theories, but a basic grasp of aspects of middle-range theory is useful in order to assess the strengths and weaknesses of different interpretations.

To make sense of the archaeological record and assess the significance of particular remains, archaeologists need to understand why some things have survived while others have not. Data can appear in historic records or as abandoned remains but is largely recovered through excavation or surface survey. The processes by which it comes to us and we recover it leads to variability in the overall record. In order to interpret data, archaeologists have to know which materials go together and can be used to provide evidence of past behaviour. For example, a clustering of broken pottery, burnt stones and processed animal bones could represent a cooking area or it could be the result of people spreading their domestic rubbish on a field as fertiliser. This is where archaeology becomes detective work. To determine which explanation is most likely to be correct we need to understand the processes by which data reached us. Sometimes these are referred to as 'taphonomic processes' although it may be more useful to understand them as several stages.

TRANSFORMATION PROCESSES

These processes include all the stages by which human behaviour from the past is translated into the data recorded in archaeological reports and all the human and natural forces that shaped that data.

Formation processes

Archaeological data can be used to explain past human behaviour because people helped create that data. Although ecofacts may be an exception, this assumption is generally a good one. The formation of archaeological materials is a complex process involving four broad stages. These need to be understood since evidence can enter the archaeological record at any point. A flint tipped arrow provides an example in Figure 5.3.

 KEY TASK

Understanding formation processes

Produce your own table or diagram to show your understanding of **formation processes** using one of the following examples:

1 Remains of a hunted animal

2 A Roman amphora

Stage of formation process	Example	We need to know	May enter the archaeological record as
Acquisition	Collecting flint, feathers and resin, cutting wood	Where and how the materials were gathered? Why were they chosen?	Flint mine
Manufacture	Shaping the flint, feathers and wood to make an arrow Heating the resin the make glue	What techniques and tools were used?	Waste flakes Antler tools
Use/purpose	Used to hunt animals	How it was used, which creatures it was used on?	Lost or broken points
Discard	Buried with its owner or in the remains of an animal	Was it thrown away, lost or deliberately abandoned?	Arrowhead in burial or bone debris

Figure 5.3 Example of the way in which artefacts enter the archaeological record

KEY TERM

Curation

Deliberately keeping and preserving something. It accounts for why finds sometimes turn up amid much more recent collections of finds. Artefacts might be curated for sentimental reasons, rarity, beauty or because they were particularly useful. What has been curated in your home? Curation can distort the record, for example in early medieval Europe classical pottery often continued in use while metal vessels were recycled.

 KEY TERM

Structured deposition

Most human societies, including our own, dispose of materials in ways determined by their beliefs and knowledge. By trying to uncover the patterns in which material was deliberately deposited in the past, archaeologists hope to reveal elements of past beliefs. Structured deposition has been particularly influential in recent studies of ritual practices in European prehistory, for example at Flag Fen (▶see p. 151).

Depositional processes are the ways in which remains actually find their way into the ground. If humans are responsible, we need to try and understand their logic. Why was an artefact discarded rather than being reused, recycled, repaired or curated? These questions also apply to structures.

Some historical sources were created specifically to deceive. While there have been odd instances of faking such as 'Piltdown Man', it is highly unlikely that archaeological material has been buried to fool later generations. However, there are still codes to be broken. Archaeologists carefully map buried finds to see if there are patterns. Where these exist they may indicate structured deposition which could be helpful in understanding behaviour or beliefs. Natural forces may also have caused particular deposits. These might include erosion, flooding or volcanic activity. By understanding formation and transformation processes, archaeologists learn to differentiate between what was due to humans and what was due to nature.

Post-depositional factors

Once buried, further modifications take place. The archaeological record is not a safe place for artefacts or ecofacts. The causes of these changes are usually grouped as:

■ natural forces or 'N factors,' including bacteria, acid, water, erosion, ice, worms, sunlight, roots, freezing and thawing, drying out (desiccation), silting, gnawing and oxidisation
■ human or cultural 'C Factors,' including grave robbing, looting, shelling, mining, reuse, ploughing, collecting, trampling, building and draining.

These factors can result in changes including movement, destruction, partial decay, colour loss, texture and shape changes, and alteration of chemical composition. The extent of change varies between different materials. Inorganic materials are preserved best. Stone, pottery and bronze, for example, are particularly durable. Consequently, there is a systematic bias in the

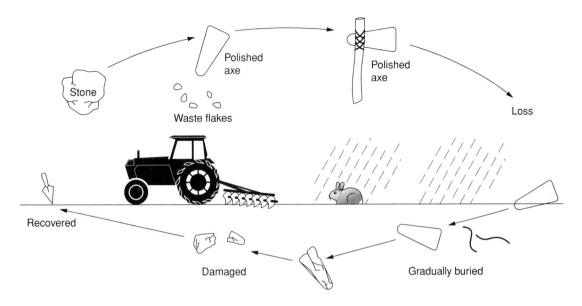

Figure 5.4 *Examples of transformation processes affecting a polished stone axe*

Proportion of sites where particular materials survive

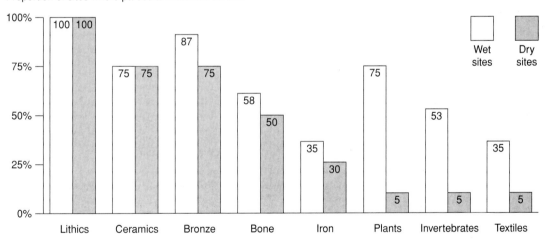

Figure 5.5 *Examples of differential survival of materials on wet and dry sites*

archaeological record towards tools made from these materials. By contrast, organic materials such as wool, wood and bodies are far less likely to survive. **Taphonomy** (the law of burial) is the name commonly given to the study of the effects of such processes on animal and plant remains. The size of buried objects; their depth of burial, climate and the nature of the soil further complicate these basic distinctions. Bones, for example, survive better in neutral or alkaline soils than in acidic ones. They will decay more slowly than normal in dry soil such as sand and in soils with little oxygen such as clay.

We can get some idea of the wealth of material that is usually lost by studying excavations from sites with exceptionally good organic preservation. In these cases remains are protected from the bacteria which normally consume organic material by climatic conditions or low oxygen levels (anaerobic conditions). While these sites remind us that absence of evidence is not evidence of absence, we cannot assume that they are typical sites from their period.

■ Arid sites, often in desert regions, can lead to remains drying out (desiccation) before they have a chance to decay. In the case of bodies, this process creates natural mummies. Classic examples include Mesa Verde in the south-west USA where wooden and leather items were preserved.

■ Waterlogged sites including lakes and peat bogs have been particularly important in European archaeology. Good examples include Flag Fen, Tybrind Vig in Denmark and the wreck of the *Mary Rose*.

■ Frozen sites have produced some incredible finds in recent years. Perhaps the most well

Figure 5.6 *Bronze Age timbers from a ritual platform at Flag Fen. They had originally been preserved in peat but began to decay once exposed to the atmosphere. Considerable expense is required to conserve and present them*

known are the bodies of Otzi the Ice Man from the Alps and the Pazyryk 'Ice Maiden' from Mongolia. Their skin has been so well preserved that tattoos and acupuncture marks can be studied.

■ Rapidly buried sites can also reveal much that is normally lost. The most famous cases are those buried by volcanic ash such as Pompeii, but mudslides such as at Ozette in the USA also preserve organic material.

KEY TASK

Group activity on transformation processes

Brainstorm ideas about what might be left for future generations of archaeologists if a disaster struck your class today. Consider what the effect of post-depositional forces would be. Present your findings in a visual format.

Recovery factors

As if these processes were not enough, there is one final hurdle for archaeological remains to cross before they can be used to explain the past. Archaeologists themselves structure the archaeological record in the way they recover data, the results in some materials or sites being better represented than others. Sometimes this may simply be due to chance factors such as discovery or whether archaeologists can get access to particular sites. Once on sites they then decide whether to excavate everything or to sample. Recovery also reflects their values. Decisions are sometimes made to prioritise certain evidence over others. For example,

excavators may dig through medieval deposits in order to concentrate on Roman layers. Similarly, while pottery and metals finds are usually recorded, animal bone is sometimes not. The techniques available for recovery are also important. Not all excavations will use flotation techniques to recover pollen and small bone fragments or have the laboratory support to analyse them. Finally there is the quality of the diggers and those recording the finds. Inevitably there are some variations. Once away from the site, the care taken in analysis and storage may continue to transform the record.

The net result of all these processes is that archaeologists do not simply piece together recorded data to produce a picture of the past. Archaeological evidence cannot speak for itself and needs interpretation. Whatever was deposited was a fraction of the material in use by people in the past. Only some elements of this will survive and only a sample of them will be recovered. By understanding transformation processes, archaeologists gain insights into what shaped the various samples. This enables them to identify which of the patterns in their data are really the result of human behaviour and to begin interpreting them. For example, human skeletons are often found with the head turned to one side. At face value this might seem significant. However, forensic science has revealed that the slumping of corpses' heads is due to natural processes of decay rather than burial rites.

Partly because of the poor or variable quality of data and the limitations of our analytical techniques, archaeological reports often contain minimal amounts of interpretation. Their writers follow a scientific tradition of reporting their findings and analysis of data but leaving interpretation to others.

Analysing spatial patterns

Having identified archaeological material and taken account of various transformation processes, archaeologists try to identify what human behaviour lies behind any patterns that they can detect. Initially this involves plotting vertical and horizontal relationships between finds, structures and sites. Patterning is taken to be evidence for behaviour. For example, a scatter of flint tools amidst the bones of an animal might indicate a butchery or kill site involving humans in scavenging or hunting. The toolkit used is termed a sub-assemblage.

 KEY TERM

Assemblage

Sub-assemblage: a repeated pattern of artefacts associated with one activity. Think of it as a toolkit.

Assemblage: the range of toolkits used by a particular community.

MAKING SENSE OF THE DATA

The next stage of archaeological interpretation tends to vary according to the ideas about knowledge held by the archaeologist. In most cases they will use **analogies** or models to formulate theories about what the data is evidence of.

Our society does not include all the rich variety of human activity and culture that has existed. To rely on it as the sole source of analogies would be limiting and lead to Eurocentric and anachronistic interpretations.

 KEY TERM

Analogy

This involves using something with which we are familiar to interpret a new thing or phenomena. It is based on the idea that if two things are similar in one way then they may be similar in others. When we describe an artefact as a hand-axe or an enclosure as a hill fort, we are using analogies. Analogies range from interpretations of how something was made or worn to what the social systems or patterns of religious belief in the past might have been. Analogies cannot prove anything about the past but they can tell us much about what was possible. They can widen our horizons, generate new lines of enquiry and provide theories to be tested against further evidence to see how robust they are.

Increasingly, archaeologists have drawn on three major sources of analogies.

Historical accounts or documents of past societies

- Classical accounts of the world such as the descriptions of Ancient Egypt by Herodotus
- Literary and artistic sources such as the poetry of early medieval Europe
- Travelogues written by the first western people to visit areas largely unaffected by European culture, for example, reports by Catholic missionaries on the peoples of Mesoamerica in the sixteenth century. These accounts are often called ethno-histories

■ Where there is continuity in population, environment and some cultural forms, the direct historical approach (**DHA**) uses studies of, or oral accounts from, current peoples. For example, Flannery and Marcus used DHA to form a hypothesis about the nature of pre-Hispanic religious beliefs and ceremonies in Mesoamerica.

Historical sources have been used particularly to flesh out the social aspects of past cultures. They have also been used to identify or interpret specific sites such as Tintagel or to explain why particular patterns of deposition might occur. Up until recently, historical sources were accorded far more weight than archaeological sources in writing the history of past societies. However, there are many problems with these sources. We don't know whether the writers had correctly identified features of the societies they describe or if our understanding of concepts is the same as that of the writers.

Ethnography or anthropology

Ethnography is the study of people in the world today while **anthropology** compares cultures to identify general principles. Amongst the most well known studies are those of the Hadza and Kalahari bushmen which were used in the 1960s to provide social and economic models for pre-agricultural people in Europe as 'man the hunter'.

■ Specific analogies have been used to explore particular archaeological phenomena. Several archaeologists have used examples of mortuary rituals from around the world to help interpret prehistoric sites (▶see p. 146).

■ General models drawing on broad comparisons across many cultures such as Service's band-tribe-chiefdom model of social evolution (▶see p. 238) have been used to categorise and describe past societies.

However, most anthropological studies come from the twentieth century when most of the world was influenced in some way by European civilisations. There is often also a huge gulf in time and place between ancient peoples and the modern groups who are the source of analogies. While taking us beyond western models, ethnography can also limit our imagination. It is highly likely that ideas, social organisations and ways of doing things existed in the past that are not present in any current societies. The greater share of variation in human societies has already been lost. Archaeologists also have to resist the temptation to select the single examples that make most sense to them.

 KEY STUDY

Iron Age Britain

Typical accounts of Britain in the first millennium draw heavily on Roman sources to interpret archaeological remains. The stereotypical view is of a warlike 'Celtic' society ruled over by chieftains who controlled trade and agricultural surpluses. This has recently been undermined by research that suggests that Iron Age society was more varied and less stratified. Archaeological data provides more evidence of productive farmers than warriors and has led archaeologists such as Hill (1996) to challenge the ideas of chiefs, Celts and hill forts (▶see p. 180).

Figure 5.8 (above) *Butser Ancient Farm. This experimental site explores the buildings, crops, livestock and manufacture of the Iron Age*

Figure 5.9 (left) *The excavator's interpretation of the 'tank traps' at the Iron Age settlement at Castell Henllys. Compare with excavation photograph on p. 28*

WHY DO ARCHAEOLOGISTS OFFER DIFFERENT INTERPRETATIONS OF THE PAST?

Since archaeologists disagree about how or whether past behaviour can be reconstructed and because the archaeological record is so flawed, it is hardly surprising that their accounts differ. Data is constantly being reinterpreted as archaeologists ask new questions, use new techniques or find new sources of analogy. They also borrow models and methods from other disciplines. In the 1970s geography provided settlement archaeology with site catchment analysis and central place theory. In the 1990s phenomenology and critical theory inspired new interpretations of beliefs and rituals. The continued debate amongst archaeologists is a sign of the subject's vitality.

 KEY SKILL

Applying your understanding to your course

Having an appreciation of how the archaeological record is formed should help you to understand archaeological reports and arguments. A grasp of why archaeologists' arguments might differ is necessary to score well on essays which ask you to evaluate a point of view. This is important at A2 and crucial at undergraduate level.

To practise, try to explore a debate between two writers who disagree about a topic you are studying. You may like to work with another student on this to halve the reading.

Start by writing down clearly what it is that they disagree about. Then, for each text list the key points that make up their argument and the key evidence they cite in support of each point. Try to identify where they are making an interpretation.

You will probably find that they will either:

- be using different data which will produce conflicting results
- differ about what the archaeological record actually shows or
- use different analogies to interpret data.

Your task is to explain the difference and then reach a conclusion about which of the explanations you consider more valid. For example, you could argue that some data is better than others for the particular question in hand or you could consult other sources to see which side they tend to support.

Present your findings briefly in bullet point form on a divided side of A4 paper. Add a visual symbol to each half to help you remember them.

Examples of debates:

 Binford vs. Freeman over whether there were elephant hunters at Torralba (Binford 1989)

 Cunliffe (1995) vs. Hill (1996) on whether Celtic chieftains ruled during the Iron Age in Britain

Chapter 6

Managing the Past

YOUR GOALS

You need to understand

- the key threats to our archaeological heritage

- the nature and effectiveness of current protection for archaeological remains

- the roles of the key agencies involved in archaeology and managing heritage

- the key debates about the preservation and ownership of archaeological remains.

THREATS TO ARCHAEOLOGICAL REMAINS

Natural processes (►see Chapter 5) account for the decay of most archaeological remains once in the soil but the overwhelming threat to surviving monuments, from field systems to buildings, comes from human activity. The rapid growth of towns and road networks since 1945 combined with more declining pasture land and more intensive forms of agriculture are largely responsible.

Since the 1960s most excavation has been of sites which were about to be destroyed through development. Despite the efforts of some government agencies, many volunteer groups and the charity Rescue, only a small proportion

were recorded. This was the key factor behind the introduction of the government policy and planning guide PPG 16 (►see p. 111).

In Britain recent debates about the destruction of archaeology have focused on peat extraction, the Channel Tunnel rail link and various road schemes. One of the most controversial is at Stonehenge and all sides of the debate can be researched at the websites below.

 http://www.britarch.ac.uk/cba/stone1.html

 http://www.savestonehenge.org.uk/

 http://www.stonhengemasterplan.org/

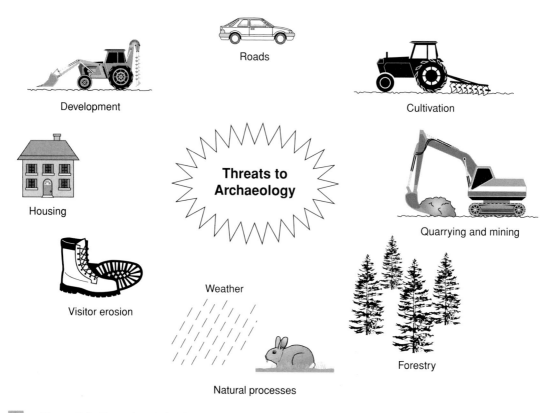

Figure 6.1 *Examples of the threats to archaeological remains*

Some high profile sites are simply threatened by increasing public interest in our past. Hadrian's Wall and Avebury are two high profile sites that have suffered badly from erosion caused by walkers. As World Heritage Sites (▶see p. 110) detailed management plans have been drawn up to try and resolve the conflict between access and preservation. Avebury's plan can be found at:

 http://www.english-heritage.org.uk/ knowledge/archaeology/new-archcommis/ archcommis9697/1.html

Naturally public attention focuses on threats to known monuments and exciting discoveries. However, a massive amount of our visible archaeological heritage has disappeared in the last fifty years with little protest. A glance at local aerial photographs from the 1940s will reveal how many hedges, water meadows and medieval field systems have vanished. To the landscape archaeologist they provide key evidence about landownership, settlement and use of the environment. Medieval field systems also provided a protective blanket over earlier sites that would otherwise have been eroded.

Global threats to archaeology

With the pace of development across the globe, huge numbers of archaeological sites are lost each year. Few countries have the resources to record what is lost and, for many, archaeology

KEY STUDY

The Monuments at Risk Survey of England (MARS), 1995

Bournemouth University and The Royal Commission on the Historic Monuments of England (RCHME) combined to survey the condition of a 5 per cent random sample of England's 937,484 recorded archaeological sites. The study, which was funded and published by English Heritage, provides a census of the nature, distribution and state of England's archaeological resources.

The study discovered that the South-east had lost the highest proportions of monuments with best survival in the West Midlands. Standing buildings and field systems are most at risk while those protected by legislation are at least risk. In total, 95 per cent of monuments had suffered some damage. Since 1945 an average of one site a day has been destroyed. Around 2 per cent of recorded sites will have been lost since the survey. The table below summarises the key causes of destruction.

Cause of destruction	Wholesale	Piecemeal
New building and urban growth	27	9
Building repairs, alterations, demolition	20	19
Mineral extraction	12	3
Cultivation	10	30
Road building	9	4
Natural processes, visitors, vandalism	5	24
Unknown	17	11

Figure 6.2 *Key causes of destruction to archaeological remains. From the MARS Report*

MARS drew on existing records plus its own surveys but inevitably will have missed many buried sites. The numbers of all sites destroyed and at risk will be higher.

 http://www.csweb.bournemouth.ac.uk//consci/text_mars/marsint.htm

Figure 6.3 *Example of a damaged site. Spoonley Wood Roman Villa was partially excavated and restored by Victorian antiquarians. Trees and visitors continue to damage it*

comes an understandable second to feeding and housing their people. An additional global problem is the looting of archaeological sites to feed the demand of western collectors for artefacts and artwork. Britain has its problems with 'nighthawks' (▶see p. 116) but looting in much of the world is on an industrial scale. At Angkor Wat and other Buddhist temples in Cambodia, power tools have been used to remove statues and reliefs which are then trucked over the border for export. In the west, the blame is often placed with corrupt local officials and the army for colluding or even controlling the trade. The Cambodian government has responded by blaming famous auction houses in London for disposing of

Figure 6.4 *Tikal, a Mayan site in Guatemala. Despite World Heritage Site status, Tikal, as are many similar monuments, is regularly threatened by looting. Gangs of well-organised (and sometimes armed) looters have removed stone reliefs and statues, sometimes with power-saws. Much of this material is bought by wealthy 'art collectors' in the west*

stolen antiquities. On a much lower scale sites throughout the world are routinely looted for coins, pottery and other portable artefacts by local people. They supplement low incomes by selling to tourists and dealers. Sometimes monuments are deliberately destroyed as has happened recently in Bosnia and Afghanistan.

 http://www.nationalgeographic.com/
features/97/copan/

 http://www.amnh.org/naturalhistory/
features/0201_feature.html

THE PROTECTION OF ARCHAEOLOGICAL REMAINS

Archaeology has not been well served in terms of legal protection. Nevertheless some protection has been provided in legislation since 1882. Some of the following laws only apply to England. There are similar laws for other parts of the UK.

Ancient Monuments and Archaeological Areas Act 1979 (AMAA)

Legislation before 1979 provided little protection. Even owners of scheduled monuments simply had to give notice if they wanted to change their condition. AMAA replaced previous laws and provided greater protection. Its key features are:

- the *consent* of the Secretary of State is required before any changes to scheduled monuments (listed by English Heritage as being of national importance) can be made
- English Heritage has the task of recording, assessing and monitoring monuments. It can recommend endangered sites and the land around them for scheduling to the Secretary of State for Culture, Media and Sport

 http://www.english-heritage.org.uk/

- Part 2 of the Act allowed Areas of Archaeological Importance to be designated where development could be delayed for proper assessment and excavation (paid from government funds)
- the National Heritage Act (1983) amended AMAA to also include works, gardens and 'areas' as Monuments.

Pros

- It gave legal protection to some visible monuments after years of destruction.
- The English Heritage monument protection programme is listing other key monuments. Currently about 15,000 are listed (only 2 per cent of known archaeological sites).
- Part 2 established the use of mapping as a tool to protect sites by warning developers of sites where their plans might be slowed down or halted.
- Some landowners have accepted funding and signed management agreements to protect sites.

Cons

- Sites which are not scheduled as being 'of national importance' (around 98 per cent of known sites) are not protected.
- Newly discovered sites are not protected, so these can be lost in development. The process of scheduling is slow (for example only 40 of 40,000 known shipwrecks are scheduled).
- It doesn't cover landscapes.
- It often protects a visible monument but leaves hidden, related features at risk of further damage. Many barrows survive as tiny islands in ploughed fields. This is vividly illustrated at the Knowlton Henge site.

http://www.csweb.bournemouth.ac.uk/
consci/text_kn/knhome.htm

- Landowners and developers can appeal and can also plead ignorance as an excuse for damaging sites.
- Few towns had areas of archaeological importance designated. The second part of the Act was never brought properly into force.
- The cost of work fell on local or national government, which did not always see this work as a priority!
- Ploughing of monuments can continue as long as the depth of ploughing isn't increased.

Other protective legislation for sites

Most of these laws were not drawn up with archaeology in mind, however they do provide some protection for unscheduled sites including archaeological landscapes.

- *The National Parks Act 1949 limited* development within the parks and designated other 'Areas of Outstanding Natural Beauty'. MARS found that survival in these areas was better than elsewhere.
- *The Wildlife and Countryside Act 1981* required local authorities to assess rural areas and draw up plans for their management. Archaeology *can* be taken into account.
- *The Town and Country Planning Act 1971 allowed* local authorities to take Archaeology into account in planning applications and *required* them to produce structure plans for future development. Further legislation in 1990 created conservation areas.
- *Capital Transfer Tax 1984.* Landowners are exempted from this if they sign (secret)

 KEY TASK

Group exercises assessing local monuments

- Visit a sample of local monuments to try and assess the condition and threats to them. You may be able to obtain a list from your local SMR. Compare your findings to the MARS study.
- Investigate what the impact of PPG 16 has been in your area. This could involve interviews with some of those involved and examination of the role of local organisations such as units, SMR, etc.

Either of these tasks would make a good personal study project.

management agreements to maintain and preserve the land and ensure reasonable access.
- Additionally there are clauses on archaeology in legislation on a number of industries including coal mining and electricity. There are also a growing number of non-statutory categories of designation such as Parks and Gardens and the Battlefield Register. None of these provide secure protection and none ensures funding for archaeological work.

International protection

The United Nations Educational, Scientific and Cultural Organization (UNESCO) has drawn up a World Heritage list of 630 sites of outstanding international value.

Governments of most UN member states have signed up to protect these sites. In itself this provides some protection since it would be embarrassing for a government to authorise development on a listed site. The scheme also enables funds to be channelled to conservation and restoration projects on endangered sites in poorer countries. However, it does not guarantee preservation and only covers a fraction of sites worldwide.

 http://www.unesco.org/whc/nwhc/pages/ sites/main.htm

Countries vary widely in how they manage archaeological resources. This chapter has focused on England but Australia provides an interesting alternative example:

 http://life.csu.edu.au~dspennem/ VIRTPAST/VIRTPAST.HTM/

PROTECTION OF ARTEFACTS

Legal protection of artefacts focuses on those few examples of high monetary value. The old laws on treasure trove in England and Wales were replaced by the Treasure Act in 1996. It defines objects and coins as treasure which are over 300 years old and either over ten per cent precious metal or at least ten in number. Items substantially composed of precious metal and less than 300 years old are treasure if it can be shown that they were deposited with the intention of recovering them.

 http://www.hmso.gov.uk/acts/acts1996/ 1996024.htm

 www.finds.org.uk

Apart from general legislation on theft and trespass, the law neglects other materials (for example pottery) which may be of greater archaeological value. In the case of treasure, it also means that the archaeological record/archive can be broken up.

PROTECTION THROUGH THE PLANNING PROCESS: PPG 16

Planning and Policy Guide note number 16 (1990) is not a law. It one of several guidelines issued by the government to help local planning officials in England when they consider applications to develop land. Another note, PPG 15 (1994), deals with changes to buildings of historic interest. However, while PPG 16 is not law, planners need to have good reasons for not following its advice. It advises planners to consider archaeology at an early stage of the development process and to favour the preservation of archaeological remains where possible. PPG 16 advises that the developer should be responsible for funding any archaeological work deemed necessary. It also provides guidance on appeals that can be made to the Secretary of State for the Environment.

PPG 16 broadly divides archaeologists into two groups.

Curators

Local authority (LA) archaeologists advise planners on the sensitivity of each site, following a desktop survey (►see Chapter 1) drawing on information held by the LA Sites and Monuments Record (SMR). They will draw up the brief for any archaeological work needed and check that it is done to required standards. Most of the finds from development work are usually deposited with the LA museum service.

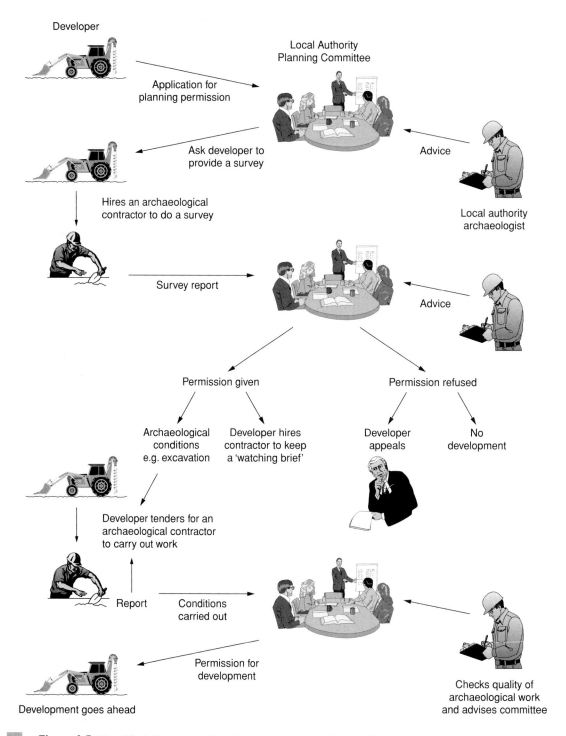

Figure 6.5 *Simplified diagram to show how archaeology is involved in the planning process*

Contractors

Developers will put out a contract for
exploratory archaeological work or excavation
to competitive tender. They may also hire
archaeological consultants to contest the local
authority positions. Independent archaeological
trusts or commercial 'units' do most of this
work. LA units or amateur groups carry out
some work but this is becoming increasingly
rare.

 http://www.britarch.ac.uk/info/contract.html

The effects of PPG 16

PPG 16 has had an enormous impact on
archaeology in England and there is considerable debate amongst archaeologists about its
positive and negative effects. To gain a taste of
the debate, look in the archives of the
archaeology email discussion group Britarch.

 britarch@jiscmail.ac.uk

Key points include the following:

Positive
- The past is now recognised as a finite
  resource, which requires management and
  conservation.
- Rescue archaeology is funded by what
  amounts to a tax on development.
- Archaeological remains are considered by
  planners and those which are destroyed are
  often 'preserved by record'.
- It provides increased employment for
  professional archaeologists
- It encourages the development of
  SMRs because of the need for detailed
  records.

Negative
- Sites for excavation are dictated by
  development rather than research needs.
- It results in decreasing opportunities for
  amateur enthusiasts to become involved in
  excavations (▶see p. 116).
- Archaeological units tended to price
  themselves too low in bids during the early
  1990s with the result that many struggle to
  pay staff well.
- The costs of post-excavation work,
  including the use of specialists and storage
  of remains, tends to be overlooked and may
  have suffered. Some museums are now
  'full'.
- Excavation reports are the property of the
  developers, who do not have to publish
  them.
- Some local authorities have used PPG 16 as
  a way of reducing funding for archaeology.
  LA archaeologists often spend most of their
  time on planning matters.

The language of PPG 16

PPG 16 has generated a new range of
terminology, which needs to be understood in
order to follow archaeologists' discussions:

- *Archaeological assessment or appraisal*:
  usually means a desktop survey and a look
  at the site.
- *Field evaluation*: a survey of the site, which
  usually includes trial trenching to establish
  the depth, nature and condition of remains.
- *Watching brief*: literally that. An archaeologist will watch as the bulldozers go in to
  see if any archaeological remains are
  unearthed and to report on them.
- *Preservation in situ*: PPG 16 favours
  preserving archaeological remains where
  they are. This can mean putting a raft of
  concrete over deposits or resting buildings

Other forms of protection

The protection of archaeological remains is a key aim of many of the organisations listed in the next section. Official agencies such as English Heritage or Historic Scotland have statutory responsibilities and advise ministers on policy and decisions affecting archaeology.

http://www.english-heritage.org.uk/

http://www.historic-scotland.gov.uk/

Campaigns, including lobbying, use of the media and advice for developers and farmers, are also part of the roles of independent organisations, charities and learned bodies such as the Council for British Archaeology (CBA), Rescue and the Prehistoric Society. There is also the Institute of Field Archaeologists which promotes (but cannot enforce) high standards amongst those engaging in excavations and acts as a professional body for the sector.

http://www.britarch.ac.uk

http//www.rescue-archaeology. freeserve.co.uk/

http:www.britarch.ac.uk/prehist

http://www.archaeologists.net

Figure 6.6 *Developer-led archaeology. This major excavation in Cheltenham by the Cotswold Archaeological Trust was the result of a contract tendered by the developers as part of planning permission for a new superstore. The small team of professional archaeologists dressed in safety gear and working to tight deadlines at any time of year (this was January) is the face of most modern archaeology*

on piles driven through deposits. This method is controversial. In Norway, piling, which damages and interferes with the drainage and stratigraphy of sites, is viewed as destruction rather than preservation.

■ *Preservation by record*: the site is destroyed but a proper archaeological record is made through a detailed site report.

WHO ARE THE ARCHAEOLOGISTS?

Within archaeology in the UK there is increasing debate about who should engage in practical archaeology. Archaeology's roots lie with the work of enthusiastic amateurs but it has become increasingly professionalised.

Beginning with the antiquarians from the seventeenth century onwards archaeology provided a hobby for landed enthusiasts. This continued until the 1950s. Some early diggers were little more than grave robbers but by the twentieth century other amateurs, such as Sir Mortimer Wheeler, had pioneered modern excavation techniques.

Learned and excavation societies

By the late Victorian period most parts of the country had societies devoted to gathering archaeological information and communicating it to their members and to the wider public. Most undertook excavations and began journals, many of which continue to this day. Some even established museums where their collections could be displayed. As before, it was largely an upper-class activity, undertaken by those who could afford the time to take part in research excavations. The societies did,

however, engage a wider spectrum of the public by the 1950s.

Rescue archaeology

The massive urban expansion and road building programmes of the 1960s and 1970s saw a rapid rise in rescue archaeology as teams of volunteers or low paid diggers sought to record what they could before bulldozers or ploughs destroyed remains. This coincided with a rapid expansion of higher education including the development of new archaeological departments. These developments provided many new opportunities for the public to get involved in archaeology and to follow that interest academically. However, archaeology was poorly resourced. Much of the funding came from charitable efforts. It was difficult to find full time paid work in archaeology but a pool of skilled excavators did develop from diggers who moved from site to site.

Figure 6.7 *How it used to be: amateur involvement in archaeology. The Empingham excavation (▶see p. 30) involved a small number of professionals working alongside volunteers. Since the 1970s, amateurs have been gradually squeezed out of much excavation work by professionalisation and the terms of developer contracts*

Archaeology today

In the 1980s and 1990s archaeology underwent major changes. Commercialisation came initially thorough government funding for job creation schemes run by the Manpower Services Commission, then with PPG 16 it largely came from developers. Opportunities for amateurs to be involved in digging declined. Developers expected professional workers on site and commercial health and safety regulations to be applied. Also, the need for recruits to spend their time earning a living made it difficult to supervise or train volunteers. Professionalisation was also marked in the growth of member organisations such as the Institute of Field Archaeologists, which set standards for entry and provided a code of conduct for members. Archaeology also became more specialised. The application of scientific techniques for prospecting, recording and analysing was in most cases beyond the resources of rescue committees and enthusiastic amateurs.

Most excavations now fall into the following three categories:

- Assessments and rescue excavations in advance of developments. These are largely carried out by professional archaeologists in the contracting units.
- Research excavations run by universities. These are largely open to their own students although some take paying volunteers as training excavations.
- Research excavation by specialists from government heritage agencies.

There are still amateur excavations but they are much fewer and smaller scale than previously. The Council for Independent Archaeology offers a forum for amateur archaeologists.

 http://www.archaeology.co.uk/cia/default.htm

More generally, amateurs are still able to take part in supporting roles such as pot-washing and fieldwalking but their opportunities to dig and to develop expertise are greatly reduced. For criticisms of 'official archaeology' see:

 http://www.archaeology.co.uk/gateway/thinktank/who/welcome.htm

Metal detecting

The gradual exclusion of amateurs from field archaeology has coincided with an increase in metal detecting. Some professionals remain hostile to all detectorists because of damage that has been done to sites or looting by organised gangs of 'nighthawks'. Increasingly there are also commercial companies advertising metal detecting tours.

 http://www.losttreasure.com/affiliatedtravel

However, most detectorists are not intentionally destructive or members of criminal gangs but simply people interested in the physical past. Increasingly there have been moves by county archaeologists to work with detectorists and some archaeologists do use metal detectors on excavations. Issues can be followed up at the CBA website.

 http://www.britarch.ac.uk/detecting/index.html

 http://www.ukdetectornet.co.uk/

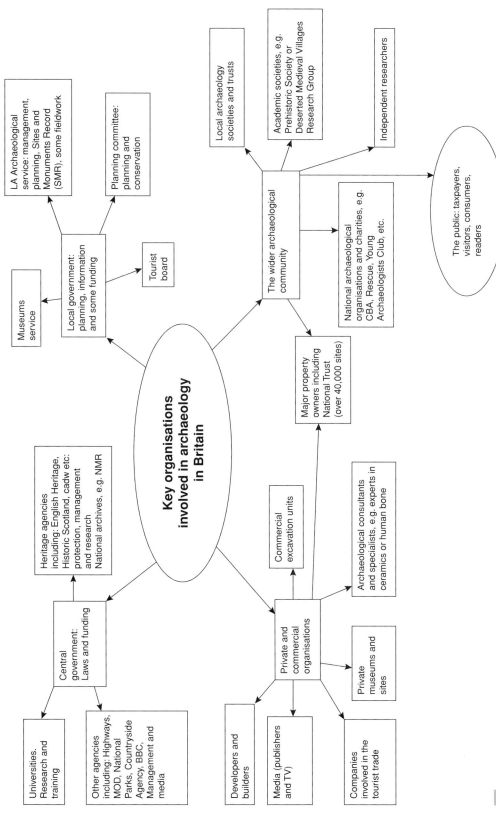

Figure 6.8 *The key organisations involved in British archaeology*

Key organisations involved in archaeology in Britain

Central government: Laws and funding

Universities. Research and training

Other agencies including: Highways, MOD, National Parks, Countryside Agency, BBC, Management and media

Heritage agencies including: English Heritage, Historic Scotland, cadw etc: protection, management and research National archives, e.g. NMR

Museums service

Local government: planning, information and some funding

LA Archaeological service: management, planning, Sites and Monuments Record (SMR), some fieldwork

Planning committee: planning and conservation

Tourist board

The wider archaeological community

Local archaeology societies and trusts

Academic societies, e.g. Prehistoric Society or Deserted Medieval Villages Research Group

Independent researchers

National archaeological organisations and charities, e.g. CBA, Rescue, Young Archaeologists Club, etc.

The public: taxpayers, visitors, consumers, readers

Major property owners including National Trust (over 40,000 sites)

Private and commercial organisations

Commercial excavation units

Archaeological consultants and specialists, e.g. experts in ceramics or human bone

Private museums and sites

Developers and builders

Media (publishers and TV)

Companies involved in the tourist trade

KEY SKILL

Starting to construct arguments

Putting together arguments is a key element in higher level essay writing. One way to approach this is to organise your notes into pro and con lists. Try this for the following question. It would work equally well as a small group task.

Outline the case for and against amateur involvement in excavation

Aim to write three sides of A4. You might like to consider the following points as starters.

■ Most archaeologists start out as amateurs.
■ Professionals are 'better' than amateurs.
■ Can standards be ensured without professionalism?

Tip

Writing pro and con assignments usually leads to one of the following structures.

A	B
Introduction and outline of issue	Introduction and outline of issue
Points and examples for	Point by point for and against
Points and examples against	Weighing up to reach a judgement
Weighing up to reach a judgement	Conclusion
Conclusion	

A is easier to write than *B*, but *B* ensures that you compare for and against on each point. *A* can become descriptive while with *B* you have to be analytical. Whichever you select, try to provide a range of points and support each with a specific example. If you only consider a few points it is difficult to reach the higher levels of markschemes, however much detail you have included. It is also vital that you say at the end how far you agree with the arguments for and against. Don't worry about what you conclude as long as it is supported by the judgements you make in the body of the assignment.

Alternative assignments:

■ Consider the arguments for and against metal detecting.
■ Consider the strengths of research archaeology against developer-led archaeology.

KEY SKILL *cont.*

Key skills opportunities

The task above provides the opportunity to meet some national level 3 communication key skills. By entering the table from the MARS report (Figure 6.2) in a spreadsheet package such as Excel you could present and interrogate the information in a variety of different formats to meet ICT key skills at level 2 or 3.

Archaeological employment

The popular view of archaeologists is that they spend their time digging. While many do, there are at least an equal number who do not. For those of you who are considering archaeology related careers, Figure 6.8 may provide helpful in identifying opportunities.

Chapter 7

Presenting
the Past

YOUR GOALS

You need to

■ understand some of the political and ethical debates about ownership and presentation of
the past

■ have a knowledge of a range of methods of communicating archaeological understanding

■ know some case studies in depth to use as examples

■ be able to critically assess the merits of different modes of communication.

WHICH PAST?

Before considering how archaeological remains
and knowledge might be best communicated it
is worth reflecting on what the social and
cultural implications of explanations about the
past might be. Archaeological knowledge and
the images of the past created by archaeologists
are not value free. As with history and
literature, the selection of what is significant
and how it should be interpreted partly derives
from the political and social values and
structures in present-day society. Archaeology
and history have in turn been used either
consciously or unconsciously to justify
present-day values and social structures.

The political use of archaeology

Extreme cases are fairly easy to identify. Recent
centuries have seen a succession of rulers who
have sought to justify their regimes and their
territorial ambitions by claiming precedent
from the past. Mussolini, the Fascist dictator of
Italy (1922–45) claimed to be following in the
footsteps of the Romans with his plans to
establish an Italian empire in Africa and to turn
the Mediterranean into an Italian lake (Mare
Nostrum). Saddam Hussein in Iraq has drawn
parallels between his regime and the ancient
civilisation of Babylon, which dominated the
region in the second millennium BC. Israel,
Bosnia and the Indian city of Ayodhya are
three of many places where archaeology is

KEY STUDY

Nazi archaeology

Archaeology was enlisted for propaganda purposes by the Nazi government of Germany during the 1930s and 1940s. At this time it was commonplace for archaeologists to associate pottery styles with distinctive ethnic groups and to identify racial differences from skeletal remains. The Nazis used this confusion of race with ethnicity to draw up racial maps of Europe and identify 'superior' races. Their excavations 'revealed' artefacts of Germanic origin in occupied Poland including some bowls marked with swastikas! Overlooking the fact that the symbol itself is an ancient Indian one, these forgeries were given a scientific stamp of approval and used to justify the Nazi conquests as retaking land that was 'proven' to be historically German.

involved in violent political conflicts. In each case the ability to control what is known about the past is used as a tool to legitimise political, social or economic power.

However, it is not just dictatorships or extremist political parties which have used archaeology for political ends. Mainstream politicians in many countries have argued over the ownership of cultural remains. The most famous of these is the dispute between Britain and Greece over the Elgin Marbles. In many parts of the world, native peoples are using archaeology to reclaim rights lost in previous centuries. In some cases this involves claims for the return of cultural artefacts taken from them by foreign museums or art collectors.

Increasingly there are also disputes over the disturbance of burials by archaeologists and for the return of human remains to their place of origin for burial. Usually at the heart of these conflicts are two fundamental issues:

■ Should (usually western) archaeologists have the right to excavate cultural remains of another culture or are their actions simply a continuation of colonialist exploitation?
■ Do excavated remains from the past provide evidence which can be used to sustain claims on the rightful ownership of land?

Archaeology and land rights

In South Africa during the colonial period, a myth was created by Dutch settlers that they had occupied an empty land. Archaeological finds proved that to be false. In Australia, aboriginal groups have been able to use archaeological evidence to prove that their ancestors inhabited particular regions and to demonstrate their right to the land or to compensation for its use by others.

Archaeology and identity

In Britain, there are also political struggles about rights and identity which involve archaeology and assumption drawn from it. In Wales, the selection of sites for preservation and particularly for promotion has generated debate about which version of the past should predominate: the past of English conquest and castle building or the tradition of Welsh independence and resistance? More generally, the way archaeologists have interpreted the past can lead to certain values and arrangements being seen as unchanging and therefore 'normal'.

KEY STUDIES

Archaeology and Native Americans

According to historical records, the Pequot Indian tribe of Connecticut died out following a war with European settlers in the seventeenth century. However, archaeologists working with descendants of the Pequots were able to establish cultural continuity between the original tribe and survivors of the war whose descendents continued to live on reservations in the area until recent times. The Pequots were able to use archaeological data to gain recognition as a sovereign nation from the US government in 1987. A treaty was signed and some of their land was returned to them.

By the 1990s the civil rights movements for Native Americans had won a series of legal and political victories. One of these was the 1990 Native American Graves Protection and Repatriation Act (NAGPRA) which provides for the return to tribes of the skeletons and religious artefacts of their ancestors. This has created problems for archaeologists. To some Native Americans, archaeology is grave robbing by an occupying power. A major conflict has arisen since the discovery of human remains at Kennewick on the Columbia River. Scientists who examined the remains dated them to 8410 ± BP and claimed that the anatomy was different from that of Native Americans. 'Kennewick Man' quickly became a political issue. Native Americans wanted the remains to be reburied, not studied. Some feared that if he did prove to be from a people who occupied the area before the current tribes, his existence might be used to challenge the right of Native Americans to that land. Attempts to perform rituals near the bones led to claims that their DNA was deliberately being contaminated. The US Army then dumped rubble over the find-site but were unable to prevent the dispute spreading. For further details on this fascinating case try the following websites:

 http://www.kennewick-man.com/

 http://www.umatilla.nsn.us/
(for the Native American perspective)

 http://www.archaeology.org/
(for the Archaeological Institute
of America's view)

Until the late twentieth century, many archaeologists associated particular artefacts with homogenous ethnic groups and attributed social changes to the arrivals of new peoples, for example 'the beaker people'. This fitted with the assumptions of many classically educated people that social and technological developments had originated in the Mediterranean and then were spread by colonists into the barbarian lands further north. It also fitted the way in which Europeans viewed their empires in the rest of the world

PRESENTING THE PAST ■ 123

 KEY SKILL

Taking notes from contradictory sources

For longer questions, including essays, you will be expected to consider more than one side to any given issue. In order to do this effectively and quickly, you need to become used to understanding arguments. If you find this difficult you could try using this structured approach. Attempt it using the Kennewick websites as your raw material.

For each point of view complete a table such as the one below. State as simply as you can the general argument or claim.

List the key points they make	What evidence do they give to support this point?	Do you find the evidence acceptable?	Does this point support their overall argument

How strong do you think this argument is?

Having done this you may now be able to distinguish between the arguments. Are some of the points in them contradictory? Are some points unsupported or supported by evidence that you feel is unsound? Is the difference one of belief or opinion for which you can only decide on a moral basis? You may find that the two parties agree on certain aspects or that you think they are both sound in different ways. This is the kind of information you will need to write down when you move on to discursive essays (▶see p. 191).

and to some extent justified their role in spreading 'civilisation' to inferior 'races'. Recent advances in archaeology and genetics have undermined the idea that pure ethnic groups existed in the past, while radiocarbon dating has shown that indigenous Neolithic and Bronze Age peoples had achieved a great deal well before the arrival of Mediterranean influences. The building of Stonehenge and the brochs of Scotland and the Northern Isles (▶see p. 185) are two cases where the achievements of indigenous populations are now recognised.

In a similar way, early archaeologists often identified burials of male and female on the basis of their assumptions about gender roles. For example, a skeleton buried with an axe *must* have been male because men fight and chop down trees, a burial with a mirror or domestic artefacts *must* be female. A largely 'female' burial with an arrowhead could be explained away as a woman who had been killed by the arrow. This kind of analysis has, in turn, tended to reinforce stereotypes about natural roles for men and women. Once again, recent discoveries such as the Pazyryk 'Ice

Maiden' and DNA analysis have tended to challenge the traditional view (see p. 247). Some museums have begun to re-label displays where the earlier sexing of skeletal remains is in doubt.

New Age and pagan beliefs and the issue of access to ancient monuments

Most books on Stonehenge feature a picture of the Druids, a nineteenth-century order who developed their own ceremonies at the monument based on their interpretation of Iron Age beliefs. Since the 1960s other groups have also sought to use ancient monuments for rituals and festivals. In some cases people have claimed the sites as sacred according to their beliefs and want the right to worship there. For others their demands to hold parties at the sites symbolise a struggle against an oppressive state. Either way, these demands have led to conflict with those responsible for managing the monuments and archaeologists concerned about damage to remains. In the case of the West Kennet Long Barrow this involves sarsen stone being damaged by candles. In the case of Stonehenge disputes over access have led to public order offences and occasionally violence. There is plenty of material available on other controversial sites including Mayburgh Henge where there was a proposal to raise a Christian millennium stone in 2000.

 http://www.stonehenge.ukf.net/edenarts.htm

 KEY STUDY

Seahenge

In 1999 a Bronze Age timber monument was discovered on eroding mudflats off the Norfolk coast. Initially there was a very public dispute between English Heritage, which felt it was not worth saving from the sea, and archaeologists, who saw it as a unique and priceless ritual site. English Heritage reversed its decision and the timbers were excavated and taken to Flag Fen near Peterborough for conservation. This provoked opposition from local people who wanted the timbers to remain near where they had been found, and from pagans who saw the excavation of the site as sacrilege. The debate continues and is extensively documented on the 2000 link at the Time Team website.

 http://www.channel4.com/nextstep/ timeteam/

Figure 7.1 *Seahenge: the Bronze Age timber circle at Holme on Sea in situ (before excavation). This unique site is to be reburied because there are insufficient funds to conserve and present it*

KEY TASK

Seahenge role play

In groups, take on the roles of the various interested parties in the dispute. Use the Time Team website and its links to research the nature and basis of the arguments used before debating the issue. If you make a presentation of your arguments, you could use this as evidence for part of your national key skill in communication.

The common thread that runs through all of these disputes is control of the past. Those who control access to sites and artefacts are best placed to interpret the past for the wider public. It is their values which will be reflected in accounts of the past and their values which in turn are supported by those accounts.

COMMUNICATING ARCHAEOLOGICAL KNOWLEDGE

Figure 7.2 gives you some idea of the range of modes of communication used within archaeology. Some of these will already be familiar to you but some may not be. Try to have a look at a couple of examples of each of the unfamiliar modes so that you can comment on them and provide examples in the evaluation exercise that follows. The websites

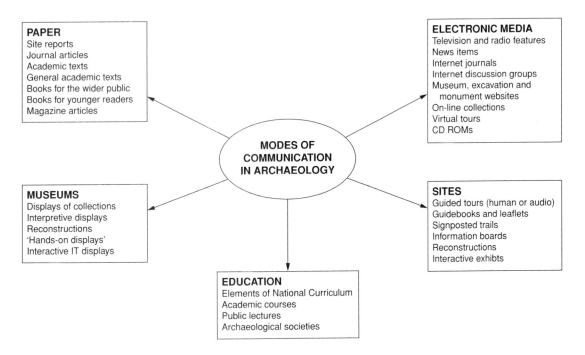

PAPER
Site reports
Journal articles
Academic texts
General academic texts
Books for the wider public
Books for younger readers
Magazine articles

ELECTRONIC MEDIA
Television and radio features
News items
Internet journals
Internet discussion groups
Museum, excavation and
   monument websites
On-line collections
Virtual tours
CD ROMs

MODES OF COMMUNICATION IN ARCHAEOLOGY

MUSEUMS
Displays of collections
Interpretive displays
Reconstructions
'Hands-on displays'
Interactive IT displays

SITES
Guided tours (human or audio)
Guidebooks and leaflets
Signposted trails
Information boards
Reconstructions
Interactive exhibts

EDUCATION
Elements of National Curriculum
Academic courses
Public lectures
Archaeological societies

Figure 7.2 *The communication of archaeological information. These are the main modes of communication used in archaeology. There is overlap between some categories, for example some museums also provide education services and have their own websites*

KEY STUDIES

Different modes of communication

A specialist pottery report within a site excavation report

The audience is largely other professionals, particularly pottery specialists. Only a few hundred copies have been printed, so the report is expensive to buy and you can probably only obtain it from a university library or a specialist archaeological bookshop. Some of the data may only be readable using a microfiche reader. The report may contain little or no overall interpretation, leaving the expert readers to draw their own conclusions. The precise, scientific nature and language of the report makes it fairly inaccessible to the general public but it is an essential reference for pottery specialists and for researchers who can access the published report instead of having to examine the pottery. In the future, an electronic version might increase accessibility for specialists while 3D reconstructions might make the report interesting to a wider audience. However, this would be expensive.

A Time Team excavation on television

Some professionals despair at the idea of a three-day excavation against the clock but they are not the intended audience for this programme. Its main function is to provide entertainment to a general audience whilst educating them in some aspects of archaeo-logical methods and interpretations. The format of a time-limited challenge to a group of personalities is well established in popular television through house and garden makeover shows. Technical language and ideas are communicated simply through computer-generated images while the routine or time-consuming aspects of excavation and post-excavation work are edited out in favour of action involving celebrity diggers. Its entertainment value is attested to by its high ratings. It has raised public awareness of

Figure 7.3 *Using computer aided design (CAD) to reconstruct pottery in 3D*

Figure 7.4 *Time Team: probably the most successful vehicle for bringing archaeology to a wide audience*

KEY STUDIES *cont.*

archaeology in a way few other media can equal. In addition, its website and publications provide opportunities for people to develop their understanding and explore links to educational sites. However, the programme may raise unrealistic expectations about

archaeology and the possibility of public involvement that may ultimately frustrate its audience.

 http:///www.channel4.com/nextstep/ timeteam/

---

listed in this text and the bibliography provide examples to get you started.

One of the reasons for such diversity is that there are many differing audiences for archaeology and their requirements vary. Consider how your requirements of a site or museum might differ from those of a researcher or of a class of 5 year olds. As a result, what is a perfectly adequate mode of communication for one person may be inaccessible or too shallow for another. The contrast between a specialist pottery report and an episode of Time Team illustrates this point well.

Archaeological communication and new technology

Before 1990, most archaeological knowledge was communicated via lectures and the printed word. While these are familiar mediums, it is expensive to produce reports and books and there is often a considerable timelag before new ideas and discoveries are widely disseminated. Developments in communications technology present a great opportunity to archaeology and practice is rapidly changing.

Virtual reality displays and GIS systems (►see p. 9) are still expensive but digital photography and basic websites are now

accessible to most people. This has enabled a much wider range of people to produce and disseminate archaeological information. A look at some good examples illustrates this:

- Individual enthusiasts, for example the Stone Pages:

  http://www.stonepages.com/

- Groups of enthusiasts, for example the Megalithic Society:

  http://www.stonehenge-avebury.net/

- Local surveys, for example Thetford Forest:

  http://harsner.fsnet.co.uk/frames.htm

- Individual excavations, for example Stanway:

  http://www.hullcc.gov.uk/archaeology/ flixboro.htm

- University projects, for example Gardoms Edge

  http://www.shef.ac.uk/~geap/

- National sites, for example the Coa petroglyphs in Portugal:

  http://www.ipa.min-cultura.pt/coa/homeuk/ homeuk.html

KEY SKILL

Assessing modes of communication using the 4 As

Assessing particular modes of communication and display is usually done in relation to specific case studies, for example 'How might archaeologists best communicate the results of a particular excavation?' or 'How could a specific site be better presented to the public?'

In order to address these issues you should consider the following criteria:

- *Audience*: who is it for and what might they hope to get from it?
- *Accessibility*: does its design and location enable it to reach its intended audience(s)?
- *Adequacy*: is it useful for that audience?
- *Alternatives*: would another mode of communication be more effective?

Select several examples such as a local museum display, a TV programme or a site report. Copy out the grid below on a large sheet of paper and complete it, using yourself as a student on your particular course as the intended audience. Pay particular attention to your reason for using the sources and why it was useful or not.

Examples	Audience	Accessibility	Adequacy	Alternatives
	Research for my essay on . . . (insert topics in boxes)	Could you get it and understand it?	How did it meet your needs or was it of limited use to you?	How might an alternative mode have worked better?
Local museum				
A local site				
Site report on X				
An academic text				
A website				
A guidebook				

Now repeat the exercise taking the part of a different audience, for example a tourist visiting the area, a primary school group. You should start to gain an awareness of the difficulties of meeting diverse needs within one mode of communication.

■ International research projects, for example Catal Huyuk:

 http://catal.arch.cam.ac.uk/catal/catal.html

■ Museums, for example National Museums of Scotland at

 http://www.nms.ac.uk/

■ Government agencies, for example Cadw at

 http://www.cadw.wales.gov.uk/

■ American archaeology videos at

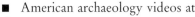 http://www.archaeologychannel.org/

The time between recording and presenting to an audience is much reduced. Many excavations now offer daily diaries or web cams on their websites. Shapwick (►see p. 15) illustrates this well. The numbers visiting most site websites far exceed the numbers of site reports sold. Moreover, the audience is now global rather than largely national.

The use of hyperlinks in text offers the chance to satisfy more than one audience at the same time. A basic account can be supplemented by detailed discussion in other linked documents. Similarly, this can be applied to maps and site plans through point and click options as at Kilmartin.

 http://www.kilmartin.org/

Not only does digital imagery readily offer high quality colour photographs where their use was previously rationed, it also goes beyond the limitations of two-dimensional illustration on A3 sized paper. Maps and plans can be presented at a much larger scale and three-dimensional modelling is possible as at Wroxeter.

 http://www.bufau.bham.ac.uk/newsite/ Projects/BT/default.htm

The online journal *Internet Archaeology* is exploring the wider potential of the internet for archaeological publishing.

 http://intarch.ac.uk/

Finally there is the potential for discussing ideas and seeking help from fellow archaeologists through discussion groups such as the CBA's Britarch list or the archaeology teachers group Ed-arch-uk.

 http://www.jiscmail.ac.uk/lists/britarch.html

 http://www.jiscmail.ac.uk/lists/ed-arch- uk.html

Problems with using the internet for research

There are, of course, some drawbacks to the new technology. The sheer volume of material available means that you have to be selective but it is often difficult to immediately see what might be relevant. A particular problem for students is that referencing conventions are not applied to the same degree as in printed material. It is often hard to tell what is opinion, fantasy or based on evidence. Often there is no way of checking. If you cite internet sources in essays at undergraduate level, be sure to appraise them thoroughly. A further problem, admittedly more for your lecturers, is plagiarism. It is easy to cut and paste someone else's work into your own. Resist the temptation. If you are caught, the penalties can be severe.

Figure 7.5 *An example of poor presentation of an archaeological site. This is the view from the avenue into Stonehenge. It was a likely processional route in the Bronze Age. Modern visitors are prevented from entering the monument in the 'right' way by a fence and busy road. The new plans for the monument may correct this*

Applying communication issues on your course

By now you will appreciate how hard it is to successfully communicate in ways that reach all possible audiences. Some sources will have clearly targeted particular audiences. Others, such as sites or museums, will probably have changed their methods to reach wider audiences. This may have involved diversifying the types of presentation or a wholesale change in the way collections or a site are displayed. If you wished to follow up this topic as a major project on a particular site you should be able to find one of their staff who can explain their thinking on this.

A second approach to this topic on some courses, including A Level, is to ask you to consider how to present a site which may currently be inaccessible, or has little existing display material. This might typically include sites under excavation or a site that has no upstanding features. In these cases you need to not only draw on your knowledge of different types of communication and their suitability for particular audiences but understand some of the other issues facing museum and site management staff. These include:

■ *funding*: the latest high-tech displays might be nice but how realistic is a budget to provide, maintain and secure them?

KEY STUDY

The 'reconstructed' Anglo-Saxon village of West Stow

West Stow in Suffolk uses a variety of different means to present an excavated and recorded site to the public.

Excavation of this site revealed traces of a number of features including rectangular grubenhauser. The materials used had not survived in the sandy local soil but postholes, pits and beam slots were preserved, as were a range of inorganic artefacts and a quantity of animal bones. The site reports catalogue and interpret the finds for the archaeological profession and also highlight the problem of interpreting the above ground structure of the buildings.

Rectangular pits with domestic rubbish are common on early Anglo-Saxon sites. These grubenhauser had previously been interpreted as pit dwellings, in part reflecting the view amongst classically influenced archaeologists that their inhabitants really were barbaric. With increasing knowledge of Anglo-Saxon carpentry and construction techniques, experimental archaeology has developed alternative models. At West Stow several versions were constructed over the excavated features. It is now thought likely that gruben-hauser had suspended floors with the rubbish entering the pit after the building's abandonment.

There is also a debate about the internal decoration and use of buildings. The site, which includes a display centre through which visitors enter a recreation of the settlement, addresses these issues and the problem of multiple audiences in a number of ways.

Figure 7.6 *An excavated grubenhaus at Lechlade*

■ Several different versions of the buildings were built on the sites of the originals so that visitors could enter each and judge them against the plans in guidebooks and the visitors centre.

■ Artefacts are displayed in the visitors centre with pictures and reconstructions alongside to show how they were used.

■ Activity areas allow visitors to see how artefacts might have been made.

■ Demonstrations by experts in fields such as green woodworking are available to those interested.

■ Audio tours offer the alternative of a populist commentary by 'a Saxon', which

KEY STUDY *cont.*

discusses the way of life. or a 'serious' archaeological tour, which discusses the evidence.

■ Publications are available at a variety of levels ranging from infant school to professional.

Figure 7.7 *Experimental Anglo-Saxon houses at West Stow based on excavated remains similar to those in Figure 7.6*

■ *impact*: modern interactive displays take up more room than traditional displays of exhibits. In a finite space, what would you have to remove from display? Visitor centres and display boards may be useful, but will they alter or ruin the visual impact of a site?

■ *Accuracy*: reconstructions are popular with the public but may be misleading. It may be possible to reconstruct the wooden handle of an iron tool with a reasonable degree of accuracy but rebuilding a Neolithic structure from a mass of postholes will be more problematic. Is it better to show how something was used, even if it may be inaccurate, or provide the evidence and ask people (who are not specialists) to try to make up their own minds? The websites in

KEY TASK

Outlining a presentation of a site or landscape

Consider a site or a landscape that contains archaeological remains with which you are familiar.

a) Briefly describe the site and outline the types of evidence available. (200 words)
b) Produce a visual presentation to show how it could best be presented to visitors to the area. (800 words)

Your account should include a justification of your selection of key methods of communication and use sketches, diagrams and plans where appropriate to illustrate it. Remember to consider the 4 As.

Key skills opportunity

This activity offers the chance to meet some national key skill communication objectives at level 3.

Figure 7.8 *The Roman Villa at Kingscote cleaned up after excavation for viewing by visitors*

this section illustrate a variety of responses to this issue.

 http://www.archaeolink.co.uk/home.htm

 http://www.history.maelmin.ukf.net/

The world heritage site at Lascaux provides a good example of what can be done with a large budget. The very presence of visitors in the caves was damaging the delicate Palaeolithic wall-paintings there. The response has been to close the cave but to construct a copy nearby for visitors whilst producing an interactive website to enable virtual exploration of the real thing.

 http://www.culture.fr/culture/arcnat/ lascaux/fr/p

Part Two
Studying Themes in Archaeology

The content of archaeology courses can be arranged in many ways. All include methods but they are selective and often include an element of choice in their areas of archaeological knowledge. Some focus on particular parts of the world, following continuity and change over time, e.g. 'British prehistory'. Others may focus on change but take a whole world perspective, looking at topics such as 'human origins' or 'the origins of farming'. Some concentrate on particular cultures in more limited periods such as 'the classical world' while others, including A Level, are organised around themes. Whichever course you take you will need to use case studies. In fact the same case studies might be relevant to all these courses. For example, the Iron Age settlement at Hengistbury Head could be used to study:

- the emergence of elites and trade in Iron Age Britain
- the development of towns and commercial trade
- the influence of the Roman Empire
- settlement function, exchange and manufacturing.

We have chosen to organise this section thematically partly because it mirrors the A Level syllabus and partly because an understanding of the themes is more transferable. A study of Maya temples may not be immediately useful to a student studying Neolithic Britain and vice versa, but an introduction to concepts of religion and ritual will be useful to both. We have included content, but its function is to illustrate. It may well be in just the right size chunks to put into essays but it is there to provide examples of archaeological ideas and debates.

Chapter 8

Religion and Ritual

YOUR GOALS

You need to understand

■ the key concepts drawn from sociology and anthropology that archaeologists use to help define and explain past beliefs and rituals

■ the techniques and sources archaeologists use to interpret evidence of religious belief and practices

■ case studies from your area of study, which illustrate religion and ritual from that period or culture

■ how to use evidence to support longer pieces of writing.

For periods where there are written sources such as Ancient Greece or medieval Europe, archaeologists have tended to use texts as the means to interpret and understand past belief systems. For cultures where there are no written sources, many archaeologists have held the view that uncovering the nature of past religious belief from material remains is beyond their ability. In the 1950s Hawkes argued that there was a hierarchy of inferences which archaeologists could make from their sources. Using material remains they could say a great deal about technology and economics, much less about society and very little about belief. How can you understand thoughts from bones, sherds and postholes? His

argument has become known as Hawkes' ladder of inference (see Figure 8.1).

Since the 1960s there has been an explosion of interest amongst the general public in past religions, especially those of the later prehistoric period. The reluctance of many archaeologists to discuss religion left a gap that was filled by a range of other explanations, which fed on public interest in ancient monuments. Often these involved projecting current concerns onto evidence from the past. The most famous was Von Daniken's depiction of god as an astronaut. This view attributed great monuments from the past to aliens. For example, the Nazca lines in Peru became alien

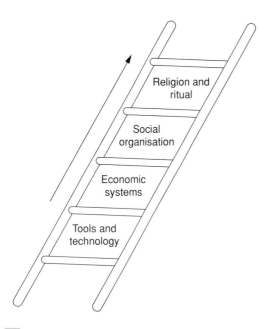

Figure 8.1 *Hawkes' ladder of inference (after Hawkes 1954). The higher one goes up the ladder the harder it is to make inferences on the basis of archaeological evidence*

landing strips. More recently a New Age version of prehistory has linked together sites from various periods as evidence of a universal cult of an earth goddess. Partly in response, archaeologists have borrowed a battery of analytical techniques and concepts from other disciplines including ethnography, sociology and critical theory to explore religion and ritual. It is now a core element of study for many periods. A particularly influential idea has been the fact that for many cultures religion cannot neatly be separated from social organisation or even economics. It influences the way people behave and therefore leaves traces in their material culture.

The analytical power of computers is increasingly enlisted in searching for patterns, particularly in the disposal of artefacts and the siting of monuments. Use of these techniques has in turn

led to criticism of written sources for what they omit and because they are often ambivalent. Archaeology may have much to offer the study of religion in the classical period after all.

In this chapter we have tried to explain some of the more unfamiliar concepts which archaeologists have adopted in depth. We have also provided examples of the methods and insights used by archaeologists to tease out clues about belief and ritual from material remains.

WHAT IS RELIGION?

You are most likely to be familiar with modern world religions. These are atypical. Christianity, Judaism and Islam, for example, are all **monotheistic** (one god) religions which provide codes of conduct for life, have permanent religious institutions and offer life after death to believers. There have been religions that have differed on each of these points. At the other end of the scale from the **states** (▶see p. 239), which have promoted world religions, are hunter-gatherer societies. They tend to see themselves as part of, rather than in control of, nature and their religion may be simply one part of their daily life rather than something done on special occasions. There is far more variety in those small-scale societies which survive today than in world religions, and they may provide better insights into the wealth of lost belief systems. After all humans have spent most of history hunting and foraging for food rather than growing it.

Giddens (1989) provides a broad definition of religion which you may find useful: 'a set of symbols, invoking feelings of reverence or awe . . . linked to rituals or ceremonials practised by a community of believers'. These symbols may be of gods and goddesses, ancestral or nature spirits, or impersonal powers. Rituals can consist of prayers, songs, dances, feasting, drug taking, offerings and sacrifices. People often use them to try to influence supernatural powers and beings to their advantage and to deal with problems that cannot be solved through the application of technology. However, there are some religions without objects of worship. In Confucianism and Taoism, for example, the individual attempts to attain a higher level through correctly following specified principles.

WHAT IS THE FUNCTION OF RELIGION?

Archaeologists are more interested in how religion affected the people practising it rather than whether a particular religion accomplished what its believers hoped. All religions cater to basic human social and psychological needs. Some of these, such as the need to explain what happens when people die, may be universal if we are correct in our interpretation of the archaeological evidence for burial and associated activities since at least 40,000 years ago. Common functions include:

- Explaining the unknown in order to provide meaning and reduce anxiety. A belief in a divine force can provide hope and comfort in difficult times. The death of a family member may be easier to cope with if they are believed to exist beyond death. Ritual at a time of crisis may give people the confidence to cope with problems, for example, praying before a battle.
- Establishing rules and models of behaviour. Most religions put divine power behind definitions of what is right and wrong. They may tell believers the 'right' way to live. Religion can be used to enforce obedience to a ruler (e.g. medieval kings) or even to justify rebellion.
- The maintenance of social solidarity was seen as the primary function of religion by

the sociologist Durkheim. His study of **totemism** (▶see p. 148) amongst Australian aboriginal societies suggested that what was being worshipped represented society and its values. By holding collective ceremonies people reinforce their sense of togetherness and social cohesion.

- Transmitting memory, especially in non-literate societies, by the learning of oral traditions and through repetitive rituals. The classic example of this is the telling of creation myths. Myths are explanatory narratives that rationalise religious beliefs and practices. Myths invariably are full of accounts of the doings of various super-natural beings and hence serve to reinforce belief in them. The building of religious monuments can literally set collective memories in stone.

Figure 8.2 *Drawing of the Wakah Kan or 'Raised up sky' from Copan. This 'world tree' linked the underworld, the realm of the living and the sky. The king would dress in the image of the Wakah Kan to emphasise the special relationship between the ruler and the spirit world and his ability to move between the different realms*

Figure 8.3 (left) *Bust of Rameses II at Luxor. Many rulers have used statuary and images of themselves in ritual places to emphasise their special links with the gods and to reinforce their claim to power*

 KEY SITE

The Temple of Karnak at Luxor

In Egypt, Amun's great temple of Karnak, through the physical symbolism of the building, offers key insights into the creation myth, the role of the priesthood and the nature of rituals. Every pharaoh felt bound to leave his mark on this temple by lavish construction works of his own such that over time it extended over an area that would encompass more than a dozen medieval cathedrals.

The layout of Karnak was designed as a microcosm of the world at the time of its creation by the god Amun. Its high walls and huge gates or 'pylons' excluded ordinary people. Only priests could enter the temple and they, like all other things dedicated to Amun, had to be pure and clean. They shaved off all their body hair, bathed daily in the Sacred Lake in the heart of the temple and dressed in spotless robes. Rituals depicted in hieroglyphics include the journey of Amun's sacred boat from Karnak to Luxor with attendants singing and dancing. The desire for the maintenance of order is also featured symbolically in the temple reliefs. Battle scenes show foreigners as disorderly mobs until they have been conquered and brought within the civilising influence of Egypt. Then they are shown in neat lines. In the nearby Luxor Temple this contrast is very clear: the Egyptian infantry and chariots at the Battle of Kadesh are immaculately organised in geometric squads while the opposing Hittites are in total disarray.

KEY SITE *cont.*

The myth at the heart of the temple is that of the original creation of the world from the waters of chaos. The 'Hypostyle Hall' represented the 'Swamp of Creation' with its forest of columns whose capitals were carved in the shape of plants such as papyrus. Amun came into being in this chaos. He lifted himself out of the water and masturbated himself to produce the two constituent elements of all life: wet and dry. From this act comes the first

Figure 8.4 *Entrance to the Temple of Karnak. The massive first pylons (gates) completely obscure the religious areas inside, while mythical creatures lining the approach signify the ritual nature of the site*

land in the form of the 'primeval mound' (the temple) and then the sky and later the first inhabitants of that Egyptian 'Eden': Isis and Osiris. In the hidden depths of the temple was the cult statue of Amun. The exact nature of the statue is much disputed due to the damage inflicted on the portraits of Amun in antiquity and the desire of previous generations of scholars to play down the sexual nature of Egyptian iconography. For the Egyptians this statue was a house for the god, a place where he could take up residence to interact with mortals. Through his divine presence it became 'alive' in a very real sense. The priests would anoint the statue, dress it and entertain it each day as they would the pharaoh himself. One relief shows a group of females playing musical instruments while others clap rhythmically. They are led by a woman who is identified by the hieroglyphs as 'the Hand of God'. On a balance of probabilities scholars believe that the statue of Amun was shown in a state of sexual excitement grasping his erect penis and that the reliefs are picturing a ritual re-enactment of the original moment of creation induced by the rhythmic music and hand clapping. The central question here is whether the ritual was essentially a metaphorical act that happened in people's minds or whether it had some sort of physical reality enacted by the chief priest of the temple or by the pharaoh himself once a year.

 Strudwick and Strudwick 1989

 http://www.memphis.edu/egypt/ luxortm.htm

http://www-ceg.ceg.uiuc.edu/ ~haggag/luxor.html

Detecting evidence of past beliefs and practices

When examining material evidence a standing joke amongst archaeologists has been the idea that anything that can't immediately be explained must be ritual. While there has been some overenthusiasm in what is still a relatively new area of archaeological interpretation, most studies are based on far more than an odd shaped building or one figurine. Egyptologists

---

 KEY STUDY

Zapotec religion

Flannery and Marcus used three key methods in their exploration of beliefs from the Zapotec civilisation that flourished in the Oaxaca Valley of southern Mexico between 200 BC and AD 700.

There was evidence of great continuity in local populations from Zapotec times until the Spanish conquest in the sixteenth century. The archaeologists were able to use what they termed a direct historical approach (**DHA**). Spanish priests had documented local 'pagan' customs that were used to form a hypothesis for testing by excavation. The archaeologists predicted that anything with breath (pee) would be sacred and that ancestors would be worshipped. The burning of copal incense and sacrifices of blood, jade, living things and exotic goods would be made to petition elemental forces such as earthquake and lightning. They expected to find evidence of priests who lived in two-roomed houses with sacrifices made in the inner room and who used drugs to reach ecstatic states.

Excavations at San Jose Mogote revealed a series of two-roomed buildings with the same east–west axis superimposed upon them. The inner rooms had been kept scrupulously clean although there were traces of repeated burning in them. Tiny pieces of debris in the corners were frequently from obsidian blades or stingray stings, used for bloodletting until historic times. Buried in the floor were tiny statues, jade beads and the bones of quail; a bird believed to be pure. The Spanish hadn't recorded this aspect of religion. Underfloor offerings also included effigies of the lightning clouds, hail and wind. Research amongst local people revealed that they called the statuettes 'little people of the clouds'. Ancestors were also known as cloud people.

Through a mixture of historical records, analyses of excavated architecture and artefacts, and ethnography, Flannery and Marcus were able to reach conclusions about Zapotec reverence for ancestors and natural forces and the types of ritual practice involved in worship.

 Marcus and Flannery 1994

 http://www.angelfire.com/ca/
humanorigins/religion.html#zapotec

have the advantage of the Book of the Dead to draw on but for other cultures different approaches are required. Analogies drawn from ethnography have been particularly useful. Not for direct parallels so much as to demonstrate a range of possible options and influences and to prevent simplistic interpretation. It may appear common sense that a burial with many goods was that of a wealthy person, yet ethnography has provided examples where this is not the case. Studies have often focused on repeated patterns. These include symbols that recur in similar places or on specific types of artefact; non-random patterns of deposition of particular artefacts or animal remains and the distribution of deposits and monuments across the landscape. The treatment of boundaries in the past has been a focus of many studies.

WHAT KINDS OF RELIGION WERE THERE?

Most known religions include a belief in supernatural beings and forces through whom appeals for aid may be directed. For convenience we may divide these into three categories: deities, ancestral spirits and nature spirits. While some societies have only believed in one of these categories, it has been common for belief in several or all of them to co-exist, for example belief in evil spirits in medieval Europe.

Major deities

Gods and goddesses are great and remote beings who are usually seen as controlling the universe. If several are recognised (**polytheistic**) each often has charge of a particular part of the universe. Hinduism, the oldest major world religion, is around 6,000 years old and is polytheistic. Its contemporaries included the gods of Ancient Greece: Zeus was the lord of

the sky, Poseidon was the ruler of the sea and Hades was the lord of the underworld and ruler of the dead. In addition to these three brothers there were many other deities of both sexes. Each embodied characteristics seen as typical of male and female roles; each was particularly concerned with specific aspects of life and the workings of the world, or indeed universe. Pantheons or collections of gods and goddesses, such as those of the Greeks, were also common in non-western states such as Egypt or the Maya. States that grew through conquest often incorporated the local deities of conquered peoples into the official state pantheon. For example, the Romano-British

Figure 8.5 *An example of a deity: the Egyptian god Horus at Edfu*

 KEY STUDY

Copan

The acropolis of Copan in Honduras exemplifies the way in which religious beliefs can be embodied in material culture. The layout of the city reflects the cosmology of the Maya in a general sense and some special buildings have more particular symbolic meaning. The temple pyramids symbolised mountains, the surface of the plaza the waters. Temple interiors were caves or magic portals to the world of the supernatural and stone statues of kings (**stelae**) were symbolic world trees. These depict the kings bridging the upper and lower worlds. They reveal the source of the kings' authority to be their power to intercede with the gods and ancestors on behalf of the people. **Glyphs** (carved reliefs), architecture, burial and iconography all help piece together the beliefs and rituals of the Maya.

Structure 22 is a temple building with commanding views over the whole acropolis and the valley beyond. Steps rise to its entrance, which was carved to look like a mask of the earth monster. The fragments remaining include the stone fangs of the monster's lower jaw. Entering here, watched by his people below, the king symbolically died and was reborn when he emerged. He would be wearing an elaborate costume of feathers,

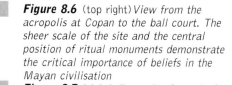
Figure 8.6 (top right) *View from the acropolis at Copan to the ball court. The sheer scale of the site and the central position of ritual monuments demonstrate the critical importance of beliefs in the Mayan civilisation*

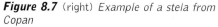
Figure 8.7 (right) *Example of a stela from Copan*

✎ **KEY STUDY** *cont.*

jaguar fur and heavy ornaments of jade when he confronted the gods and his ancestors inside the temple. Weak from days of fasting and blood loss through sacrifices, he may well have been in an altered state of consciousness when he appeared before the inner portal. This has a row of stone skulls as its bottom step and above it arched a writhing two-headed serpent in whose coils swirled the figures of his ancestors and which was supported at each end by a skybearer god. Glyphs depict maize plants and remind us that stone, water and vegetation collectively suggest the other function of the temple as 'the mountain of sustenance'.

Figure 8.8 *Photograph of a panel from altar Q at Copan. The iconography seamlessly links history, rulers and the gods*

 Schele and Miller 1986

 http://www.virtualpalenque.com/

site at Bath or Aquae Sulis may have been the centre for a cult combining the local deity Sul and the Roman goddess Minerva. Specific deities are identified from repeated images on buildings or artefacts ranging from mosaics to statues.

Belief in gods, goddesses or both, often seemed to parallel what we know of the gender relationships between men and women in everyday life (▶p. 245). In societies in which women have less power than men, the nature of 'god' is defined in masculine terms. This is commonest in societies where the economy is based upon herding animals or on intensive agriculture, which would have been largely male activities. In such societies men must often have been seen as rather distant authority figures to their children. Goddesses, on the other hand, appear more often in societies where women make the major contribution to the economy, enjoy some measure of equality with men and in which men are more involved in the lives of their children. Such societies often depend on horticulture or specialised craft production, which is done by women. You might compare the central role of the production of vegetables to feed pigs in Papua New Guinea, which underlie the 'Moka' ritual, with the evidence for rich female grave goods in early Thai society at Khok Phanom Di. The masculine god figure that replaced various goddess cults amongst the Hebrews during the late 2nd millennium BC may have helped establish gender relationships in which women have traditionally been expected to submit to the rule of men. This in turn shaped Jewish, Christian and Islamic society. Gimbutas (1991) took up this theme in her book *The Civilisation of the Goddess* and argued that world religions developed to legitimise the replacement of early agricultural societies in which women played leading roles.

Ancestral spirits

A belief in ancestral spirits has its origins in the widespread idea that human beings are made up of two parts: the body and some kind of vital spirit, which in Mesoamerica for example resides in the blood. For example the Maya Indians have always maintained that each person had a 'spirit-companion' that could leave the body and move around during sleep. The 'spirit-companion' was envisaged as an animal. One inscription tells us that 'the watery jaguar is the "way" of the Lord (King) of Seibal'. Given such a concept, it is only a small step to believe that the spirit could be freed by death from the body and have a continued existence. It has something in common with recent accounts of 'out of body experiences'.

Where people do believe in ancestral spirits, they are frequently seen as retaining an active interest and even membership in society. For example the 'ghost ancestors' of the Wape

might either provide or withhold meat from their living descendants. Like living persons, ancestral spirits may be well or badly disposed towards the living, but they are often capricious and unpredictable, hence the need to appease them with offerings. Is this the explanation behind some of the ritual behaviour observed in Neolithic societies at long barrows and causewayed enclosures? Many authorities believe that it is, and recent ethnographic parallels have been sought in Madagascar along these lines.

Whatever the involvement in particular past societies, belief in ancestral spirits provided a strong sense of continuity. These beliefs seem to have been particularly strong amongst early farming communities. Ancestors may have linked past, present and future generations and ownership of particular land.

Animism

One of the most common sets of beliefs about the supernatural world is usually referred to as animism. This centres on the idea that the living share the physical and spiritual world with all sorts of spirits. Animals, plants and people may all have their own individual spirits, as may springs, mountains, or other natural features. Roman statues of the rivers Tyne and Thames exemplify this belief very clearly.

People who believe in animism are inclined to see themselves as being part of nature rather than superior to it. This includes most hunter-gatherers, as well as those food-producing people who see little difference between a human life and that of any growing plant. Gods and goddesses may have created the world and perhaps provided the main physical fabric of that world but it is spirits to whom

KEY STUDY

Neolithic tombs

A range of hypotheses have been put forward about the nature of the religion of the builders of the passage graves, cairns and long barrows of western Europe. Although these monuments are similar in some ways there are significant differences in their contents. In long barrows there was a gradual change from individual articulated burials to collections of **disarticulated** bones as at Hazleton or re-sorted bones as at West Kennet. However, this pattern is not universal and suggests some variety in beliefs. The tombs that hold the remains of the dead are often massive while remains of the settlements of the living are more fleeting. If a semi-mobile, pastoral economy (▶see p. 198) dominated at the time this may not be entirely surprising. However, the importance of the dead is suggested by the way the location of their remains are permanently marked on the landscape. Most writers conclude that there was some sort of ancestor worship or at least belief in their spirits.

Analogies have often been made with the Merina of Madagasgar who continue to build and use chambered tombs. While they are radically different societies there may be some interesting parallels. The Merinas use a communal tomb even when they live away, to emphasis their community and kinship. Skeletons are wrapped in the tomb but are periodically taken out and re-wrapped. This is an occasion for feasting by the family of the dead. Passage graves and some barrows could also be re-entered and there is evidence of food remains and human remains around many of them. Perhaps the living and the dead continued to mix to emphasise continuity and community.

Graslund in a comparative study of Scandinavian tombs from the Neolithic to Viking periods concluded that settled societies share a belief in some sort of afterlife and in souls or spirits. There are two models. The breath soul leaves the body with its last sigh and goes to join the ancestors. The free or dream soul is active when the body sleeps. After death it remains with the body until the flesh is gone. Graslund argued that the treatment of the body after death corresponds to the soul belief. Where **excarnation** or disarticulation (▶see p. 153) had occurred before placing in a tomb it suggested a breath soul. The tomb served as an **ossuary**. Where decomposition occurred inside the tomb it was a grave. The evidence for this is the presence of small bones that would have been lost during excarnation, skeletons in sitting positions and beads that may have come from clothing. There are also fatty deposits in the

Figure 8.9 *A replica of the inside of a Neolithic tomb with disarticulated human remains. There is nothing to stop modern visitors rearranging the bones. A modern example of taphonomy!*

soil in some tombs. For a dream soul the corpse would have to be cared for as if it were alive and this would also account for the presence of grave goods. The shape of passage graves with their narrow entrances and the east–west orientation of many (towards the sun) suggest a womb from which the soul is reborn.

Those who support the idea of an earth or fertility goddess have also explored the tomb-womb idea. For farmers, fertility is a crucial issue and reseeding mother earth with the bones of ancestors may have been a symbolic gesture to ensure good crops or plentiful livestock. Other archaeologists have noted the similarity between some of these monuments and the longhouses of the first farmers of central Europe. Although there seems no direct link between the two groups there may be some link in terms of associating ancestors with a specific place of origin, perhaps to establish land rights. Either way, the dominant metaphor seems to be of ancestors.

The transformation of bodies and the mixing of bones in many tombs may have other significance. The disarticulated remains in some cases are also associated with a variety of sherds of pottery, often with fresh breaks. Perhaps the purpose was to downplay individual differences and mask inequalities amongst the living. The remains therefore could both reflect and reinforce social reality. They also offered a symbolic resource both to the community whose ancestors' remains were held in them and those who were able to enter the tomb. Some tombs were used for over 1,000 years and beliefs may have changed over that period. It is also worth noting that the bones represent a relatively small proportion of Neolithic populations.

Graslund 1994

Parker-Pearson 1999

Thomas 1991

Tilley 1996

Whittle 1996

one turns for the ordinary needs of daily life and whom the ordinary hunter may meet during the hunt or while out roaming the woods. Many of the indigenous peoples of North America subscribed to this view of the world and would pray to the spirits of their 'brothers and sisters' the animals for success in the hunt. They asked animals to give up their lives for the good of people and apologised to them when they were actually caught. You may have seen the Hollywood version of this at the start of the film *Last of the Mohicans*.

Totemism is a label sometimes attached to animistic forms of religion. Here animals or plants with special powers may be worshipped or there may be complex rules about their treatment. Totemism has been used as an explanation for some of the non-human finds in prehistoric tombs. Hedges noted that Isbister Tomb on Orkney contained the remains of sea eagles while other nearby tombs held dog or deer bones. However, these may have been food or in some case scavengers which entered the tombs independently.

Figure 8.10 *Sea eagle talons from the cairn at Isbister on Orkney*

Animatism

Some societies believe in a supernatural power that exists independently of deities and spirits. The people of Melanesia, for example, believe that 'mana' exists as a force inherent in all objects. In itself it is not physical but it can be revealed through its physical effects. When a warrior experiences success in battle this will not be as a result of his own strength but directly attributable to the 'mana' carried with him in the form of an amulet that hangs around his neck. In much the same way, in farming societies an individual may know a great deal about the right way to treat plants, about soil conditions and the correct time for sowing and harvesting, but still be dependent on 'mana' for the success of his crop. He may build a simple altar for this power at the end of the field, as often seen in the rice fields of Bali. If the crop is good, it is a sign that the farmer has in some way acquired the necessary 'mana'. The possession of objects containing such power may provide the owner with confidence. For example, in going into battle. Confidence might then lead to

fearlessness and victory. This would then 'prove' the power of the 'mana'. The Sioux followers of the Ghost Dance cult provide a less successful example. They believed their magical shirts would stop bullets in their final conflict with the US army in the late nineteenth century.

Belief in magic has some similarities with animatism. Magic involves individuals influencing events through potions or chanting. It can also involve divination, astrology and curses such as those found at Aquae Sulis and on the walls of Pompeii. The wearing of charms to bring good fortune and ward off evil combines elements of magic and animatism and has survived in a watered down way in societies which have been Christian for hundreds of years.

Havilland 1994

RELIGIOUS CHANGE

Comparative studies over long periods often reveal changes in the evidence for religion. This can be useful as the contrasts often suggest much about the nature of beliefs. The overlap between paganism and Christianity revealed in the changing grave goods and orientation of bodies from Anglo-Saxon cemeteries such as Lechlade and Sutton Hoo are well known. On Cranborne Chase very different monuments spanning over 1,000 years are oriented or physically linked to earlier ancestral monuments. This suggests that while the precise beliefs had changed, ancestors were still venerated although their identity may have been redefined. The continuing power and importance of earlier beliefs can also be seen in the reuse of some religious sites. At Cairnpapple an open monument associated with a range of burials was filled with an individual cairn in the Bronze Age, suggesting that some people had a better claim on ancestral spirits than did others. At Stanton Drew magnetometer surveys have revealed that the stone circles replaced earlier timber monuments. The nature of the religious changes of the reformation can be seen in the study of structural and decorative changes in churches. This is most evident when medieval wall-paintings are revealed under puritan whitewash as at Baunton. The total abandonment of earlier beliefs appears to be evident in the way later Bronze Age field systems cut across earlier monuments whose faint traces had been respected for over 1,000 years, as at Stonehenge.

 Bradley 1998

RITUAL ACTIVITY

Much of the value of religion comes from religious activities. Participation in ceremonies enables people to relate to higher forces; it is religion in action. Ritual involves repeated performance of religious activities, usually at a particular place. It can reinforce the social bonds of a group and reduce tensions. Participants can feel a wave of reassurance, security and even ecstasy and a sense of closeness. Although the rituals and practices vary considerably, even those rites that seem to us the most bizarrely exotic can be shown to serve the same basic social and psychological function. Anthropologists have classified several different types of ritual, a major division being between '**rites of passage**' and '**rites of intensification**'.

Rites of passage

Rites of passage are ceremonies to mark crucial stages in the life cycle of the individual. These might include birth, puberty, marriage, parenthood, and advancement to a higher class, occupational specialisation and death. Anthropological analysis of ceremonies, which help individuals through these potential crisis points, has often identified three stages: *separation*, *transition*, and *incorporation*. The individual would first be ritually removed from the society as a whole, then isolated for a **liminal** period and finally returned to society with a new status.

Van Gennep (1909) observed this pattern amongst Australian aborigines. When boys were to be initiated into manhood, elders led them to secret locations in the bush. Women cried and pretended to resist their removal while the boys pretended to be dead. In the bush the boys were taught the culture and stories of the tribe but also went through ceremonies including minor operations, such as circumcision, to teach them to bear pain. During this period the boys were 'dead' to the tribe. On returning they were welcomed with ceremonies, as though they had returned from the dead. The ceremony highlighted their new status as adults and reminded existing adults to act towards them in the appropriate ways. They skipped the ill-defined status of 'teenager', which causes problems in western society.

In the same way female initiation rites prepared Mende girls in West Africa for womanhood. When they begin to menstruate, they were removed from society to spend weeks, or even months in seclusion, usually on the grounds that their menstrual blood would 'contaminate' that with which it comes into contact. There, they are trained by experienced women and change their appearance, setting aside the remnants of their childhood and undergoing surgery to remove their clitoris. Mende women returned from their initiation as fully adult women in control of their sexuality and ready for marriage and childbearing.

Rites of intensification

Rites of intensification mark crises in the life of the group. Whatever the precise nature of the crisis (war, disease, etc) mass ceremonies are performed to mitigate the danger. Because these rites are carried out at a group rather than an individual level, the effect is to unite people in a common effort in such a way that fear or confusion are replaced by optimism and collective action and the natural balance is restored. In regions where the seasons differ enough to force changes in human behaviour patterns, annual ceremonies develop. (Christmas replaced midwinter festivities dating back at least to the Iron Age.) Participation in such ceremonies cultivates the habit of reliance on supernatural forces through ritual activity, which can be activated in other stressful circumstances.

A growing body of evidence from late Bronze Age and Iron Age sites suggests rites of intensification. At Flag Fen the building of and maintenance of a very large structure is associated with the sacrifice of dogs and deposition of ritually smashed valuable artefacts into water. Contemporary evidence of water sacrifices against the context of environmental change and social conflict suggests rites of propitiation, perhaps in appeals to a water or underground deity. The widespread deposition of metal artefacts in water and the discovery of apparently ritually killed bodies in bogs in Britain and Denmark suggest that these practices and perhaps the associated beliefs may have been widespread.

The act of monument building may be ritualistic in itself. It unites people and their

 KEY TERM

Propitiation

Making offerings or sacrifices to a spirit or deity. The widespread burials of human and animal remains in grain pits, as at Danebury, are often interpreted as such offerings.

 Cunliffe 1995

collective resources in pursuit of a shared, and subsequently memorable, goal. Recent work on the Cleaven Dyke in Scotland has revealed that it was constructed in stages and that the monument may not have ever been totally visible. The process may have been more significant than the monument.

Funerary ceremonies

Funerals blur this neat distinction. The death of an individual can also be a crisis for an entire group, particularly if the group is small. The survivors must readjust, take up new roles and work out how to behave towards one another. They also need to reconcile themselves to the loss of someone to whom they were emotionally tied. This can take extreme forms. One of the **funerary rites** of the Melanesians was ritual cannibalism. This was felt to be a supreme act of reverence, love and devotion. Funerals offer the opportunity for outpourings of emotions without disrupting society. They can also emphasise that the values of the group outlive the individual. Burials are just one part of the funerary process but they are the most archaeologically visible. This does not mean they were the most important part.

KEY STUDY

The Yaxchilan Lintels

These huge sculptural slabs which once occupied prominent locations above doorways in temples offer us many insights into Maya belief and ritual, particularly in the area of autosacrifices or bloodletting. Blood was analogous with water and thus vital for the fertility of crops and for the maintenance of good relations between god and men – a repayment for the sacrifices made by the gods on mankind's behalf at the time of creation. An example of these lintels can be seen in the Mexican gallery of the British Museum. It shows Lady Xoc perforating her tongue and collecting her blood on paper strips to be burnt as an offering. She is rewarded by the subsequent appearance of one of their ancestors in the form of an armed warrior dressed as the 'Vision Serpent'.

Figure 8.11 *Drawing of Shield Jaguar making a sacrifice of blood from his penis. Taken from the Yaxchilan Lintel*

 Renfrew and Bahn 1991

Mortuary rituals

The treatment of the dead can overlap with funerals. The dead may be prepared in advance for funerals and their remains may need further ritual treatment afterwards. Much has been learnt from studying the treatment of the corpse, particularly its final disposal. There is a range of possibilities.

Inhumation (burial) is a deliberate setting of the dead outside the world of the living. Where this occurs it may be indicative of attitudes to the dead. Roman and Christian cemeteries are placed apart from the living while some Upper Palaeolithic burials, as at Franchthi Cave, were kept close to the living. The orientation and position of the body – flexed, extended or contorted – may be significant. For example, foetal positions may indicate some belief in rebirth.

Cremation is more complex. Funeral pyres can leave several kilos of charred bones. The fire may destroy the body and release the spirit but these remains may have to be dealt with in a secondary ceremony. This can involve burial.

Excarnation is also likely to be part of a process. It involves exposing the body for scavengers and the decay process to clean the flesh from the bones. Parsees practise 'Sky burial' today and there is increasing evidence of excarnation from Neolithic times. The human bone evidence at Hambledon Hill was particularly persuasive. Cleaned bones may be used in other rites or stored in an ossuary.

Figure 8.12 *A pot being excavated from grave 5 at Empingham. Were grave goods such as these the possessions of the dead, offerings to them or the gods, or food for their journey to an afterworld?*

Mummification is often an elaborate process, which can involve removing some parts of the body. It may be believed that the body can be used by the person's spirit in another world or the future. The use of certain types of coffin or funeral vaults that may slow down natural decay processes may reflect similar beliefs.

 Parker-Pearson 1999

Sometimes the dead are hard to find. This may be because they are totally consumed. The Yanomano grind the cremated remains of their dead to a powder that they then drink. The dead thus remain in the living. There are also ethnographic examples of bones of ancestors being worn by their descendants. Bruck's (1995) study of human remains on Iron Age sites revealed that bones occurred in many locations not necessarily thought of as ritual, including huts and pits. Again, relics may have been a part of everyday life.

Funerary monuments and grave goods

Both of these categories may tell us more about the mourners and society than they do about their religious beliefs (▶see Chapter 11). However, elaborately decorated tombs such as those in the Valley of the Kings or the reliefs carved on Maya tombs may provide detailed information about both beliefs and rituals.

Gravestones provide many insights for a variety of cultures, not least about the setting aside of respected areas for the dead. Goods buried with the body or which were consumed in a funeral pyre are suggestive of an afterlife but this is not necessarily the case. Goods may be placed in the grave by mourners as tokens of affection or because they belonged to the deceased and are considered unlucky or taboo.

Tools used to prepare the dead, such as razors or tweezers, may fall into this category. There may also be important offerings of food or organic materials that have not survived. The absence of grave goods doesn't mean that there was no belief in an afterlife. It may suggest a belief in an afterlife where people are equal and provided for or it may reflect an idealised picture of society that masks differences in wealth.

Figure 8.13 *The Pyramids. Probably the best known funerary monuments in the world*

IDENTIFYING RITUAL AND RITUAL SITES

Most essays on this topic rarely stray from Renfrew and Bahn's list of indicators. In most cases their key points – focus of attention, boundary zones, symbols or images of the deity, and participation and offerings – can be ticked off. Tombs and temples are obvious places but one can also apply the list to monuments such as henges and ghats.

However, there may be exceptions. Their indicators work best for communal rather than individual ritual acts, many of which leave no traces. They also rely on there being a distinct area set aside. Even if it is in a dwelling special zones can be identified. For example, the altar or 'lararium' mounted on the wall of the 'House of the Vettii' in Pompeii, which depicts the gods of the house, where small offerings would be made as a daily ritual to ensure their continued favour and protection. However, there are societies today where there is no clear demarcation between ritual and the everyday. The layout and structure of houses as far apart as Bali and the Amazon jungle are determined by religious beliefs. Their orientation, where domestic activities occur and the direction particular people can move around them are all subject to religious rules. This kind of ethnographic insight has led archaeologists of the Neolithic in particular to question whether what were thought to be houses are domestic or at least partly ritual sites. Detailed study has revealed that many are associated with unusual artefacts, for example Ballygalley, and the structures do not look domestic. The massive timber house at Balbridie appeared to have a screen just inside the door, which would have made the inside dark and restricted access. Another at Balfarg is unlikely to have been

roofed and held finds of grooved ware (often associated with ritual) which contained traces of narcotic substances.

 Darvill and Thomas 1996

 http://museums.ncl.ac.uk/archive/mithras/intro.htm

The orientation of sites also suggests that the ritual and the everyday may be intertwined. The orientation of some major monuments towards the rising or setting sun, phases of the moon or particular constellations has been widely studied. In some cases this can clearly be established, for example the 'lightboxes' in tombs at Newgrange and Crantit.

 http://www.iol.ie/~geniet/maeshowe/

These may link ancestors with the heavens. However, some domestic sites also had very patterned orientation. Hill's (1996) comparative study of Iron Age sites revealed a tendency for houses to face south-east. This may have been to do with light, although in Britain south is the best direction to face to maximise daylight entering a hut. Light cannot have been a factor with enclosures. These tend to face south-west even if local topography and defensive considerations might suggest other directions. It may be that there was a 'right' direction from which to enter or perform activities.

Identification of objects with known religious links such as **votives** provides powerful clues. Objects cannot be seen as ritual simply because they are exotic. However, the form and find sites of particular artefacts have been used to suggest ritual objects for most periods. In some cases the material is important. Amber is associated with burials from the Mesolithic

Figure 8.14 *Ritual monuments such as Rievaulx Abbey are found throughout Britain. A visit provides a good opportunity to test out the indicators of ritual sites*

KEY TASK

Identifying ritual sites

This is a simple exercise designed to get you using and applying the terminology of ritual. List Renfrew and Bahn's (1991) indicators of ritual sites down one side of a piece of paper. Visit two different local centres of religion such as a church or mosque and see how well the indicators apply. Jot down what you find against each point. Next take studies of two archaeological sites from your area of study and apply the same test. You may find that this gives you almost enough material to support an essay on the subject.

ritual in the everyday. Hill's (1996) statistical analysis of the relationship between different classes of material culture in pits from Iron Age Wessex revealed patterns of **structured deposition** that are non-random and therefore deliberate. These are possibly ritualistic. Similar analysis has been undertaken on **middens** from several periods. In particular Scottish and Danish middens from the Mesolithic with their deposits of artefacts and human remains may not have been simply rubbish heaps. Even apparently economic sites such as flint mines may have had some ritual function. In the past the distinction between ritual and practical may have been irrelevant. Actions may have been informed by belief.

onwards. Its colour of blood and fire with slight magnetic properties perhaps marked it out. Pottery vessels with particular designs such as beakers or grooved ware are often seen as ritual artefacts. In some cases these have been repaired but not sufficiently to make them useable. Figurines and statues such as the 'Venus figurines' of Palaeolithic Europe and non-functional artefacts such as copper axes are more ambivalent unless their context can link them with other indicators.

Feasting falls into a similar category. The sharing of food is a powerful social unifier and is likely to feature in many rituals, but it can also be secular. The great halls of most castles were places of feasting for social rather than religious purposes. However, where there is other evidence, the remains of feasts can help identify ritual functions.

Evidence of other apparently waste material has also been used to suggest the embedding of

 KEY STUDY

The West Kennet timber enclosures

Whittle's (1998) excavations revealed two massive egg-shaped enclosures. They had comparatively short lives and there seems little doubt that they were places of ritual. There was extensive evidence of feasting such as a large number of meat bones that had been discarded without being fully processed. There were considerable amounts of grooved ware, a pottery type associated with ritual sites. The circles were located very close to other ritual and funerary monuments and the boundaries of the site had been given special attention. In particular, the entrances had non-random deposits of grooved ware, bone and artefacts. These features have been noted at other timber enclosures throughout Britain.

KEY STUDY

The Temple of the inscriptions at Palenque

The stone temple-pyramids at Palenque, in north central Mexico advertised the special magical authority of the reigning king. The Temple of the Inscriptions has stucco figures on the outside showing the child king Chan-Bahlum (Snake-Jaguar) as a child inheriting power from his ancestors, including Pacal whose body lies in the tomb below. The child king has a prominent umbilical cord that links him to his famous ancestors and echoes another feature of the temple known as the 'psychoduct'. Other carvings show captives who were sacrificed when the new heir was presented to the people or later when the building itself was dedicated. The costumes worn by Pacal and his relatives are full of symbolic elements such as the net skirt that shows that Pacal personifies the 'First Father'.

Inside, a passage covered with inscriptions and a staircase lead down to the burial chamber of Pacal. The floor of the passage contains the remains of five sacrificial victims. The chamber is almost filled by a huge stone sarcophagus, decorated with

Figure 8.15 (above right) *The temple-pyramids at Palenque*

Figure 8.16 (right) *A Mayan ritual stairway carved with hieroglyphics. Structure 26 at Copan*

KEY STUDY *cont.*

portraits of Pacal's parents and ancestors. The body is dressed in exotic costume items, many of jade, which is associated with water and life, and maize, which represents rebirth. The central scene on the lid of the sarcophagus shows Pacal falling backwards at the moment of death into the mouth of the earth monster, which symbolises death. Underneath the king is a 'bowl of sacrifice' with its bloodletting equipment, which the Maya believed to open up a portal into the other world. A smoking axe, a symbol of divinity, pierces Pacal's forehead and he is wearing the jade net skirt, which tells us that at the moment of death he had become the 'Maize God'. Behind Pacal rises the World Tree or Wakah Kan (▶see p. 139) which connects the three realms of Underworld,

Mortal World and the Heavens. The moment that the tree was raised aloft signifies the moment of creation to the Maya. The branches of the tree are shown as a double-headed serpent symbolising the serpent of life and death, the Milky Way and the sceptre of kingship held by the Maya Divine Lord. Snaking into his coffin and extending all the way up the side of the staircase to the temple above is the 'psychoduct', a tube which allowed the king's spirit to travel abroad at night in the form of his 'spirit familiar', usually a jaguar. It also allowed the priests to communicate with Pacal now that he had joined the ancestors.

 http://www.virtualpalenque.com/

Art and symbolism have also provided indications of ritual. Some such as the example of Palenque are undoubtedly ritual, others are disputed. Palaeolithic cave art and the swirling abstract patterns of Neolithic rock carvings have been particularly hotly debated. Other approaches to ritual symbolism have focused on repeated patterns including pairings such as left/right, male/female, in/out. This technique has been drawn from media and critical theory. Recent examples have been studies of the colours of stone used to construct cairns. On Arran red boulders were chosen to face the setting sun with white granite facing the rising sun. Red, the colour of blood, flesh, ochre and amber and white (bone and flint) are often associated in graves.

The sequential nature of the buildings at Palenque and Copan provides a good opportunity to study the continuity of ideas over time. Here one ritual structure would be ceremonially decommissioned and another structure, which was physically and iconographically related to its predecessor, would be built on top. The same rich symbolism in these temples is also found in graves below household patios, which connect commoners with the ancestors and the great cycle of heaven and earth.

LANDSCAPE RITUAL AND BELIEF

A combination of the development of landscape archaeology and a growing awareness from ethnography of the ritual significance of landscape has led archaeologists to look

KEY STUDY

The Clava Cairns

This group of monuments illustrates many of the different features of ritual sites. Two of the cairns are aligned on the midwinter sunset so that when viewed from the passage of the north-eastern cairn the dying sun disappears over the south-western cairn. The rays of the setting sun fall on

Figure 8.17 View of the Clava Cairns looking down the main alignment. Note the way the internal kerbstones in the first cairn have been graded

reddish boulders while the rising sun would have sparkled on white quartz. The kerbstones of the cairn were carefully graded in height from the south-west. Rock carvings both inside and outside the cairns follow the same conventions as others in Britain and Ireland.

The monuments also seem to represent a change in ritual practice. Excavation by Bradley revealed low platforms covered in seashells and flat stones surrounding the cairns. 'Rays' or ridges of stones led out through the platform to standing monoliths. Excavation showed that these were all integral to the cairns rather than add-ons. These monuments seem to have been a midway stage between ordinary passage graves, where the views of mortuary rituals would have been very restricted, to stone circles, where ritual may have been much more public and perhaps on a larger scale.

Figure 8.18 View of a standing stone linked by its 'ray' to the platform of a cairn at Clava. This integral relationship could only be established by excavation

 Bradley 2000a

beyond burials and individual monuments. Studies from Australia, for example, reveal that to the aborigines the whole landscape had a mythical dimension and they in turn inscribed it with meaning, including the use of rock carvings.

The term 'ritual landscape' to denote a whole block of land dedicated to gods or spirits was first coined for Cranborne Chase where the 7-mile long **cursus** monument was the focus for burials over several thousand years. Field-walking has revealed more exotic artefacts and less sign of everyday activity the closer you get to the cursus. Similar observations have been made for other Neolithic and Bronze Age complexes. The way in which many monuments make reference to much earlier ones is also often very evident. At Ballynahatty a cluster of monuments around the Giants Ring appear to be focused on one small passage grave.

 Green 2000

 http://www.qub.ac.uk/arcpal/ballynahatty. htm

 http://csweb.bournemouth.ac.uk/consci/ proj_cran/titles.htm

At Dorchester later monuments respect the line of the cursus and are aligned on it even though it would have been barely visible when some of them were built. Loveday's (1998) work on Dorchester suggested that the cursus itself might have been aligned on a natural feature: a twin peaked hill known as Mother Dunche's Buttocks. This illustrates the point that Neolithic monuments may have related to places that already had special meaning in Mesolithic times. The discovery of traces of earlier structures underneath barrows, as at Hindwell, adds weight to this idea.

The study of sacred geography involves examining the relation between monuments and landscape and the ways in which the building of monuments affects the way in which people may have moved around or viewed the landscape. Amongst the range of techniques are studies of intervisibility, which examine whether monuments were sited in view of each other. This has been assisted by the use of GIS and has been particularly applied to rock art and barrows. Attempting to 'read' the way monuments structure experience of the landscape borrows from the sociological approach known as phenomenology and has been pioneered in case studies in Britain by Tilley (1994). This approach has led to a reappraisal of linear monuments. These clearly structure movement in a particular order and direction but may themselves be permanent inscriptions of earlier movements or processions. Barnett's (1998) study of the stone rows on Dartmoor noted how many lead from the valleys onto the moors, perhaps marking a route for spirits or the dead. Similar suggestions have been made for Avebury and Stonehenge with pathways linking ritual areas for the living and those of the ancestors. A powerful concept increasingly used in many discussions of ritual is liminality. It has been particularly used in relation to boundaries and evidence of concentration of ritual activity on entrances and the margins of settlement areas.

 Tilley 1994

RELIGIOUS SPECIALISTS

In all societies there are certain individuals especially skilled at contacting and influencing supernatural beings and manipulating supernatural forces. They assist or lead other members of society in their ritual activities.

KEY TERM

Liminal

A boundary, space or time which is literally between two worlds. It may be between land and water as at Flag Fen or between the living and the dead. **Liminal** areas can be dangerous and therefore are likely to be marked by ritual. Most well known ritual sites have well defined boundaries.

Their qualification for this role may be certain distinctive personality traits or they may have undergone special training. A body of myths may help explain how and why they are different from those who lack such powers.

Priests and priestesses

Priests and priestesses are found mostly in complex societies that can afford to support full-time specialists of all kinds. He or she will be ceremonially initiated into a religious organisation and given a rank or office similar to those held before by others. They interpret

Figure 8.19 *Aerial view of the Roman Temple at Uley. The distinctive shape of the main ritual building on the right with a number of buildings, possibly used as accommodation for pilgrims, beyond it*

their wishes or commands for other people but may also appeal to deities on behalf of believers. This may be for a fee or for payment in kind. The priest and recently the priestess are a familiar figure in western society. Priests may be recognised archaeologically through objects placed in burials, through special equipment and clothing, through literary and epigraphic evidence and through artistic evidence of persons involved in ritual activity such as Shield Jaguar and Lady Xoc at Yaxchilan. Their presence could also be inferred from the structure of monuments from Stonehenge to medieval churches. In most cases monuments physically divide people into those who are in and those who are out, those at the head of a procession and the followers.

Shamen

There have been societies without full-time occupational specialists for much longer than those in which one finds priests and priestesses. However, there have always been individuals who have individually acquired religious power. This often happens in isolation and may involve bodily deprivation, even self-torture, to try to induce shamanistic visions. It can also involve trances induced by hallucinogenic drugs or repetitive dancing and chanting. Through contact with a spirit or power, or visits to the land of the dead these persons acquire special gifts, such as healing or divination and the ability to deal with supernatural beings and powers. When they return to society they are frequently given another kind of religious role: that of the '**shaman**'. Faith healers and some evangelists in our own society are similar in some respects to this definition of the shaman.

Definitions of shamanism vary. Some writers reserve it for Siberian culture but it is widely applied, particularly to herding, hunter-gatherer and mobile **horticulturist** societies. Shamen are sometimes characterised as magicians rather than religious leaders. In some situations they may coexist. Unlike the priest or priestess who represents deities on earth the shaman is essentially a religious entrepreneur, who acts for their client. Sometimes shamen are paid in kind but usually the increased status that their activities bring is sufficient reward.

A shaman in action may put on something of a show. Frequently shamen enter a trance-like state in which they can see and interact with spirit beings (Lewis-Williams 1988). The shaman enters a dangerous contest to impose his or her will on those spirits, as in faith healing or exorcism. In many groups trancing is accompanied by conjuring tricks, including the use of elaborate masks (for example in the Pitt-Rivers Museum) and ventriloquism. Shamen know, of course, that they are tricking people, but at the same time most shamen really believe in their power to deal with supernatural powers and spirits.

The drama of the shaman's performance promotes a feeling of ecstasy and catharsis for the individual members of society. Psychological assurance is the key to the role of shamanism in society. The shaman may claim to be able to manipulate super-natural powers, and promise such things as protection from enemies, success in love, or a cure from some illness or mental affliction. This treatment may not be effective in any medical sense that we would acknowledge, but the state of mind induced in the patient may nevertheless play a large part in his recovery. The shaman may also help to maintain social control through the ability to detect and punish evildoers. This can backfire on the shaman. If they are believed to work evil as well as good, or are unsuccessful, shamen may be driven out of their group or even killed.

In societies without iconography shamen are most likely to be detected through burials. Siberian examples have been buried face down, tied up and covered with rocks. Prehistorians have tried to identify shamen from burial goods. The Birdlip burial had a mirror and various amulets including some made from amber. Originally this was classified as a woman's grave but some researchers have suggested that these goods may be shamanistic. The Upton Lovell burial in Devizes Museum is another such instance. The goods here include some that are similar to those of goldworkers. However, metalworking involved (magical) transformations and its practitioners are linked to divination in many cultures, including that of Gypsies.

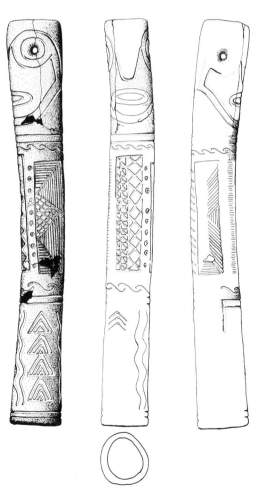

Figure 8.20 *A ritual artefact? This Neolithic flute carved from a human bone comes from the Trentino region of Italy (▶see p. 173). The anthropomorphic designs and the material itself suggest that it might have been used in shamanic rituals*

KEY SKILL

Developing an argument in longer pieces of writing

When faced with an open-ended question it is useful to break it down into manageable chunks. A title such as 'How far is it possible for archaeologists to identify ritual for your period of study?' provides a good example. First, you might want to distinguish between periods that have written sources and those that do not, although it is a good idea to ask about the reliability of sources. For the rest, you could subdivide using sub-questions based on the '4 Ws':

- *What*: can we identify the kind of ritual, which took place (for example, feasting, sacrifice)?
- *Where*: can we identify places where ritual took place, how, what evidence and examples?
- *Who*: can we identify who was involved (for example, individuals, groups of pilgrims)?
- *Why*: can we identify the purpose of the ritual (ancestor worship, rite of passage, etc.)?

In each case you will come up with an answer somewhere between yes and no depending on the techniques used and the quality and survival of evidence. This provides you with a structure and, taken together, the basis of an argument about the extent to which it is possible to detect ritual.

In writing up each section you need to argue. If your tutor keeps writing 'assertion' on your work then you are not doing this. You must support each point you make with evidence from relevant studies. There are several models or gambits for integrating supporting material:

- Using authorities to support statements: '. . . as Prior (1991) demonstrated at Flag Fen'.
- Cross-referencing: 'The possibility of the Dorset Cursus being used to structure movement was enhanced by Green's (1990) discovery of avenues of postholes leading from it to later round barrows. Analysis of the Stonehenge landscape by Parker Pearson (1998) also suggested movement along the avenue between the zones of the living and the ancestors.'
- Using evidence to choose between competing versions: 'Renfrew (1978) suggested that long barrows might have been territorial markers. Recent studies by Tilley (1998) and Barnett (1998) suggest otherwise. They found that . . .'
- Juxtaposing evidence to assess it: 'Deposits of cattle bones and smashed pottery near many entrances may suggest feasting but similar evidence inside is more ambivalent. Is it debris from feasting, gifts to the ancestors or the remnants of food the dead took with them?'

It is useful early on in your course to build up a vocabulary of *link words* and phrase such as 'however', 'for example', 'on the other hand'. These will prevent you from becoming repetitive and remind you to always back up your statements.

Finally you need to conclude. You should revisit the conclusions of each sub-question and see what the balance of your argument was. Use this to make a tentative (try to avoid certainty) judgement in response to the main question.

Chapter 9

The Archaeology of Settlement

YOUR GOALS

You need to

■ become familiar with a range of case studies of different types of site, settlement and structure

■ understand and appraise techniques archaeologists use to interpret the function and status of sites and structures

■ understand some of the methods used to study the relationship between human activity and the environment

■ develop your use of case studies and plans to help you with essay writing.

WHAT DOES THE ARCHAEOLOGY OF SETTLEMENT COVER?

Whether you are studying a range of different cultures or following a thematic course, settlement is likely to be a central topic. However, the term itself can mean several things.

Today, when we think of settlements we usually mean cities, towns and villages. However, for most of human history none of these existed. For periods when the population was mobile rather than sedentary humans created a range of temporary camps and sites for processing raw materials and food.

Sometimes caves or rock shelters were repeatedly used for occupation and rich deposits remain. Other sites consist of scatters of flakes from stone tool making (debitage) or animal bone remains from a butchery site. It is likely that these people identified with an area of the landscape, through which they may have moved on a seasonal basis, rather than living in one fixed place as we do.

For many past societies, off-site areas that we sometimes detect as flint-scatters or field systems were as important as the 'sites' which archaeologists have tended to excavate. The work of Binford in particular demonstrates that individual sites can provide a rather biased

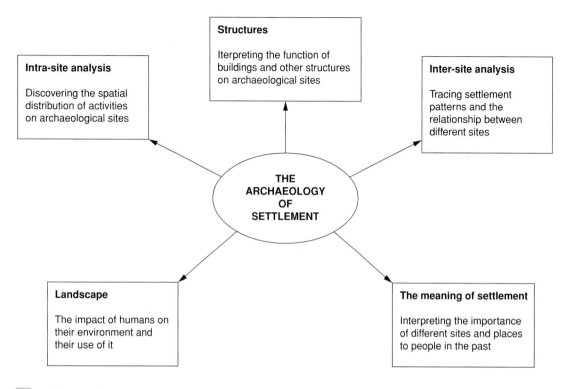

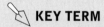 **Figure 9.1** *The archaeology of settlement*

KEY TERM

Site

A broad definition is useful here. The term is applied to field monuments, such as round barrows, to concealed evidence, such as cropmarks on aerial photographs, and even to towns.

A **site** is any place where traces of human activity are found. Usually these traces include artefacts but depending on the period studied they might include remains of structures, faunal remains or modification of the landscape such as a quarry. Boundaries make it easier to define sites, but many sites appear as unenclosed scatters of material. The recent emphasis on the significance of natural places in the ritual life of past peoples in the works of Bradley (2000b) and Tilley (1994) stretches the definition still further. The duration of use of a site might range from a few hours for a hunting site to centuries for a village or town. A settlement is just one type of site. The specific forms of site will vary according to period: kill-site, barrow, motte, mill, etc.

KEY TERM

Sedentary

Essentially **sedentary** means living in one place. It used to be thought that hunter-gatherers were mobile or nomadic and that people 'settled down' with the advent of farming. Evidence from archaeology and anthropology suggests that the reality is more complex. Many cultures have existed whose settlement pattern lies somewhere between the two poles of mobile and sedentary. A wealth of terms such as semi-sedentary, radiating or tethered mobility have been used to describe these patterns.

 KEY STUDY

Nunamuit ethnoarchaeology

Binford's (1978) classic ethnoarchaeological research project amongst the Nunamuit Eskimo examined the dynamics of their settlement pattern through seasonal movement from an archaeological perspective. His studies revealed the huge range of territory covered and the variable factors that influenced the location and timing of campsites. Specialist camps were established for hunting, carcass processing and sexual liaisons while non-residential sites included caches of meat and deadfall traps. While careful not to draw direct parallels between Nunamuit and Palaeolithic hunters, Binford was able to argue convincingly that since humans do not confine their behaviour to identifiable sites, we should study sites as part of a wider context. Drawing an analogy with the parts of a car engine he showed that in order to understand the activities of a mobile society we need to fit all the parts of the system together to see the whole picture, from hunting stands to skinning sites. Within the sites he put great emphasis on the spatial relationship between lithic and bone evidence.

picture of activity in the past and that there is a need to consider the whole settlement 'system'.

Settlement archaeology, therefore, includes the study of both permanent and temporary sites and the interaction of humans with their landscape in order to understand how they adapted to it. Human impact on the landscape from forest clearance to division by boundaries into territory is therefore a vital part of settlement study. Archaeologists also try to understand the ways in which people in the past understood their landscape through ideas such as ownership, territory and status. To do this they need to identify and explain the spatial distribution of past human activities. This might mean understanding the location of sites within a landscape or the placing of structures or other features within a settlement. At a micro level it includes studying activities within a room or living floor. The key questions asked usually revolve around identification of functions or the reasons for patterns in their distribution. Artefacts, ecofacts and features are the key evidence base in studying of distribution of ancient activities.

RECONSTRUCTING ANCIENT LANDSCAPES

Huge progress has been made in recent years in our ability to research and understand past landscapes. By attempting to reconstruct local

KEY TERM

Feature

The term **feature** is used to describe traces in the soil of human activity. Sometimes these are obvious, such as the foundation trenches of a building or a surviving built structure such as a kiln. Often the traces are more fleeting and less easy to interpret. Confusing masses of postholes and pits are found on many sites from the Mesolithic onwards. A distinction can be made between:

■ constructed features which were deliberately built, such as a fish trap or the postholes of a roundhouse
■ cumulative features, which are the accidental result of repeated human activity. The shallow gullies known as drip rings, which encircle houses, are good examples, as are holloways.

Figure 9.2 *Sites contain, and are made up of, features. This stone-built feature is a kiln or grain dryer from Kingscote Roman Villa*

environments, archaeologists hope to understand how sites developed and were abandoned, and how people adapted to their surroundings. To do this, archaeology uses intensive regional surveys that borrow from geology, biology and environmental science.

The land surface

Today's landscape has been shaped by human and natural activity on top of a geological base. Observing the morphology (shape) of the modern landscape is the starting point for research. Major investigations will also use GIS to produce digital maps and 3D models of past environments, for example that of Roman Wroxeter.

http://www.bufau.bham.ac.uk/newsite/ Projects/BT/default.htm

However, while the (post-glacial) topography and mineral resources may be similar, much else is different. Today's environment has been shaped by many sequences of human activity on top of a geological base. For the Palaeolithic and Mesolithic, understanding of geological changes is essential. For example, sea levels and the courses of rivers were often radically different. At Elveden in Suffolk geophysical survey was used to track ancient river channels running west-east through a series of narrow gorges. Today the land is flat and drains north-south. For most periods, data on soils is essential both to understand the environment it may have supported in the past and to track changes in its composition due to human activity (▶see p. 67). For example, the soils of many upland areas, including Dartmoor, show that they were once wooded but that clearance and agriculture in the Bronze Age contributed to degradation of the soil and the formation of 'iron pans' which have prevented their use for

crops since then. Studies of eroded layers of soil from the highlands of New Guinea around Kuk Swamp enabled Baylis-Smith (1996) to identify the start of slash and burn agriculture in the surrounding forests.

The environment

Climatic data can be obtained from international studies of deep-sea cores, varves and ice cores. These methods involve the examination of annual layers, which reflect climate at the time. In the case of sea cores the tiny organisms trapped in sediment were sensitive to contemporary oxygen levels. Strata of ice laid down at the poles reflect the temperature and salinity of the ocean at that time. Varves are layers of sediment at the bottom of lakes. Their thickness reflects the extent of annual thawing and the length of summer. Local climates can be inferred from ecofacts including animal bones, invertebrates and plant remains. Pollen is the most widely used (▶see p. 76). Living trees and the type of plants growing on specific soils can also provide evidence of past microclimates, for example, bluebells and oxlips indicate where ancient woodland stood.

For more recent periods a wider range of evidence becomes available. The texts by Aston, Fleming and Muir in the bibliography provide a wealth of examples. Their research has revealed that earlier patterns of land use are often fossilised within today's pattern of fields and woods. Some boundaries may date back to at least Roman times and the hedges that mark some of them may be almost as old. The names of fields also provide clues to what the land was used for. For example, assart refers to land cleared from woodland, wick and chester to settlements.

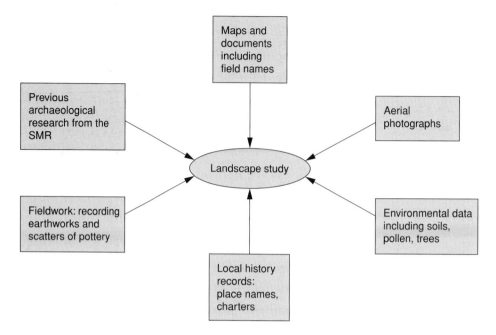

Figure 9.3 *Sources for reconstructing past landscapes*

KEY SITE

Hayley Wood

Rackham's (1990) study drew on estate documents from the fourteenth century onwards and fieldwork to show how this ash and hazel woodland was managed as a renewable crop. Timbers were felled and replanted on a thirty-year cycle and coppiced on a seven-year rotation. His work demonstrates the range of evidence available to the woodland archaeologist including monuments, banks and the trees themselves. Coppiced and pollarded trees still remain from managed woodland.

Seasonality

Ecofacts have been used on many transitory sites to identify periods of occupation. The settlement patterns around the Palaeolithic sites of Ambrona and Torralba were identified by the bones of migratory birds while occupation periods of the Mesolithic midden at Cnoc Coig were estimated from the ear bones or otoliths of fish. These methods are not without controversy. The antlers found at Star Carr have been used to argue for its use in almost every season.

IDENTIFYING HUMAN USE OF THE LANDSCAPE

The term 'cultural ecology' has been used to describe the relationship between people and landscape. Humans are part of the ecosystem like other living organisms and climate, environment and natural food sources impose some limits on human populations and how they live. However, unlike that of other mammals, human movement around and use of the landscape cannot be explained solely in terms of biology and the physical environment. Humans adapt to their environment through the use of cultural technology. They can extend the range of resources and territory they exploit beyond their natural biological limits by, for example, harvesting sea fish through the development of boats, traps and nets during the Mesolithic or using irrigation to farm arid areas. To understand the dynamics of human adaptation, archaeologists need to understand both the environment of the area studied and the technology available to the people living there. Humans can also modify their environment. Human fertility is not just determined by the carrying capacity of the land as the modern world demonstrates. However, the relationship is complex as archaeology can demonstrate. The collapse of the Mesopotamian civilisation at Mashkan Shapir provides a classic example. The city prospered in a desert area through the development of irrigation and the construction of a network of canals. At one time the city was also a port. Unfortunately irrigation contributed to the rapid salination of the soil. Crop yields collapsed and the civilisation crumbled. This process of human change provoking environmental change is referred to as feedback. Flannery (1976) identified an example of positive feedback in his study of the Oaxaca Valley in Mexico. His study showed how mobile foragers had encouraged the spread of a type of grass, which was to develop into maize. Maize flourished and as the average size of maize cobs grew, it became a major component of human diets. Maize was able to support a higher density and more sedentary human population than previously. Eventually this meant that there could not be a return to a foraging existence and dependency on maize agriculture increased.

 http://www2.learner.org/exhibits/collapse/mesopotamia.html

Site catchment analysis

In the 1970s archaeologists interested in understanding how humans exploited their environment and the extent of settlement 'territories' borrowed a range of analytical techniques from economic geography. Prominent amongst these was site catchment analysis. This assumes that settlements were not located randomly across the landscape, but were sited to maximise efficiency and minimise effort in gathering resources. By walking and analysing the area around a site, archaeologists tried to identify the resources its inhabitants would have been able to exploit and therefore understand its location. Ethnographic studies of site exploitation territories were used to determine the distance people might travel for subsistence resources. For instance, foragers such as the !Kung bushmen of the Kalahari rarely walk more than 10 kilometres (about 2 hours walk) from their base with a range of 20–30 kilometres to other sites with whom they traded and areas they occasionally visited, for example for building materials, clay or summer pasture. Studies of peasant farmers suggest that their normal limit is just 5 kilometres. Although models tend to feature circular territories around sites, in reality they would reflect local topography. This was the case with pioneering studies of early farmers in coastal Palestine.

Site catchment analysis can help understand the economic potential of a territory and perhaps generate ideas about population levels by estimating the carrying capacity of the land. It also provides a model, which can be compared with archaeological evidence such as food, remains, pollen and artefacts. Human remains can also provide some dietary information as to which resources were particularly exploited (▶see p. 72). Similar ideas can be used to understand settlements in the historic period. Mick Aston's study of Ashington in Somerset (1985) uses the idea of site catchment to illuminate the way the settlement and others like it in Somerset organised its exploitation of the local environment. Resources needed on a daily basis were produced in or close to the settlement with less frequently needed resources located further out. Aston's book *Interpreting the landscape* also shows how the landscape can be used as a text to read off past activities and relationships.

Plants are good indicators of local environments because we know the conditions that the various species can tolerate. Analysis of plant samples from sites can provide insights into the 'catchment area' beyond the immediate locality with people introducing plants into the site through plant collecting or cultivation or by accident. For example, Otzi the Ice Man was found to have cereal grains adhering to his grass cape. To have value the archaeologist must study very carefully the formation processes that led to the creation of the deposit which contains the plant remains under consideration. A good example of this sort of study was the analysis of weed seeds in the plant remains at Danebury. Weeds, like food crops, prefer specific soil conditions, such as wet lowland valleys or higher chalk pastures. From the types of weed present archaeologists were able to infer the soil conditions in which the main crops were grown before being brought into the hill fort. This information meant that the catchment area of Danebury in terms of agriculture was more clearly understood and future research could be focused on the soil types contributing to this overall assemblage.

However, site catchment analysis has serious limitations. It depends on accurate reconstruction of ancient landscapes, which is difficult since traces of changes in much of the flora and fauna may not have survived. It assumes that people in the past were aware of and could access the resources we can identify today. It also assumes that their behaviour was economically 'normal'. That is, they sought to maximise returns for the least effort. Finally, it is a rather deterministic model of human behaviour. It may well be that spiritual, cultural or political considerations were as important factors in decisions about site placement as economics. Even so, the method is valuable in exploring potential site use and in forming hypotheses to be tested against archaeological data.

Studying spatial distribution

The distribution pattern of sites and settlements across a landscape has the potential to tell us a great deal about the interaction between people and environment and the nature of social organisation. The first stage is to plot known sites of similar dates on a map and then add aerial and surface survey results if they are available. The distribution can then be analysed for signs of patterns, clustering, and relationships between larger and smaller sites. GIS is particularly useful here. Once the data is inputted, queries can relate sites to a wide range of factors including soils, water and intervisibility.

Describing the pattern is easier than explaining it. Various types of cluster analysis have been used to test archaeological site distribution against geographical models of distribution.

KEY STUDY

Ethnoarchaeology of modern camps in the Kalahari

Kent's (1989) ethnoarchaeological study of modern sites in the Kalahari tested the importance of site catchment in determining difference in size, complexity and period of occupation between different settlements. She compared the camps of different groups of farmers and foragers to see whether ethnicity or a major source of subsistence was critical, and was able to talk to the people themselves about their behaviour. There was a marked variability of data but it could largely be explained by social factors, for example the layout and range of features was determined by how long people expected to remain at the site.

KEY STUDY

Mesolithic hunters of the Trentino

Clark (2000) examined the connection between site location and subsistence strategy in the mountains of Northern Italy over a long period. Animal bone and lithic tools from well-preserved deposits in rock shelters were used to determine the type of hunting practised. In the early Mesolithic summer hunting sites at high altitude had been used to catch ibex and chamois with hunting bands retreating to lower rock shelters in the winter.

Figure 9.4 *Replica of a rock shelter in use by a group of hunters*

In the late Mesolithic the high level sites were abandoned and a range of resources were exploited in the lower woods and river valleys. Bone assemblages suggested whole carcasses were being brought to the shelter rather than selected joints removed in the field. This decrease in hunting territories coincided with an increase in forest cover which reduced the high level pasture. Human adaptation included a shift in prey and the adoption of a range of tools suited to forest hunting.

KEY STUDY *cont.*

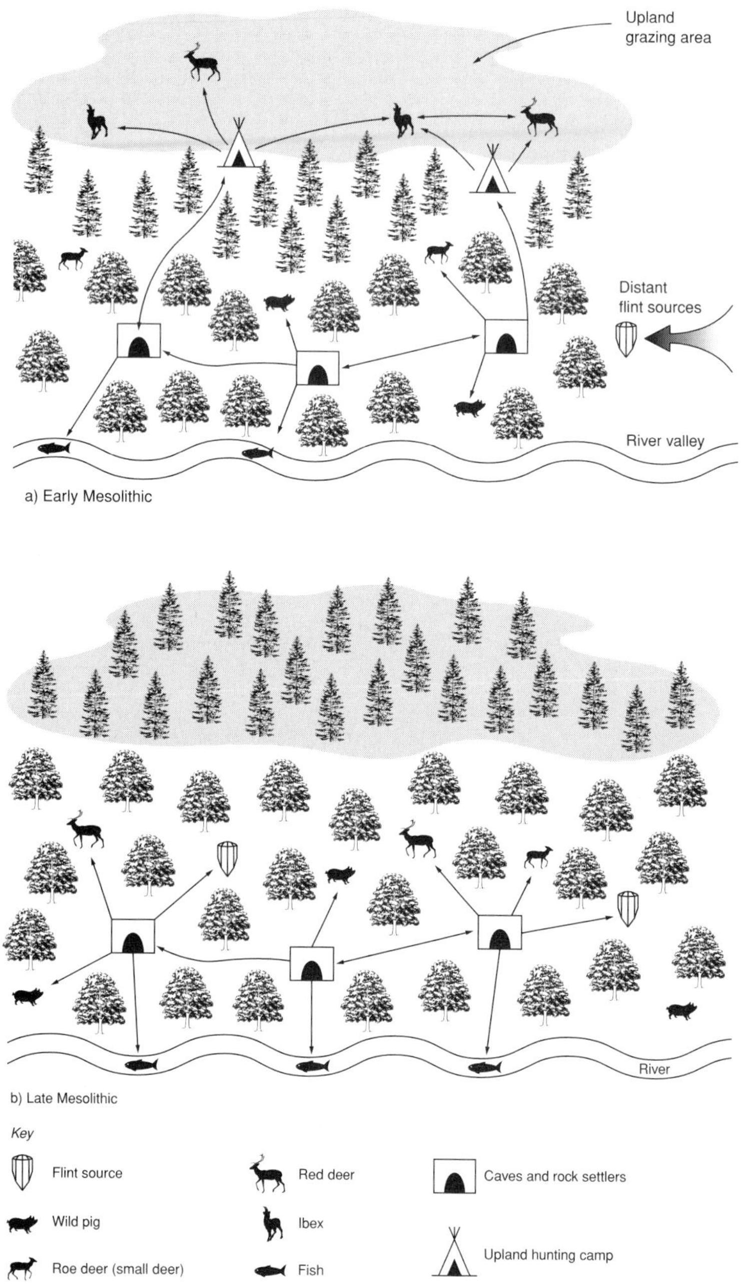

a) Early Mesolithic

b) Late Mesolithic

Key

Flint source	Red deer	Caves and rock settlers
Wild pig	Ibex	Upland hunting camp
Roe deer (small deer)	Fish	

Figure 9.5
Economic changes in the Trentino region during the Mesolithic. During the early Mesolithic bone and lithic data from the valley rock shelters suggests that bands of hunters operated over wide areas, exploiting resources on a seasonal basis. Lithic evidence from high level sites suggests small groups from summer hunting camps ambushed ibex and red deer herds through intercept hunting strategies.

By the late Mesolithic, pollen evidence suggests that trees had colonised the high pastures, pushing herd animals and ibex beyond the reach of the hunters. Evidence from the valley rock shelters suggests a switch to broad spectrum foraging within a much more limited territory. Riverine resources increasingly supplemented forest animals killed through encounter hunting strategies

Central place theory (CPT) based on the modelling of Christaller assumes that as the landscape fills up, settlements will be spaced evenly throughout it. Where settlements are more or less of equal size this reflects a fairly equal society. Where there is considerable variation in size it reflects a hierarchical society and one where the larger places perform central functions and provide a wider range of goods on behalf of a cluster of smaller satellite settlements. These will also emerge at regular intervals across the landscape. The most efficient pattern of spacing is a hexagonal lattice so areas for each central place are modelled by drawing hexagons around them. A study of medieval English market towns found that they fitted this model quite well. Each town was 4–6 miles from its neighbours and served a cluster of satellite hamlets and farmsteads. **Thiessen polygons** have been used in similar ways.

These are created by joining up the midpoints between settlements, to form irregular shaped zones of influence and exploitation.

These methods can be used to generate hypotheses to test about territory or catchment. CPT could also be used to suggest where there might be undiscovered sites. Such models have been used in a variety of regional studies including predicting the influence of Roman towns and changing social organisation in Iron Age Wessex. Cunliffe (1995) noted that a wide distribution of hill forts gave way to fewer, larger hill forts later in the first millennium. He interpreted this as representing a wider scale of social organisation with the development of tribal chiefdoms. A similar approach was used by Renfrew (1973) who interpreted the distribution of long barrows on Arran as reflecting the territories of groups of

 KEY STUDY

Early medieval settlement in the Cotswolds

Between the decline of Roman towns and villas and the emergence of known villages by the eleventh century, settlement patterns are hard to detect. The absence of dateable ceramics from the archaeological record means that fieldwalking's contribution is unusually limited and there has been no major excavation of a village. Reece's ongoing study (1998) focuses on the possibility that hedgerows may be indicative of past settlement locations. They would have been used to separate arable land from pasture and trackways and would be expected to occur along tracks and within a doughnut-shaped zone around settlement. Through examination of the species in hedges Reece has found that periods in which hedge management lapses will lead to domination by a few species and the elimination of some which grow more slowly. So the Hooper method may underestimate the age of the oldest hedges. He has used evidence of particular species such as wayfaring tree and guelder rose to suggest which might be the oldest hedges. Comprehensive mapping of richer (older) hedges may help identify lost settlement.

pioneer farmers. He found that the areas of land involved were similar to the holdings of modern crofts.

These idealised models tend to minimise the contribution of social and cultural influences and the influence of topography. CPT fits all known sites into one of the categories in a hierarchy of sites, which may not be realistic. A single pattern of settlement may be the physical expression of many different social systems. Belief, social relations and political considerations can be significant. For example, the distribution of Roman towns could reflect administrative areas for tax and law and order as well as the influence of markets. Some small sites may also have a social or ritual importance, which means they are of major importance in their region. One has to be confident that all the plotted features are related (for example contemporary) and also that no significant ones have been omitted. If not, the analysis is of the results of archaeological discoveries rather than of decisions made in the past. The key point is that these are models. Their primary function should be in helping generate questions and hypotheses that can be tested against archaeological data rather than fitting data to a model.

The social landscape: territory and boundaries

Of course, many social territories include many sites and are not obviously shaped by geography. Spatial distribution is of little use in explaining the British Empire of the nineteenth century although another geographical model, world systems theory, is useful in helping understand its workings. For state societies, written records often exist which help to identify centres and their territories. Roman inscriptions and the stone stelae of the Maya

have both been used in this way. For some states the extent of political control is indicated by physical boundaries. Hadrian's Wall and the Great Wall of China are well known from the ancient world but during the twentieth century fortified borders became the norm for nation states. The ruins of France's Maginot Line and the 'Iron Curtain' dividing East and West Europe provide classic examples. Less certainty surrounds the purpose of early medieval earthworks such as Offa's Dyke or Wansdyke. Artefacts of administration also provide clues to territories and the influence of central authorities. These include clay seals, emblems, standard weights and measures and coinage. However, influence and territory are not identical. Well-recognised currencies were used in the past outside their area of issue just as the US dollar is today. The evidence may be

 KEY STUDY

Bronze Age zones of influence in Wessex

Most sites known from late Bronze Age Wessex are small farmsteads. However, there were also several large hilltop enclosures such as Rams Hill. Ellison's (1980) study examined the distribution of a range of artefacts across southern England to see whether the patterns related to these sites. She found that they were positioned on the edge of the distribution of two or more types of finer pottery and seemed to be central to the distribution of metal ornaments. She concluded that they were centres for exchange and probably also for a developing social and political hierarchy.

KEY SKILL

Using case studies effectively

Case studies are detailed examples that will provide the evidence that supports your answer. The key sites and key studies used throughout this book are case studies and indicate the amount of detail you may eventually need to use. To reach the higher levels in any mark scheme you must use case studies. They are often the difference between a grade D and grade B response at A Level. It is a good idea to build up a portfolio of case studies throughout the course, covering each of the major topics.

Finding case studies

Your teacher will provide you with a base set of case studies but you should supplement this through your own research. There are many rich sources of additional material including television, museums and newspapers, as well as the sort of texts and websites listed in this book. Whatever your area of interest in archaeology there will be case studies available.

How to note case studies

The main points here are to avoid copying down large chunks of information and to keep in mind your purpose. You are likely to find case studies as you research one piece of work, but need to consider what other questions you might be asked in the future which they could also help with. It is sensible to adopt a thematic approach as used in the Stellmoor example on p. 204, breaking the study up into components. There are many ways to do this from simple highlighting of

the original or sets of keywords and concepts to elaborate cross-referenced, illustrated and colour-coded separate notes. You should use whichever system you find the most effective for retaining useable data. Experience has shown that the following work well:

- Condense the factual content to one third or less of the original, emphasising keywords and concepts that will trigger recall of data in an examination situation.
- Extract phrases and quotations but keep them punchy and brief.
- Use illustrations and diagrams when they convey a concept more effectively than you could do with words.
- Use the 'list' or 'brainstorming' method (▶see p. 193) to give consistency and information at a glance.
- Use highlighters sparingly in your own notes and never on the original!
- Use colour to code for methodology and for each of the big themes, perhaps six colours in all.

Managing case studies

As your folder grows it is easy to lose track of material. You should track this material by using a grid such as the one below. Enter the name of each site in the left-hand column and then indicate key aspects of the site which relate to the themes you are studying and which you may be examined upon. The grid is set up for the AQA course. This grid could usefully function as an index in your folder and help you to make links between themes.

KEY SKILL *cont.*

Study	Methods	Material culture	Economics	Ritual	Society
Gudme		Metal working	Exchange	Votives	
Boxgrove	Excavation Use wear	Lithics	Hunting		

contradictory in other ways. Zones of pottery and coin distribution have often not matched up. For early periods there may have been markers of territory which have not survived. These might have included totems or the appearance of peoples themselves.

On a local level, the landscape can also be used to explore power and status. The position of powerful social institutions such as churches and country houses are often prominent in the landscape. The traces of deserted villages on land cleared for sheep pasture in the sixteenth century or for deer parks in the eighteenth century provide insights into local control. Studies such as that at Shapwick (▶see p. 15) have revealed the way that the apparently natural distribution of villages nestling in the countryside was often a medieval creation. Powerful estate owners reorganised the landscape, creating nucleated villages from scattered farmsteads to maximise control and profitability. Modern field patterns strongly reflect the enclosure movement of the early nineteenth century, which was pursued for similar reasons.

 http://www.wkac.ac.uk/shapwick/index.html

 http://www.nottingham.ac.uk/tpau/projects/lax/

 http://www.loki.stockton.edu/~ken/wharram/wharram.htm

IDENTIFYING THE FUNCTION(S) OF ARCHAEOLOGICAL SITES

Archaeological sites are usually categorised by function. Generally this is a matter of determining the primary function since most sites have several. A castle is primarily defensive but may also have a domestic, economic and political function as well as being a status symbol. The same point could also be made about individual buildings. Archaeologists therefore try and identify what activities were carried out and whether there are any significant patterns in the evidence that might indicate that those particular spaces (areas, buildings or rooms) had specific functions. For example, was food preparation separated from storage? Taken together these enable the functions of the site to be described and assessed to determine their relative importance.

Evidence of human activities varies widely according to period, degree of preservation and the resources available to the excavators. If a site is from a historic period there may be written accounts, artistic depictions, plans and for the last few centuries maps, photographs, film and even living people! This is clearly not the case with much of prehistory. While there are cave sites and rock shelters with deep deposits of cultural material that have been sheltered from erosion, these sites are not typical. Most Palaeolithic sites have been subject to the ravages of a full range of transformation processes (▶see p. 95) and any interpretation has to take these into account. The main evidence for most sites will come from the archaeological record resulting from excavation or reconnaissance survey. Archaeologists will then try to recognise and explain patterns in the data. This relies on the comprehensiveness and accuracy of excavation recording (▶see p. 43) for its validity.

Figure 9.6 *A Mesolithic hearth at the Grotto D'Ernesto in the Trentino. The exact position of surviving artefacts and ecofacts provides clues to enable interpretation of group size and behaviour*

How are different types of activity identified on archaeological sites?

Boundaries such as internal and external walls, fence alignments or ditches are usually intended to separate different activities. This applies equally to a room, a farm or a town. Clear demarcation with boundaries makes detecting patterns of finds or space and comparing finds and features in different areas easier than on open sites. Where boundaries are identified, their shape, size and orientation can provide indications to their use although analogies will be needed to interpret them. Certain shapes and patterns (for example 'four-posters' or 'church shapes') may occur frequently. This enables interpretation of features on new sites with reference to identified examples from known ones (for example, comparing Roman features with well-preserved examples from sites such as Pompeii). Shapes of buildings and patterns can also be detected from detailed aerial photographs or by remote sensing. Archaeologists use their experience and data from excavation reports to identify connected groups of features. For example, a particular group of holes might be suggested as the postholes of a house from similarities in size, depth, fill, date and because the archaeologist recognises their pattern. Other evidence will be examined to see if the interpretation can be corroborated.

✎ http://www.rdg.ac.uk/AcaDepts/la/
silchester/

Association of artefacts and other finds with particular areas is the most common archaeological method. Detailed three-dimensional plotting of the distribution of finds across entire excavations enables patterns of activity to be identified. Examples include clusters of hide or bone working flints or the association of particular artefacts with particular features such

Interpreting Iron Age hill forts

Early studies of hill forts often started with classical sources and looked for evidence to support those historical accounts. Caesar had described chiefs and the warlike nature of the Celts. Hill forts with their massive defensive earthworks and evidence of violence at some of them, for example Hod Hill, looked to many like the strongholds of powerful chiefdoms. Cunliffe's excavations at Danebury seemed to support this view. The large number of storage

Figure 9.7 *Aerial photograph of the massive ramparts of Badbury Rings Hill Fort. To us these concentric earthworks and complex entrances look defensive, but they may have had other, more significant, functions*

pits and possible 'four poster' granaries could be interpreted as evidence of foodstuff stockpiled by a chief for redistribution or exchange. Other research has called this view into question. Danebury is still an impressive site today and undoubtably the resources that went into its construction would have given it a special status. However, there does not appear to be evidence of high status housing. Sharples' investigation of Maiden Castle also found little difference in size or artefacts between the mass of huts concentrated inside its massive earthworks. In many respects it is just a large farming community.

Hill (1996), in a series of attacks on Cunliffe's view of the Iron Age undertook statistical analysis of the ratios of finds to cubic metres of soil excavated on a range of Iron Age sites. While Danebury produced more finds, more soil was trowelled to produce them than on other sites. Comparison of the ratio of finds to volume of spoil suggested that Danebury was unexceptional in its density of craft tools. Several farmsteads such as Winnall Down produced higher densities of many finds. Hill used this kind of data to argue for a less hierarchical Iron Age. He also focused on the unenclosed and often 'richer' sites of the nearby Thames Valley to question the warlike nature of the period. Collis' (1996) work provides a further insight. He views hill forts principally as enclosures and sets them into a tradition of special hilltop enclosures in southern England stretching back to the early Neolithic. Nobody is suggesting that they were never used for defence and never occupied by a powerful leader, just that those may not have been their sole or principal functions.

 Champion and Collis 1996   Hill 1996

 Cunliffe 1995

KEY STUDIES

Palaeolithic assemblages

For the Palaeolithic, assemblages of artefacts and faunal remains are often the key to determining function. The 'living floors' of Olduvai Gorge and Koobi Fora in East Africa with their dense concentration of stone tools and animal bones have been much debated. Archaeologists who took these assemblages at face value tended to see these as kill sites or base camps where groups of hunters butchered carcasses or shared meat from their prey. This idea has been challenged on the grounds that the 'sites' were unsafe for humans and that microscopic analysis of the bones suggests that humans scavenged the bones after other predators had processed them. Further studies have questioned whether we should consider these as 'sites' at all. Taphonomic studies of bone distributions from predator kills and experimental work on site formation processes affecting tools and bones in the region suggest that the sites might be **palimpsests**, that is, accumulations of material from different times caused by natural forces as well as human activity.

 Schick and Toth 1993

 Binford 1989

as loom weights in a hut doorway. However, one has to be careful not to assign function on the basis of a few finds.

Computers make sophisticated density analysis possible such as comparing ratios of finds to area or volume of earth excavated. This can suggest which areas were most used for particular activities and may counter the bias created by large finds or raw numbers of finds. Similar analysis has been used on pits to suggest that they were not used solely for refuse disposal.

Areas with few finds present more of a challenge. The apparent deliberate clearing or 'purification' of an area can be a signature of ritual activity (for example the ditch at Avebury or the Zapotec temples of San Jose Mogote). However, absence of finds alone

 KEY TERM

Signature

To help identify features and their functions, archaeologists use mental templates for common activities in the period they are studying. There will be certain recurring patterns at sites, which have already been studied, which are associated with particular activities. For example, fires or hearths usually colour the earth reddish-orange while smelting or metalworking leaves slag and other waste products.

Alternative inferences can be made through the use of analogies drawn from experimental archaeology, ethnography and ethnoarchaeology (▶see p. 102).

should not be taken as proof of ritual purification!

Analysis of soils or other environmental evidence has been used successfully on some sites to determine activity. Phosphate or heavy mineral analysis can indicate where animals have been penned and there is some suggestion that different animals may have different chemical 'signatures'. Other environmental data including the remains of invertebrates with specific habitats can also provide clues. For example, grain beetles were used to identify particular buildings as granaries in Roman York.

The immediate context of a site can also provide clues to its general function and the activities that may have occurred there. A site surrounded by arable fields is likely to have had areas for processing and storing crops while evidence of watercourses may help to identify the remains of a building as a mill. This is least easy to do in towns where a picture of overall patterns can only be built up over a long time through a series of 'keyhole' excavations.

There are, of course, limits to the conclusions that can be drawn about any site. Archaeologists are usually investigating at the end of lengthy post-depositional processes and need to understand the impact of these on the evidence. For example, is it a site or a palimpsest? Partial survival, partial recovery, accuracy of find identification and the quality of sampling will also influence what is there to be studied, for example not all excavations will have recovered environmental evidence. Beyond this there is the quality of the insights and interpretations of the archaeologists. While the above provide clues, other insights will be needed to interpret them and test ideas. Analogies can be drawn from experimental archaeology, ethnography and ethnoarchaeology (▶see p. 103). Studying patterns of deposition from known activities may reveal signatures, which can help unravel evidence from the past. Conclusions will also reflect the values and assumptions of the archaeologists as well as their skill and knowledge. This is even more significant if one hopes to identify areas associated with particular gender, status or age groups.

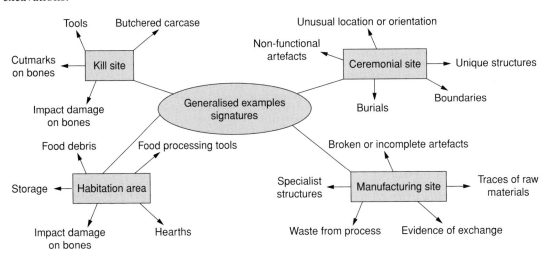

Figure 9.8 *Examples of signatures*

KEY TASK

Linking signatures to sites

To familiarise yourself with these concepts and the issues relating to identifying settlement function for the period(s) you are studying, produce your own version of the signature diagram (Figure 9.8). This will provide a useful aide-memoir for when you write evaluative essays on this topic.

- Insert three or four additional, relevant categories in boxes, for example military site, port, extraction site and high status site.
- Enter one or two sites from your study in each of the boxes, for example Boxgrove as an example of a butchery site. You may find that some sites fit several categories.
- Around the box list indicators of function which could serve as signatures from these sites.
- Finally, try to identify any problems you have encountered such as contradictory or ambivalent evidence. For example, some archaeologists have identified Neolithic houses as dwellings, others as ritual structures. It is possible that they had several functions.

THE USE OF SPACE ON ARCHAEOLOGICAL SITES

The reasons why sites within the same area differ in their internal layout have been explored by archaeologists drawing on ethnoarchaeology. Binford's work with the Nunamiut (▶see p. 167) provided insights into the complex reasons for differences. He showed that it was wrong to expect the same group of people to produce homogeneous sites. Sites differed due to their role in the overall settlement system. For example, hunting and residential sites used space differently, but even hunting camps might differ widely. The site of a successful hunt might generate many additional activities to the site of an unsuccessful one.

Ethnoarchaeology has identified some of the problems that can occur if the distribution of artefacts and features on a site are interpreted as a direct record of economic decisions and activities. Site maintenance, the practice of disposing of rubbish, may create misleading patterns in the archaeological record. Different materials are treated differently, some being thrown aside while others are recycled or deliberately taken to dumps. Some activities are deliberately sited to be near heat and light while tasks that require a lot of space are rarely in areas where people socialise. In Clarke's (1972) study of Glastonbury Lake Village he used artefactual evidence in relation to spaces marked by boundaries to identify a series of zones which went beyond economic activity. Distinct compounds for carpentry, leather and iron working were identified and interpreted as male working areas while zones for spinning and baking were interpreted as female areas. Clarke also identified some differences in the value of artefacts in different huts, which he saw as evidence of a ranked society with differences in wealth.

The distribution of activities can be most clearly seen where buildings remain. Distinctive features such as ovens, drains and traces of fixings provide important clues. Decorative features, the size of the room and the nature of doors and windows provide hints to both

KEY STUDIES

The Mask site and Pincevent

Binford's observations of behaviour and the use of space around a hearth by Nunamuit caribou hunters at the Mask site have been particularly influential. He identified an irregular doughnut-shaped distribution of material. He divided this into drop and toss zones according to the way the hunters disposed of rubbish. For example, larger pieces of debris were thrown behind the hunters or across the fire. He was able to detect differences in distribution patterns caused by differing numbers of hunters. He also noted that hearths tended to be spread by people searching for food in the ashes and that when the wind changed direction, the hunters would turn around and start another hearth. Binford contrasted this behaviour with observations inside structures where hearths and resulting ash are usually surrounded by stones to prevent the spread of fire and to provide working surfaces. People also tend not to throw rubbish over their shoulders indoors.

Binford (1983) used these insights to challenge Leroi-Gourhan's (1978) interpretation of the Upper Palaeolithic site of Pincevent. Excavation here had revealed rings of stone associated with a number of hearths. Leroi-Gourhan had interpreted these as tents with the stones used to hold the edges of the tents down. Binford suggested that it was an open-air site with the stones used to hold down hides for working on. People built new hearths in response to changes in wind direction.

 KEY STUDY

Black Patch

Drewett's (1982) excavation of part of this Bronze Age farmstead drew on ethnography and detailed analysis of different categories of finds to suggest the functions and social organisation of the site. The largest hut, which had its own compound and pond and contained finer pottery and evidence of a loom, was the home of the headman. The smaller huts were for food preparation, storage and accommodation for the rest of the headman's extended family. Detailed study of finds within the huts was related to likely sources of light to identify areas for weaving, leather working and storage.

function and status. Surviving buildings also enable greater exploration of the social use of space than on excavated sites. This involves analysis of what the use of space meant and how social relations were structured by the architecture. For example, the household is the fundamental organisational unit for most known societies but there are exceptions where more extended social groups live under one roof. Physical space between clusters of huts may represent social distance while a building that physically dominates others may be the home of a social leader. The architecture of the houses reflects this differentiation. This type of analysis has been applied to the search for ritual specialists (▶see p. 161) and investigations of gender relations. Gilchrist (1995) has suggested that the layout of domestic areas of medieval castles reflects and reinforces contemporary views on the differences between men

KEY STUDY

Gurness

Brochs are double-walled, drystone tower houses surrounded by clusters of other buildings. Recent studies of this Iron Age broch on Orkney by Historic Scotland have challenged the idea that it was simply a defensive site. The great tower of the broch dominated the settlement and the smaller houses were ranged either side of the single passage leading into the broch itself.

 Figure 9.9 *The broch at Gurness looking down the entrance corridor to the central tower. This was the only way in or out and the view would have been dominated by, and observed from, the tower*

The architecture controlled movement around the site and constantly drew attention to the tower. The broch provided a home to a chieftain and protection for his followers. However, it also made his dominance of the people and the area visible. In helping to build it and living under its shadow the local people accepted his authority.

Figure 9.10
 An example of a smaller building at Gurness. Were these the houses of the clan members of a chieftain? Note how these buildings are all linked and cluster around the larger tower. They all open out onto the main corridor

http://www.brad.ac.uk/acad/archsci/
field_proj/scat/

Figure 9.11 *High status sites are often indicated by important buildings. Major Roman towns had a range of civic buildings. This is the Amphitheatre at El Djem in Tunisia*

and women. In the analysis of space, boundaries are of particular importance and archaeologists are careful not to see ditches and entrances as simply functional.

On a larger scale the differing size and elaboration of buildings may suggest a stratified society while controlling elites might be inferred from settlements structured along gridlines or with fixed orientations. The layout of Teotihuacan in Mexico is an example where the existence of a directing elite can be substantiated from other evidence.

The status of different sites is also determined by examining patterns. Elite sites or buildings are expected to be larger and richer in finds and decoration than humbler versions. Key features such as unusually large storage facilities and

Figure 9.12 *High status buildings may be marked by exotic or unusual features which would have required considerable expense to purchase or build. This beautiful Venus mosaic from Kingscote illustrates the status of the villa*

KEY SITE

West Heslerton

Around AD 450 a typical Romano-British settlement which had been joined by distinctive Anglo-Saxon grubenhaus was abandoned. (▶see p. 132) A short distance away a large, new settlement replaced it. This too combined Romano-British and Anglo-Saxon elements but was a very different settlement. It included post and plank built buildings and a long hall. The whole site was laid out in an ordered way with distinct zones for farming, housing and industrial activity. The evidence of buildings and pottery suggested much continuity of population but the planning and Scandinavian origin of the larger buildings suggested that the site had new, foreign leaders.

Figure 9.13 *Wooden structures rarely survive. They have to be 'constructed' from traces left in the earth from their construction. This grubenhaus from West Heslerton illustrates this point. Experiment (▶see p. 102) will be needed to interpret the superstructure of the building*

exotic finds are also indicators of status. The Minoan capital Knossos provides a good example of this. Extensive permanent storage and valuable finds from throughout the eastern Mediterranean testify to its importance.

UNDERSTANDING STRUCTURES

Many of the points made in relation to sites and features also apply to structures, but you also need to understand how archaeologists interpret structures from buried traces. Key questions revolve around why particular designs were selected and the technology and materials used to construct them. Structures range from traces of a windbreak around a hearth or stakeholes from a tent through to recent industrial or military buildings. Faced with pits, slots and postholes, archaeologists have to make imaginative leaps to reconstruct buildings from the past. Early examples reflected modern perceptions of people in the past or were drawn from ethnography.

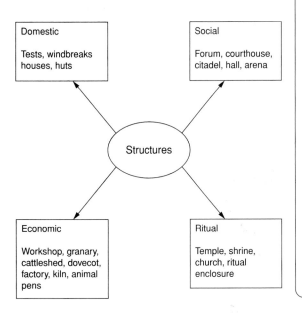

Domestic	Social
Tests, windbreaks houses, huts	Forum, courthouse, citadel, hall, arena

Structures

Economic	Ritual
Workshop, granary, cattleshed, dovecot, factory, kiln, animal pens	Temple, shrine, church, ritual enclosure

Figure 9.14 *Structures in archaeology*

KEY SITE

Butser Ancient Farm

Butser is well known as an open-air laboratory for testing ideas about Iron Age technology including farming and the effectiveness of tools. Its buildings are designed according to the floorplans of excavated sites. The walls, beams and roof itself are the product of experimentation based on knowledge of Iron Age carpentry and engineering. Building roundhouses has enabled the exploration of ideas about roof slope, light, efficiency of fires and whether a smoke hole is needed. It has also answered questions about how long a roundhouse might last and the amount of woodland needed to build and maintain it.

Figure 9.15 *An Iron Age roundhouse at Butser Ancient Farm. 'Constructs' such as this have been immensely valuable in exploring many aspects of past buildings including roof shape, potential function, construction techniques and useful lifetime*

http://www.butser.org.uk/

Figure 9.16 *Reconstruction of Central European mammoth bone house. A number of sites have been excavated in central Europe and the Ukraine dating from the Upper Palaeolithic with large quantities of carefully arranged mammoth bones. Although there is some controversy over the nature of possible structures, the dominant interpretation is that modern human hunters used the tusks, long bones and skulls of mammoths as substitutes for wood in contructing huts. Skins were probably tied over the bones to provide weatherproof shelter. If accurate, this provides a classic example of human adaptability in harsh climatic conditions. It may also indicate a very specialised economy*

The development of experimental archaeology has been particularly important in investigating structures from prehistoric and medieval times. While ground plans can be estimated from hearths and postholes or foundation trenches, the walls and roofs are problematic. However, we have developed an understanding of building and materials from sites with unusual preservation. Woodworking capabilities from the Mesolithic onwards have been informed by finds at waterlogged sites such as the Sweet Track in Somerset. They have provided insights into construction techniques, tools and the type of wood used and have hinted at the extent of woodland management. Experimental structures such as those at West Stow (▶see p. 131) and Butser Ancient Farm have used this information to test hypotheses about the design and materials used to make the walls and roofs and then about the use and function of the buildings. It is important to remember that while everyone refers to these buildings as reconstructions they cannot be reconstructions. We cannot be entirely sure what an Iron Age roof was like, so modern versions should properly be called constructs or models. Similarly we cannot know if the house was decorated or whether people slept on the ground or on platforms that lay across the roof beams. Experiment can only show what might have been and then test it to failure.

Experimental archaeology is, of course, weighted towards technological understanding. There may be social or religious reasons for particular designs and materials being used which reconstructions cannot directly address. Therefore other sources of analogy and analysis of the symbolism of designs are also studied. The predominant orientation of Bronze and Iron Age roundhouses and enclosures towards the south-east may be such a case. Experiment has shown that a southerly orientation would maximise light. The choice of south-east or west may reflect beliefs linked to the rising or setting sun.

Where archaeologists are investigating standing buildings a wide range of insights can be gained into the technical skills, communications and prosperity of the societies and individuals that created them. For instance, petrological examination (▶see p. 62) to identify the sources of building stone used for Roman villas or medieval cathedrals tells us about contemporary geological knowledge and hints at the nature of markets for materials and the transport system necessary to move them.

 KEY SKILL

Planning successful archaeology essays

For essays in any subject the same essential rules apply. Accurate statements well linked to the question and supported by relevant and detailed examples lead to success. Essays are generally marked according to 'levels-of-response mark schemes'. This means that the markers will have a hierarchical series of statements that describe essays. Each statement or band has a range of marks allocated to it. Generally, speaking, the first third of the mark range are for descriptive accounts or essays that argue but provide no evidence. These are fails. The second third combine the two and are low-level passes. The top level requires arguments well supported with case study material. Often the mark awarded within a band is influenced by the amount of relevant detail. The commonest reasons for underperformance are not supporting your statements and being irrelevant. To avoid this, most successful students plan their essays.

A plan can help you to:

- focus on what you need to do
- make sure you include all key points
- avoid wasting time on irrelevant points.

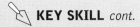 **KEY SKILL** *cont.*

The three stages of essay planning

Skeleton	*Muscles*	*Flesh*
Basic structure	Paragraph content	Depth and detail
Order of points	Major ideas	Content from case studies
Levels of importance	Links backward and forward	Theoretical concepts

Having planned what you need to include, you then need to write up the essay with a logical and appropriate structure. There is no single right way to do this. You will need to vary your response with different types of question. Archaeology essays follow three broad patterns:

■ *List-type essays* that ask you to focus on a process or methods. For example, what can archaeologists learn from human soft tissue remains?

■ *Evaluative essays*, which ask you to weigh up how far something can be supported by evidence. For example, how far is it possible to identify settlement in the Mesolithic?

Model A: *Compare* the evidence for *complex* settlement from *two* areas that you have studied

Introduction: define *key terms* in the title	
Aim for *breadth* in considering similarities and differences	
Region 1 Case study of Oaxaca Valley	Region 2 Case study of Valley of Mexico
Make explicit links to command words	
Discussion tries to identify common ground and major differences by reference to clear criteria such as size, specialisation, planning, etc.	
Conclusion: some/a lot/a little etc.	

Figure 9.17 *Planning an essay*

■ *Discursive essays* ask you to explore all sides of an issue and reach a conclusion. They are often posed as a quotation followed by the instruction 'Discuss'. You can respond to these with an argument but you do need to consider other interpretations as well as your own.

While these require different structures in the body of the essay, there are several common points, which you could use as a checklist.

1 Introduction
■ Define terms mentioned in the title.
■ Outline types of sources to be used.
■ Make a statement about the issue in the question, even if it is pointing out that there are several dimensions to it.

KEY SKILL *cont.*

2 Main body of the text

- Generalised answers are not appropriate and will not score high marks in essay questions. You must root your response firmly in archaeological contexts, selecting specific data and explaining how it is relevant to the original question.
- Link your answer to relevant theory.
- Do not be afraid to use anthropological or geographical terms and concepts where appropriate, for example Christaller, kinship, reciprocity.
- Explain conflicting or opposing theories which account for the same phenomenon where appropriate.
- Select the relevant parts of some of the bank of case studies you have at your disposal.
- It is usually better to use fewer case studies in depth than to attempt a broader approach, which runs the risk of being superficial.
- Length is important – it is difficult for your ideas to develop sufficiently or for the examiner to be able to reward you fully if your essays are very brief. You should aim for at least three sides of A4 for a 25-mark question in a formal essay.

3 Conclusion

- Don't just repeat what you have already said.
- Sum up your main arguments.
- Express a view where appropriate.
- Answer each part of the question. It is acceptable to give different responses to different aspects of a question. Most conclusions will be a variation of 'to some extent'.

List-type essays

There are many ways of producing plans. The models you select will suit your style and the amount of time you have available. These three examples are all in response to the same list-type essay: 'How does material culture change over time?'

Example 1: a detailed plan

Introduction: Define material culture and the context for *your* examples of 'over time'.

Body text: Theories related to environment, population, human evolution, innovation, diffusion of ideas, invasion. Case studies on:

- Franchthi Cave (long time depth and transition from hunting to farming)
- Stone tool development from Oldowan to Neolithic (links to evolution, innovation and environment).
- Upper Palaeolithic spearpoints (focus on one period, links to economics and functional efficiency).

![trowel icon] **KEY SKILL** *cont.*

Conclusion: Use statements such as 'on the balance of the evidence it seems that . . .' And phrases such as 'Knecht's (1990) work with upper Palaeolithic spears shows clearly that . . .'. Don't be afraid to go for one explanation if the evidence warrants it. Otherwise explain the interplay of several causal factors. Relevant quotations can be used effectively here.

Example 2: a tree diagram

![image] **Figure 9.18** (right) *A tree diagram*

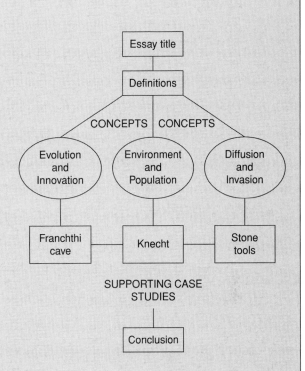

Example 3: Brainstorming

![image] **Figure 9.19** (below) *Brainstorming*

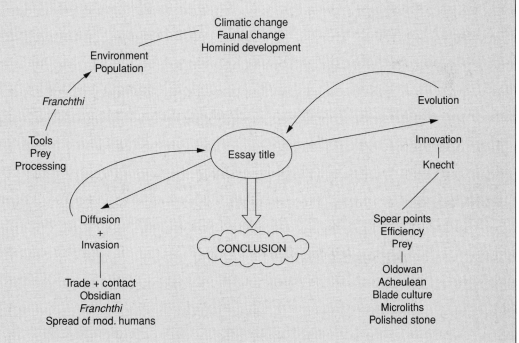

KEY SKILL *cont.*

Discursive essays

Different types of essay can be planned using similar methods although their structure may be different. Here is a plan for a discursive essay. Rather than expecting a list, the examiner is allowing you to range widely for content but to structure it tightly in response to the following question: 'The majority of material from the past is archaeologically invisible' Discuss.

Introduction: the nature of differential survival. Discussion of types of evidence available and introduction of arguments on both sides.

Ordinary sites: link to case studies to review the quality of data and its limitations. Look at how new techniques can expand data available.	*Special sites*: link to examples to support complementary nature of these sites and their limitations

---

Discussion: draws the two arguments together. Comment on overall effect of limitations. Consider how we would cope if most things did survive! Does it vary by period or theme? (See Figure 8.1, p. 138.)

Conclusion: respond to the question. To what extent and with what significance?

Evaluative essay

All essays require some evaluation. Some, however, particularly focus on the evaluation through comparison of strengths and weaknesses of a number of competing ideas. The trick is to identify good material that allows you to demonstrate your grasp of the ideas and use it to support judgements about which arguments you find most persuasive. For example consider the question 'How far have archaeologists been able to establish whether environmental or human factors best explain major change in the period you have studied?'

This has some similarities to the task on farming (▶see p. 209)

KEY SKILL *(cont.)*

Introduction: major concepts and type of sources available for each hypothesis

Elaboration of theories linked to command words

Hypothesis 1 case study material which supports environmental factors, for example Maya collapse, Mashkan Shapir.	*Hypothesis 2* case study data which supports anthropogenic factors: Baltic standstill, origins of farming.

Judgements: which arguments best fit the facts? Synthesis of ideas. Is there one solution or the interplay of many causal factors?

Conclusion: to what extent?

 KEY SKILL

Improving your essays

Experiment with the detailed plan and the structure outline above with your next assignment. If style has also been an issue for you, also check p. 227.

Chapter 10

Material Culture and Economics

YOUR GOALS

You need to

■ understand, define and use the key concepts associated with these themes

■ be familiar with a range of relevant case studies for your period which each cover several topics

■ be able to synthesise ideas and data from case studies to respond to a variety of types of questions

■ write well-structured and relevant essays.

Although material culture and economics are different themes, there is considerable overlap in relevant case studies. Economics is concerned with how people manage the cultural and natural resources available to them. Material culture is concerned with the things (in their broadest sense) that people made and what they signified.

Material learnt for one theme can usually be applied to the other. There are also strong links with the post excavation analysis covered in Chapter 3. You need to link your grasp of methods to your case studies in order to be able to appraise their strengths and weaknesses. Other major links include interpretation

(Chapter 5), particularly the use of ethnographic and experimental analogies, and the use of geographic models to interpret distribution patterns and site function (p. 178).

SUBSISTENCE: HOW DID PEOPLE IN THE PAST FEED THEMSELVES?

This is a fundamental question in most periods. Many writers have assumed that the type of economic system used largely determines the nature of society. Indeed, archaeologists define many societies according to how they acquired their food. If your course is thematic, you need to ensure that you have case studies from a range of societies. '**Hunter-gatherer**' is a label

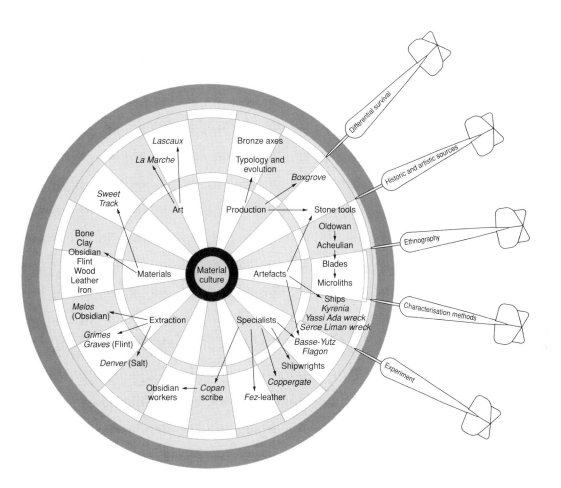

Figure 10.1 *Use of a target diagram to link the content of these topics*

used to cover a wide range of societies across over 90 per cent of human history. For the earliest period humans were not hunters at all. Hunting developed following a lengthy period of scavenging and gathering. Archaeologists are divided about when hominids began proper hunting. Estimates have ranged from over 1 million years ago to about 100,000 years ago (p. 000). The Mesolithic saw diversification into a broad range of animals, fish and marine foods. In most parts of the world this was followed by agriculture which provided the economic basis for life up to the Industrial Revolution. Societies

that herd animals are called **pastoralists**. Rearing animals for food is also known as animal husbandry. Sedentary *farmers* are usually associated with societies from the last 10,000 years. In some regions they were pre-ceded by mobile *horticulturists* whose pattern of farming was very different to those of **arable** (crop) agriculturists of historic times.

Direct human exploitation of animals takes many forms. *Hunting* may be random (you kill the first animal you encounter) or selective (you take only young males or old females,

KEY TERM

Material culture

At a general level, this term is applied to the artefacts and structures produced by a given people. They can be studied in a biographical way, for example, what raw materials were used, how they were obtained and worked and how the finished products were used. However, increasingly material culture is used in a second way. This is based on the idea that the beliefs and values of a culture are expressed to some extent in the material things it produces. People operate according to particular beliefs, ideas and knowledge and these in turn shape or structure everything that people do. Studying material culture involves 'reading' the symbolic meanings embedded in artefacts and structures (▶see p. 183). At university level you will need to understand some of the debates on this topic. Below undergraduate level you just need a basic outline. In essence, archaeologists study the context material things are found in and look for repeated patterns between them. For example, similarities in design have led some archaeologists to argue that Neolithic tombs symbolised houses. They also explore the way symbols in material things may have, in turn, structured the way people thought and interpreted their world. For instance certain artefacts may be used to express social identity. Pottery (for example beakers) has been particularly studied in this respect.

leaving breeding age females and hence maintain the effective breeding population). Intensive hunting may also include human manipulation of the vegetation environment to make conditions more favourable for a particular species. Pastoralists may herd the animals and exercise some control over reproduction by selective culling of the stock. Finally, they may control all aspects of an animal's life, dictating where it feeds (by the creation of fields), dictating its mate (by creating single sex herds) and so on. Wherever an economy lies between hunting and *stock rearing* it will leave slightly different signatures in the archaeological record. Interpretation of this will depend on an understanding of local taphonomic processes.

The direct contribution of animals to human economy takes four main forms:

- as a source of food products such as meat, blubber, fat or marrow
- as a source of secondary food products such as blood, milk, cheese, butter
- as a source of raw materials for artefact manufacture, light and fuel including antler, bone, skins, grease, dung, hair and wool
- as a source of traction, haulage and transport.

Primary products are all those which require the killing and butchery of animals such as meat or bone. **Secondary products** include all those that involve utilising the products of living animals such as dung and wool.

Identifying the nature of exploitation

The interpretation of the contribution of animals to the economy of a site is dependent upon the recovery of a sufficiently representative sample of the animal population and the

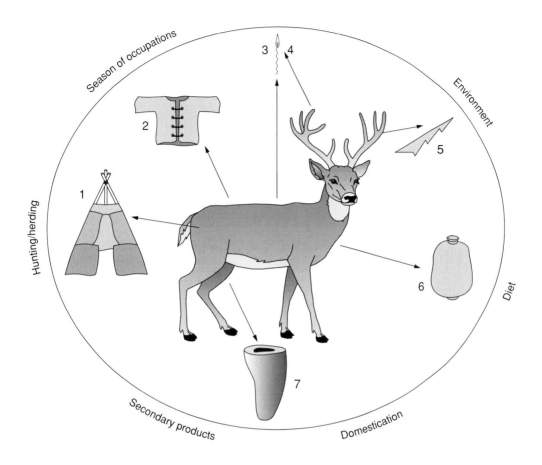

Key to primary use of animal

1. skin for tent
2. skin for clothes
3. sinew for thread
4. bone for needle
5. antler for harpoon
6. intestine for water container
7. meat

Figure 10.2 *Human exploitation of animals and areas that archaeologists can explore using surviving evidence*

identification of its age and sex structure (▶see p. 69). Kill ratios are indicative of particular strategies. **Catastrophic profiles** of the age and sex of dead animals, where whole herds were killed, suggests unselective hunting, for example using stampedes. Over-representation of particular animals provides evidence of more selective hunting. The type of damage caused to animal bones by hunting tools can help corroborate this. Natural predators tend to pick off the old, young and sick and early human hunters were probably similar. This does not endanger the survival of the herd and creates an **attritional bone profile.** More sophisticated hunters will manage herds, producing indistinguishable patterns of kills to

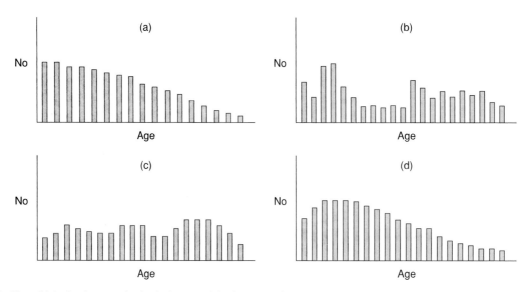

Profiles which plot the age of animals from surviving bones against the number found in each age group.

(a) The age profile of a modern herd of similar animals. This provides the norm for comparison.

(b) A profile caused by selective butchery or hunting. A disproportionate number of animals are killed as they reach maturity (probably male) and when they are beyond breeding age. Animals in their prime, particularly females, would be spared.

(c) A dairying herd. There is a rise in the proportion killed as they cease to supply milk.

(d) A catastrophic profile. The whole herd has died. Possibly caused by stampeding over a cliff.

Figure 10.3 *Simplified diagrams to illustrate catastrophic and attritional profiles in animal bone assemblages*

many farmers, for instance culling young males but not the females needed to reproduce the herds. Amongst pastoralist peoples, a predominance of older female bones may indicate dairying. The presence of very young or migratory animals provides clues to seasonal patterns of exploitation.

Bone assemblages also provide insights into preferred food sources, although the archaeological record has a preservation bias towards larger bones. Fish and bird bones in particular are under-represented in the archaeological record as are invertebrates. Inferences about their importance can be made from the remains of fish traps, specialist fowling tools or even art, as in Egyptian tomb paintings. **Isotope analysis** of human bones and teeth can indicate the proportion of diet from animal, marine and plant sources. Modern excavation techniques have also added to our knowledge. Animal fats have been recovered from Upper Palaeolithic cave sites and phosphate analysis has been used to identify stalls and paddocks. Tools, once they have been interpreted, are used to make inferences about hunting and processing animals. Use wear marks (▶see p. 65) and traces of blood on tools can also be examined. Experimental archaeology can show the capability of tools and provide insights into the

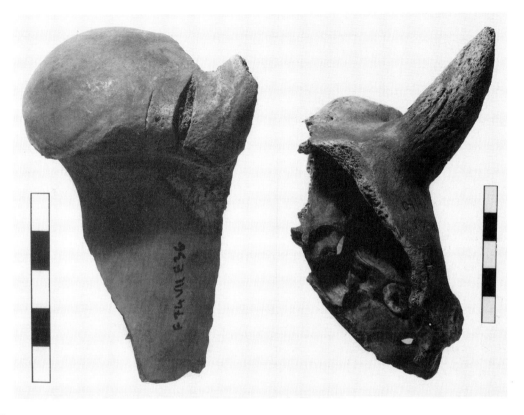

Figure 10.4 *Neolithic animal bone with evidence of human butchery. The cattle bone on the left has cut marks while the sheep skull on the right has been split open with a sharp tool*

ways that they might have been used. It can also indicate how the animal was processed through comparison with modern butchery practice and experimental observation of scavenged carcasses. Cut-marks near the joints may indicate butchery for meat while smashing the mid-section of long bones suggests marrow extraction. Similarly, angled cut-marks on animal skulls may indicate skinning. The assemblages comprised of particular meat bearing bones possibly indicate storage. Their absence on sites suggests that consumption occurred away from the butchery site.

Tracing developments in human exploitation of animals

Hunting or scavenging?

There has been continued debate amongst archaeologists about when hunting began. Evidence from hominid bones suggests that more protein was needed as brains enlarged. On the other hand, the long digestive tract in humans is not suited to meat processing and we are slow and lack cutting teeth. This does not point to a long adaptation to hunting. Other clues to humans consuming meat include bones and tools found next to each other on 'living floors'. Even when the site is not a palimpsest, association does not prove whether

KEY SITE

La Cotte de St Brelade

La Cotte is a Middle Palaeolithic site in Jersey dating to around 150,000 years ago. It has produced some Neanderthal teeth and some stone tools, but its main interest lies in possible evidence for hunting of large mammals. The site is on a promontory close to the sea but during its earlier occupation the sea level was lower. Then it faced onto an open plain leading down to the sea. The archaeological material was found during the excavation of a gully behind two isolated 'stacks' of rock, at the foot of a sheer cliff.

Apart from the human remains and tools there was a considerable quantity of faunal remains mostly consisting of mammoth and woolly rhino bones of both adults and juveniles. Some of these bones seem to have been deliberately arranged against one wall of the gully in at least two separate episodes.

The excavator's explanation was that the site functioned as a 'drive site' for hunting, in that the animals would have been carefully herded into position on the slope leading to the cliff and then stampeded to their deaths in the gully below where they could be butchered at leisure. There is a considerable body of ethnographic evidence for similar practices involving bison in North America such as at 'Head smashed in'. This suggests a very organised and concerted group effort perhaps using firebrands to frighten the animals and groups of people or stones as guide lanes to steer them towards the cliff. The end result would have been large quantities of meat to be processed and the arrangements of large parts of skeletons against the gully wall may suggest storage practice in the form of a **cache**.

---

humans were hunters or scavengers. Marks from human butchery are distinctly 'V' shaped when compared to the 'U' shaped irregular scratches of carnivores. Analysis can show who got to the bone first. Analysis of the bones from Olduvai Gorge suggested that hominids began as scavengers.

A growing body of evidence supports unselective hunting by the Middle Palaeolithic. A series of sites, such as Combe Grenal, that feature the butchered remains of large numbers of animals have been excavated. The catastrophic bone profiles suggest stampeding or similar forms of mass slaughter. The discoveries at Boxgrove (▶see p. 224) and

recent finds of spears in Germany appear to provide evidence of hunting technology.

Selective hunting

Modern human hunts are more persistent than the charges of predators and involve human culture. Hunters often work together, exchange information and share food in base camps. Knowledge is needed, for example how to create balanced, aerodynamic spears and where to penetrate large animals to kill them. This requires communication and the debate about modern hunting is closely linked to debates about when human social attributes developed. The evidence for selective hunting includes **specialisation**. On some Upper Palaeolithic

Figure 10.5 *What a mammoth trap might have looked like. If only . . .*

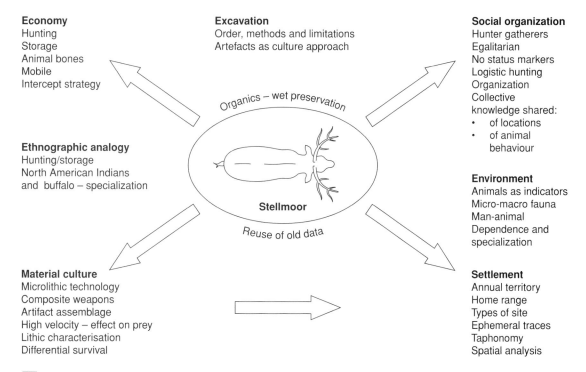

Economy
Hunting
Storage
Animal bones
Mobile
Intercept strategy

Excavation
Order, methods and limitations
Artefacts as culture approach

Social organization
Hunter gatherers
Egalitarian
No status markers
Logistic hunting
Organization
Collective
knowledge shared:
• of locations
• of animal
  behaviour

Ethnographic analogy
Hunting/storage
North American Indians
and buffalo – specialization

Organics – wet preservation

Stellmoor

Reuse of old data

Environment
Animals as indicators
Micro-macro fauna
Man-animal
Dependence and
specialization

Material culture
Microlithic technology
Composite weapons
Artifact assemblage
High velocity – effect on prey
Lithic characterisation
Differential survival

Settlement
Annual territory
Home range
Types of site
Ephemeral traces
Taphonomy
Spatial analysis

Figure 10.6 *Stellmoor. Diagram to summarise key aspects and links*

KEY SITE

Stellmoor

This site on the North German Plain dates from the last ice age of 9000 BC and was occupied briefly by groups of hunter-gatherers who specialised in hunting reindeer with bows and arrows. Their hunting method is known as an *intercept strategy* (see also p. 174). Reindeer travelled along a regular path on their seasonal migration to the northern tundra to graze vegetation during the brief 'arctic summer'. Excavation produced well-preserved organic material including arrow shafts. An extensive range of stone tools was recovered including arrowheads. The arrows appeared designed to cause maximum damage and blood loss to enable a quick kill. Analysis of damage, or lesions, caused by the arrows to the reindeer bones suggested a pattern of arrow shots which concentrated on the vital organs, avoiding the ribs. Analysis of the sex and age of kills provided evidence for selective culling of young males. This indicates a very purposeful and organised approach to hunting in this period, and knowledge of the animals' behaviour that is perhaps to be viewed as a stepping stone towards domestication. The huge quantities of bone dumped in a nearby lake margin suggest the hunters were processing more meat than they could consume. Ethnographic analogy suggests storage practices could have included caching, drying or making pemmican.

sites in the Dordogne 99 per cent of the bones are from reindeer. The kill profile is more attritional while specialised artefacts indicate sophisticated hunting technology. Spear throwers, blades, bows and a variety of traps for fish were all developed during this period (see also p. 225). Humans used material culture to transform their position in their environment. Some aspects of this may be reflected in their art (▶see p. 232). Sadly, no mammoth traps of the type pictured in children's archaeology books have ever been found.

Broad spectrum foraging

Humans have been hunter-gatherers for most of their existence although this was rarely studied until quite recently and, even today, hardly at all below university level. In the 1960s attempts were made to explore hunting through ethnography. A surprising finding was that even in hostile environments, hunter-gatherers spent much less time working than did farmers. Although some have questioned the romantic view of hunter-gatherers as the original affluent society (they were time-rich whereas we are rich in consumer goods), sites with good organic preservation have revealed that they often had rich diets and rich cultures. Where a diverse range of food resources were exploited, many archaeologists now use the term **foragers** to describe the economic strategy. Foragers are not usually nomadic, tending to move around a defined area to maximise resources. Mobility is a strategy to minimise the risk of seasonal shortage rather than being random. However, not all foragers need this mobility.

KEY STUDIES

Baltic foragers of the late Mesolithic

Sites in Denmark and Scania (southern Sweden) have produced remarkably well-preserved evidence of foraging peoples. Continuity in flint technology and skeletal shape suggests stable populations, while site density and the absence of much disease from human bones suggest that they were well nourished. Their 'broad spectrum' foraging economy drew on many different resources. Quantities of nuts and water chestnuts and residues of porridge made from seeds testify to the importance of plant food. However, isotopic evidence from human bone and a range of specialised equipment suggests an **intensification** in focus on marine foods.

The submarine site at Tybrind Vig included traps, nets and hooks along with a canoe with an on-board hearth. This was possibly for nocturnal eel fishing. Specialist prongs for eel have been found elsewhere, as have fish-weirs and harpoons. Remains of whales and sharks in coastal middens may indicate offshore fishing although they could represent strandings. The faunal assemblages on some sites suggest some specialisation, possibly on

a seasonal basis. They may have hunted seals for their fat. Large numbers were killed and sites often had exotic artefacts that may have been traded for seal oil. Other sites such as Ringkloster included the processed bones of fur-bearing animals such as pine martens. Analysis of faunal assemblages indicates selective hunting of deer, pig and aurochs, possibly even herd management of smaller species.

Quantities of data were sufficient for Mithen (1990) to use computer analysis to compare real assemblages with predicted assemblages based on different models of hunting behaviour. His research suggested that hunters were being highly selective in animals they stalked and killed and were under little pressure to bring back meat from every trip. The key sites such as Ertebolle, Vedbaek and Skateholm had hearths, pits, various structures and their own distinctive pottery. Some even had cemeteries. They could afford to become semi-sedentary and develop a rich culture because their subsistence strategy was so successful.

Herding and the domestication of animals

It used to be thought that domestication could be identified from morphological (shape) changes in animals such as smaller horns. Domesticated animals were also smaller and their bones less thick than their wild ancestors. However, climate can produce similar changes and in any case the changes take place slowly. Where archaeologists have dated domestication from changes in the size of animals or certain

features such as horns, they may have underestimated the date at which farming began. Herding was probably the end point of a long period of parasitic herd management during which humans acquired knowledge of animal behaviour.

For areas where domesticated species were not native the dating of farming practices is easier. However, care has to be taken that a few exotic

✎ KEY SITE

Tell Abu Hureyra

A **tell** is an artificial mound up to 60 metres in height composed of mudbricks from generations of houses combined with domestic rubbish. This tell in northern Syria was excavated in advance of the building of the Tabqa Dam. Faunal remains were used to explore hunting strategy and to trace the shift to pastoral agriculture in the region. Specialised hunting had focused on ambushing the Persian gazelle that migrates in herds along predictable routes. They were herded into 'desert kites', landscape features used as traps, and then dispatched with spears. After several thousand years of this activity the numbers of gazelle being caught decreased dramatically. Sheep and goats took their place. These two species are often lumped together and referred to as 'ovicaprids' since it is difficult to distinguish between their bones at this early stage of domestication. This change in the bone evidence coincides with a period known by archaeologists in the region as PPNA (see p.207). Later morphological changes in ovicaprids such as shape of horn changing from curved to curly make the distinction much easier. The gazelle of the region would never have been domesticated through specialist hunting because they lacked traits of behaviour which made the ovicaprids more manageable.

✎ Fagin 1995, Moore 2000

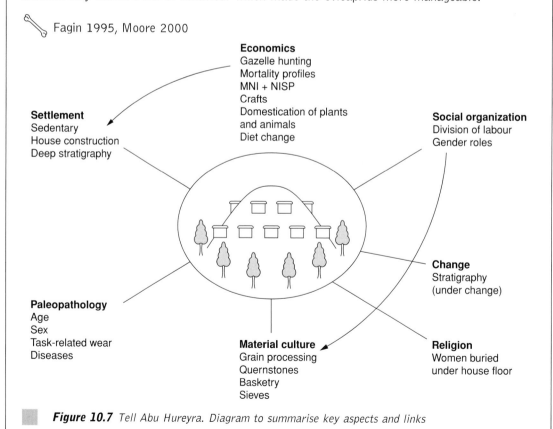

Economics
Gazelle hunting
Mortality profiles
MNI + NISP
Crafts
Domestication of plants
and animals
Diet change

Settlement
Sedentary
House construction
Deep stratigraphy

Social organization
Division of labour
Gender roles

Paleopathology
Age
Sex
Task-related wear
Diseases

Change
Stratigraphy
(under change)

Material culture
Grain processing
Quernstones
Basketry
Sieves

Religion
Women buried
under house floor

Figure 10.7 *Tell Abu Hureyra. Diagram to summarise key aspects and links*

KEY TERM

Neolithic

The first descriptive blocks of time used by archaeologists were based on changes in material culture, for example Iron Age. Further refinements added sets of economic and settlement criteria. The Neolithic 'package' includes domesticated crops and animals, sedentary 'village life', agricultural tools such as grinding stones and polished stone axes, and pottery. However, reality is rarely clear. At Near East sites such as Jericho layers revealed settled villages with domesticated animals but no pottery – hence the term Pre-Pottery Neolithic Age (PPNA). The Danish sites on p. 206 featured foragers with some 'Neolithic' artefacts but not domesticates.

food or sacrificial imports are not mistaken for farming. The same applies to cereal grains.

Post-domestication studies focus on what purpose the animals were exploited for. The 'secondary products revolution' is used to refer to rearing animals primarily for purposes other than food. This can be difficult to detect even in the bone record. Fleece, for example, rarely survives and leaves no physical trace on the skeleton. Deformity from use in traction can provide a useful indicator, but not always.

Identifying human exploitation of plants

For foraging peoples, research has focused on identifying which plants they used from plant remains and specialised artefacts such as

digging sticks and grinding stones. Site catchment analysis has been used in conjunction with environmental data to suggest possible resources. Glimpses of the range of non-food uses of plants have been obtained from sites with exceptional preservation. Nets, boats and clothes (Otzi the Ice Man's grass cape) have been recovered from later prehistory and probably represent only a fraction of plant uses. With the development of pottery, twisted cord was used for decoration, suggesting that the use of rope was well known. In the historic period, the economic importance of agricultural produce means that there is considerable historical documentation of various sorts and artistic sources that provide information on techniques, organisation and productivity.

Most attention has centred on the transition to agriculture because of the impact it has had on social development. Almost all civilisations have been based on wheat, barley, millet, rice, maize or potato.

Identifying the change to food production

Much early research on farming tried to identify where the first domesticates appeared. The Near East is generally acknowledged to have been the first, with wheat, barley, goats/sheep and cattle as its staples. However, it seems that a number of 'hearths' appeared in different parts of the world based on a different range of crops including maize in Mesoamerica and rice in East Asia. Horticulture involves modifying the growth cycles of plants, most simply by weeding, to increase productivity and usefulness. Arable agriculture is associated with a specialised and systematic approach to crop production, ultimately including fields. However, in its early stages agriculture involved minimal changes in the toolkit of late Mesolithic peoples, which makes its detection difficult. Most of the evidence comes from seed crops, which can give a somewhat distorted view. Cereals are genetically malleable and domestic varieties eventually became morphologically different from wild varieties. For example, domestic maize cannot disperse its seeds. The way they were processed meant there was more chance of grains being preserved through carbonisation than other plant foods. Furthermore, other crops such as legumes (peas and beans) seem to have changed more slowly while root crops are almost archaeologically invisible. The spread of arable farming is easiest to track in regions where the species were not native as long as original distributions are known.

In Britain and Ireland there was a lag of hundreds of years between the appearance of the first sign of arable crops and evidence of widespread farming. Most of the early finds of cereals and cattle come from ceremonial sites, suggesting that economics may not have been the main reason for importing them. Relatively few settlement sites have been excavated for this period which has led many writers to suggest that the population was mobile rather than sedentary and that wild resources were still important.

Once arable agriculture was established, its traces are relatively easy to detect archaeologically, particularly through changes in pollen sequences. Field and irrigation systems, storage pits and specialist equipment from ploughs to sickles become common from the late Bronze Age. Interest then shifts to the productivity and use of agricultural products. For classical civilisations, art and written sources have provided data on consumption and types of crops. For other areas, experimental archaeology has been valuable. Butser Ancient Farm has demonstrated the kinds of yield possible with ancient crops and explored their

response to a range of growing conditions. Detailed analysis of plant assemblages to examine weed types and ratios of weeds to grain and grain to chaff enable archaeologists to identify whether crops were grown and processed on-site and suggest where the fields were.

Identifying the causes of domestication

For 70 years, since Childe labelled it the Neolithic revolution in the 1930s, archaeologists have competed to explain the development of agriculture. Most of the theories seem plausible but all have limitations and exceptions to the rule.

Most works on the origins of agriculture make the assumption that a sedentary, farming life was superior to foraging. Certainly the wave of pioneer farming which spread (diffused) through south-eastern and central Europe at a steady rate seems to support this view. However, recent work on successful foragers (▶see p. 205) provides an opposing view. For up to a thousand years the Mesolithic peoples of north-west Europe did not adopt farming in what is termed the 'Neolithic standstill'. There were farmers to the south with whom they occasionally traded so the ideas and crops were available, but they chose not to adopt them. Why should people give up economic strategies that produced a wide variety of foodstuffs and other resources and may have provided surpluses? Farming is hard work and would have produced a monotonous diet.

 Harris 1996

Eventually agriculture did spread and this raises another question, why then? Theories include environmental change, the prestige attached to cattle and grain and the possibility

KEY TASK

Contextualising the domestication debate

1 Take each of the seven explanations below.

2 List them in the first column of a three-column table.

3 For your area of study insert evidence that supports each theory next to it in the second column and evidence that contradicts it in the third.

4 Use this to rank the explanations for your area.

5 Your analysis and evaluation would provide a skeleton for an essay (▶see p. 191) on this topic. A problem with each argument appears in italics.

Agriculture developed:

a) when climatic changes led to humans and future domesticates being concentrated in particular areas. *Climatic data does not support this idea*

b) as increasing knowledge of plants and animals led via a series of stages to domestication. *This doesn't explain why it happened in some areas and not in others*

c) in areas that were rich in the right resources where people had time to innovate. *This doesn't explain why it didn't happen in all the 'right' areas or, if wild resources were so good, why people should bother with farming*

d) in areas where there was population pressure and less wild food. Farming develops to minimise risk. *Population levels do not appear to have been high enough to force this*

e) in areas where foragers had been successful and become less mobile. Agriculture and storage are developed to reduce risk in lean periods. *Again, this does not happen in all successful areas*

f) when successful broad-spectrum foragers in good areas spread into more marginal regions. Food production began in these regions to supplement foraging. As population levels were raised farming spread. Eventually the environment was changed so that there could be no return to foraging. *This positive feedback model works best with maize and beans in Mesoamerica but is more difficult to fit with evidence elsewhere*

g) when hierarchies developed in successful foraging societies. They turned to agriculture to produce surpluses for trading and prestige reasons. *This may work best with the adoption of agriculture rather than its initial development*

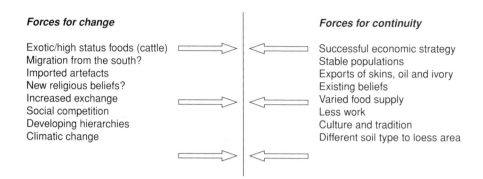

Figure 10.8 *A force field diagram illustrating factors influencing the transition to agriculture around the Baltic in the late Mesolithic*

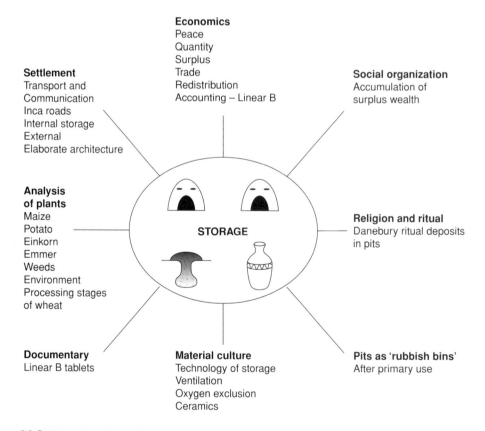

Figure 10.9 *The archaeology of storage*

of conversion. What is clear is that the transition to farming was not a simple process and that a variety of economic strategies were selected by people according to social requirements as well as ecological pressures. Increasingly, archaeological studies have examined the social significance of different models of food acquisition including gender relations and social structure.

STORAGE

Archaeologists study both the methods of storage and the social and economic reasons for it. Storage can be part of a wider economic strategy. It may be used to overcome fluctuations in supply or to collect a surplus to use in exchange. Storage can be linked to social power (▶see p. 244) and could be used by an elite to control the distribution of resources to gain prestige or power. The concept of storage can be used to include energy, information, and even the dead.

Direct evidence of storage comes from the containers or other features used to hold produce. The central granaries of ancient civilisations such as the Roman military granaries at Housesteads or the circular, ventilated warehouses for freeze-dried potatoes at Huanuco Pampa may still be intact, as are many more recent tithe barns. Sometimes they contain traces of their former contents or illustrations on their walls. Dumps of raw inorganic materials such as coal or stone will also leave at least small traces of minerals in the topsoil. Similarly, features such as pits or silos of arable farming communities are frequently recognised and contain pollen or carbonised grain to indicate their uses. On a smaller scale, storage vessels including pottery and glass can be examined in the same way for external decoration or residues of former contents. There may

Figure 10.10 *Four poster features are common on many Iron Age sites. They may be the signature of raised stores. These 'constructs' of four poster granaries at Butser Ancient Farm represent a way of testing this popular interpretation to see if it works*

also be written or artistic sources that illustrate storage, including tax records and tomb paintings.

Other traces of storage need greater interpretation. Drying racks and off-ground structures will only be represented in the archaeological record by postholes. Analogies and experiments were needed to interpret as raised granaries the 'four posters' common on Iron Age sites such as Crickley Hill.

Landscape features may be ambivalent or even represent different types of storage. Millponds, for example, may be stores of power, fish and water. Dense clusters of posts or ditches may represent corrals or stockyards for storing food on the hoof. Phosphate analysis is useful in confirming their function (▶see p. 15). If one approaches storage in terms of energy, one could also see herds of animals as a form of storage in themselves. It is important to remember this because there is a tendency to associate storage with sedentary societies, yet

KEY SITE

Knossos

The civilisation of early Bronze Age Crete was based on several large 'palaces'. Each seemed to have functioned as a collecting centre, which redistributed the goods and food supplies produced in its hinterland. The palaces themselves are complex groups of buildings. They often include a central courtyard, areas that have been identified as 'royal suites' and a large number of long, narrow rooms often referred to as 'magazines'. These served as storerooms. Some of them have stone-lined containers set into the floor and huge ceramic jars up to 2 metres tall, called 'pithoi', ranged along them, which would have held surplus amounts of food and other imported commodities.

Clay tablets with writing in Linear B, generally recognised as the earliest form of Greek, contain lists of commodities flowing into and out of the palace. The amount of storage capacity at Knossos reflects both its function as a redistribution centre at the heart of a large and fertile area and its status as a wealthy and prestigious palace. At Knossos power was exercised, craftsmen worked and exotic goods were traded from all round the eastern Mediterranean.

http://www.dilos.com/region/crete/minoan_pictures.html

Figure 10.11 *Pithoi (storage vessels) in a magazine at Knossos*

KEY SITE

Danebury

The Iron Age hilltop fort of Danebury shares many characteristics with Knossos, not least its huge storage capacity. This took the form of bell-shaped pits a metre wide and up to 2 metres deep, cut into the solid chalk. They had capacity of over 2 tonnes each and carbonised grains have revealed that they were used to hold einkorn and emmer wheat, staple crops of the Iron Age in Britain. Excavation and magnetometer survey revealed a large number of pits at Danebury. A magnetometer survey of the nearby hill fort of Woolbury contained very few. Cunliffe (1995), the excavator, used this evidence to support his idea that Danebury was a high status site with a redistributive function.

Reynolds (1979) tested the effectiveness of pit storage of grain through experimental archaeology. Excavation had suggested that the pits had been sealed and covered with a basketwork lid so that their contents would last over the winter. How they did this without rotting was unclear. Reynolds argued that the carbonised remains of seeds found in the bottom of some of the pits help explain how they worked. A small sample of chalk from the base of a pit together with carbonised seed remains was analysed in a laboratory. Dr Simon Hillson conducted a micro-excavation on the sample, removing and counting the seeds layer by layer until he reached the chalk at the bottom of the pit. Hillson demonstrated that there were more germinated seeds at the bottom, close to the pit wall. Using this information Reynolds dug a pit and filled it with grain. Instruments were inserted to measure humidity, temperature and gas exchange. The pit was sealed with chalk rubble and an airtight layer of clay. The results were impressive.

The grain in the pit gradually used up the available oxygen and produced carbon dioxide creating an anaerobic environment The grain around the edges, especially when it was in contact with the chalk, began to germinate and produced shoots until the point where oxygen was used up and germination ceased. Provided the seal remained intact the grain lay dormant and survived the winter in good condition. When the pit was opened the majority of the grain could be used except for grain around the edges, which was full of mould and fungi. This unusable grain had to be disposed of. Reynolds suggested that it was burnt 'in situ' in the pit, thus cleaning the pit to be ready for its next use. This would account for the carbonised grain at the bottom. It also suggested that the grain was taken out in one go, perhaps for sowing or trading, rather than used as a larder for food.

This is an elegant example of the way that excavated evidence, experiment, analysis of plants and geophysics can be woven together to produce a consistent set of ideas to be tested. Together they tell us a great deal more about life in the Iron Age than one piece of evidence in isolation.

 Cunliffe 1995

ethnography has shown many examples of storage practised by mobile pastoralists.

Other forms of storage leave only indirect evidence. Salting is often traced through distinctive containers, known as briquetage, used to transport it. On some sites inferences can be drawn from the nature of the food remains. The restricted range of bone types at La Cotte de St Brelade suggested the 'caching' of meat. At Stellmoor the sheer quantity of meat was indicative of pemmican making. Insects associated with particular foodstuffs also provide clues, for example grain beetles from Roman York.

Symbolic forms of storage are visible in the archaeological record from later prehistory. Instead of raw materials themselves being stored, they are exchanged for something which is widely accepted as symbolising a value in those materials. Coins are a particularly sophisticated method of symbolically storing value. They can be converted into goods at a later date. They have the advantage of being easily transported and concealed. Jewellery and cowrie shells have been used in a similar way. The concept of **social storage** should also be considered under this heading although it is much more difficult to recognise archaeologically. This is where one person stores value in others. In simple terms, if I give you a gift of a cow, at some point in the future you will give me something of at least equal value. In practice, social storage is often highly complex and can encompass marriages, feasting and military alliances. Social storage blurs economics with social and political affairs. However, for most of human history these areas have probably been inextricably linked.

Finally there are forms of storage which leave little or no trace. Woodpiles constitute one of the commonest types of stores but are usually archaeologically invisible. Organic containers such as baskets and skins only survive in exceptional circumstances. The same is true of some agricultural produce, particularly tubers.

INTENSIFICATION

In a general sense intensification can describe any strategy which re-organises economic activity to increase production. It could be applied to the development of traps and weirs for fishing or the use of two-piece moulds to speed up the manufacture of bronze axes. The greatest physical impact of intensification can be seen in evidence for increasing control over the productive capacity of the land. It is often associated with population pressure or social control.

The first traces of intensification of the landscape can be detected from the soil and pollen evidence for forest clearance and pioneer farming. The intensity of production including the exploitation of stock animals resulted in the construction of elaborate field systems and land divisions such as the Dartmoor 'reaves'. Environmental evidence can often establish the ebb and flow of human impact. For example, around Avebury cycles of forest clearance and later regeneration in association with fluctuations in the intensity of agricultural exploitation have been traced. Medieval attempts to intensify production by extending the area of arable land can be identifed through place names and earthworks such as strip lynchets where hillsides were ploughed. Manuring to increase yields is generally recognised from the halo of pottery scattered in the fields around settlements (▶see p. 14). The countryside has also been the scene of other forms of intensification, particularly extraction. Traces of quarrying, smelting and mining can often be seen, particularly in upland areas.

 http://www.mroe.freeserve.co.uk/

Some of the most dramatic evidence of intensification comes from areas of the world where artificial ways of supplying rainfall to crops was needed to raise yields. Tomb paintings supplement the archaeological evidence for irrigation schemes in Ancient Egypt. Here, canals had been used to extend the area watered by the annual floods of the Nile and so intensify production. Records survive of the technology developed to lift water from canals to fields including the shaduf and later the Archimedes' screw, an early bronze version of which may have been used to water the famous 'Hanging Gardens of Babylon'. In the Oaxaca valley of Mexico, field survey at Arroyo Lencho Diego located 20 metres of sediment which had accumulated behind a vanished dam. The inhabitants had used the dam to irrigate the whole of the valley in an area of otherwise unpredictable water availability. The canals and terraces that watered the fields supplying the major town of Monte Alban still survive as landscape features. Sometimes irrigation schemes are not immediately visible. In the third millennium BC a network of canals supplied water from the rivers Tigris and Euphrates to the fields and the port of the Mesopotamian desert city of Mashkan Shapir. Today they are buried under sand but were detected by satellite imaging (▶see p. 23). In other instances there was too much water for successful cultivation. At Kuk Swamp in New Guinea a huge network of drainage ditches was first revealed by aerial photography, showing as lines several kilometres long in modern tea plantations. Excavation revealed that early farmers had built them to

KEY SITE

Pulltrouser Swamp

The Aztecs developed a system of intensive agriculture based on floating gardens or 'chinampas'. Floating rafts were covered in weeds and lake mud and anchored to the lake bed in rows, with canals left between for access. In time as more and more mud was dredged onto them and the root systems of trees bound the mass together, the rafts became fertile islands. They produced two to three crops a year especially of flowers and vegetables. The system is still used in some parts of Mexico. The remains of Aztec chinampas have been revealed at Pulltrouser Swamp. Elsewhere, Aztec control over water is revealed in the elaborate canals and aqueducts around the capital Tenochtitlan, which supplied fresh water and separated saline water. The tax demands of the Aztec capital led to intensification of production elsewhere in the region. At Cuexcomate, surveying has revealed terracing used to maximise production of cotton. The importance of water to the Aztecs is underlined by the nature of their central religious buildings and the imagery associated with the god Tlaloc, which occurs all over the main plaza at the heart of Tenochtitlan.

drain the swamp in order to intensively cultivate the fertile soil and grow taro and other crops. (Bayliss-Smith 1996)

Communications

One aspect of economies, which generally develops in conjunction with intensification, is transport. The remains of permanent tracks and roads such as the Sweet Track or Roman and Inca road systems can indicate increasing traffic on routes. Intense use of these features can sometimes be inferred from wear such as rutting and evidence of frequent repairing.

Figure 10.13 *Artistic sources are valuable for providing some idea of what ancient vessels may have looked like. Not all the evidence provided by this mosaic from Ostia would be recoverable archaeologically*

The development of vehicles can be traced from burials, such as the four-wheeled carts in burials at Ur or the 'chariots' from Garton Slack, and through art and figurines. Evidence for the use of animals for riding and draught purposes can sometimes be determined by bit-wear marks on teeth or artefacts associated with harnesses. Artistic sources and shipwreck evidence (▶see p. 221) provide evidence of the evolution of shipping.

TRADE AND EXCHANGE

Early archaeological studies tended to largely interpret the movement of artefacts and materials as trade or the movement of peoples. Ethnographic examples have provided a much wider range of options with which to interpret archaeological evidence. There has also been recognition that exchange does not just involve goods and that its aims are often social rather than economic. Often the relationship is of more value than what is exchanged, for example Christmas cards. The exchange may

Figure 10.12 *Evidence of past transport. The ruts in this Roman street at Pergamon testify to the heavy use of wheeled vehicles*

also involve social obligations which help bind society together.

Exchange in its widest sense includes any transaction between people. This can include exchange of information, services and people. For instance, the spread of bell beakers throughout Europe and North Africa in the third millennium BC was due to exchange. Archaeologists have been divided over the mechanism for this exchange, whether it was through movement of people or the spread of ideas, drinking culture or religion. Trade is just one form of exchange.

Three main categories of exchange have been adopted by archaeology from ethnography. These are **reciprocity, redistribution** and **market exchange**.

Reciprocity

This involves transactions where a gift from one person creates an obligation to return something at a later date. We do this when we buy a round of drinks. Many societies have used it as the basis for social stability. In some cultures marriage involves payment of bridewealth from the husband's family to the bride's family. This is to compensate for their loss of a fertile worker. Payments may be in goods and may take place over time. Such exchange also cements the relationship between the two families. Feasting and the sharing of food with others are often a powerful example of reciprocity. It creates an obligation to return the favour at a later point. It can also be seen as an exchange of food for social prestige. A popular example for archaeologists has been the Big Man feasts of highland New Guinea where status is acquired by throwing huge feasts at which party-goers are given generous gifts of meat or livestock. A related concept is

social storage. Here a gift or favour is given which stores up future gifts or assistance for times when they will be needed. Extreme examples of this are provided by ethnographic accounts of the Potlatch and Kula Ring (Orme 1981). Reciprocity can involve an equal exchange (balanced reciprocity) but can also be positive or negative if one partner does better. Ethnography once again warns against imposing our values on the evidence. Islanders on Yap in the Caroline Islands used to gain prestige by spending their savings on huge stone discs, which they then buried under their homes.

Historical sources such as Homer and Egyptian tomb paintings have provided insights into prestige goods exchange. High status individuals establish and cement relationships through reciprocal exchanges. This continues at a more symbolic level amongst leaders of state today. These exchanges used to involve marriage partners and exotic goods or creatures. Archaeologically this sort of exchange may be recognised where special artefacts such as gems, amber, jade and ivory move long distances. In these cases archaeologists have talked of '**prestige goods chains**'. A classic example is the movement of amber from the Baltic to Mycenae during the Bronze Age and some of the fine metalwork that travelled in the opposite direction from central Europe. Grave goods and special votive deposits have often been the source of such material for archaeologists. The rich graves at Varna contained bracelets of spondylus, a Mediterranean shellfish. One interpretation is that these were exchanged for gold from sources close to Varna. However, some prestige goods such as furs, slaves, silk and feathers may be archaeologically invisible.

Reciprocity

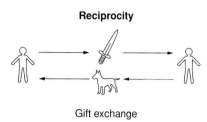

Gift exchange

Redistribution of resources

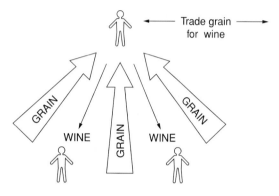

Down the line exchange

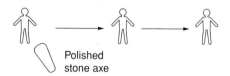

Polished
stone axe

Figure 10.14 *Some types of exchange
identified by archaeologists*

Redistribution

This model involves a central authority
collecting together resources and then
redistributing them. Our welfare state is a giant
version of this, while harvest festivals
symbolise it. In the past redistribution tended
to be operated by individual rulers to whom it
gave both prestige and legitimacy.
Ethnographic studies have tended to emphasise
this as a role of chiefdoms, particularly in areas
of economic diversity. Redistribution shares

out particular resources to areas that lack them,
for example fish to farmers and crops to
fishers. Historic accounts such as Celtic
histories suggest that rulers would use redistribution to reward their followers with weapons,
cattle and exotic goods in order to secure their
loyalty. As with reciprocity, the social aspects
of the exchange may be important and, as
before, feasting may be the vehicle for the
exchange.

Archaeological evidence includes sites with
central stores as at Knossos (▶see p. 212).
Some interpretations of hill forts such as
Danebury (▶see p. 180) have reached similar
conclusions although there is less agreement on
this. Patterns of distribution where valuable
goods have been widely distributed are also
potential evidence of redistribution to local
leaders from a central chief. The distribution of
Bronze Age swords may be such a case. The
clearest evidence comes from those sites where
records have been recovered as at Knossos and
Pylos.

Market exchange

In its simplest sense 'a market' suggests a
recognised place where bargaining takes place.
The easiest to identify are those where defined
areas or buildings exist. The agora of Greek
towns is an example. Another signature is the
development of mechanisms to regulate
amounts or to make exchange flexible. The
discovery of weights and coinage are the most
obvious examples. Of course, not all market
exchange happens in a fixed place and not all
currencies are archaeologically visible. Blankets
and carpets have been used as standards against
which value can be measured. Identifying these
instances of trade in perishable goods is
difficult. The well-preserved Pazyryk 'Ice
Maiden' from the Altai Mountains provided

such a clue. Pazyryk tribes were known to have trade links with China. When silk in her clothes was analysed it was expected to have been made of yarn from cultivated Chinese silkworms. To the experts' surprise it turned out to be characteristic of wild Indian silk. This indicated that the Pazyryk traded to the south as well as in China.

Concentrations of artefacts from many areas would be expected at a port or market. The Iron Age settlement at Hengistbury Head, with its modified harbour and apparently defensive wall, may be such an example. Finds included imported pottery, glass and figs, with evidence of metals and perhaps hides and corn being exported. However, in some cases the pattern of finds could equally represent a religious or high status site. The many interpretations of Neolithic causewayed enclosures typify this sort of ambivalent evidence. Although markets today are almost entirely about buying and selling, they too have had social functions. Ethnographic studies have noted their role in information exchange, tax collection and as places for social gatherings. Historic and artistic sources are again useful. Spanish accounts of the use of quetzal feathers and cacao beans in Mexico are supported by the images of merchants and their backpacks from the rather earlier site of Cacaxtla.

Identifying the signatures of different modes of exchange

The origins of materials used in exchange are tracked using characterisation studies (▶see p. 62). For example, lava millstones found across England in the Saxon period have been traced to quarries in the Eiffel Mountains in Germany. Roman documentary sources tell us very little about trade, but amphorae are very common finds on excavations and in shipwrecks. The fabrics of the millions of Roman amphorae that were traded all over the Empire have responded particularly well to petrology, with the result that we now know where most types were manufactured. As a result it is possible to study the sources and distributions of important agricultural products such as Italian wine, Spanish fish sauce or North African olive oil. Seals or other marks on the objects themselves may indicate their place of manufacture. For example, many Roman amphorae have potters' stamps and some even have handwritten inscriptions, written in black ink, giving details of their contents and origin. Artistic sources can provide considerable detail. Some Egyptian tombs from the second millennium have pictures of Minoans bearing goods from Crete.

Distribution patterns of artefacts from their place of origin are plotted on maps to see whether they match models for particular types of exchange. For example, clusters of Lava quernstones at centres of manufacture and ports such as Dorestadt and Ipswich have enabled the trade to be traced.

Trend surface analysis turns plots of finds on a map into contours to smooth out distortion caused by chance finds. This has been used to map the distribution of Neolithic stone axes from their source.

Fall-off analysis is used to examine the rate at which finds diminish the further one gets from the place of manufacture. A sharp fall suggests very local exchange, a smooth decline suggests 'down the line' trade while a pattern with several blips in the curve indicates secondary trading or exchange centres. This technique has been used to identify the nature of trade in copper, obsidian and pottery.

The context in which particular artefacts are found provides some clues. Shipwrecks provide insights into the nature and scale of exchange and who was trading what. **Hoards** may also provide such evidence although the motives for deposition could be more varied. A deposit of axe heads could be a votive offering, a store of scrap for manufacturing or a cache of trade goods.

Problems with exchange

Despite all these tools the nature of the movement of artefacts or exchange is not always clear. Not all of the possible types of transaction leave clear traces in the archaeological record and different processes can look remarkably similar in their spatial distribution. Sometimes only one side of an exchange can be found. The fourth-century site at Gudme in Denmark has revealed many hoards of gold which originated in the Roman Empire. Whether these represent tribute, booty, mercenary pay or religious offerings is unclear. There are also cases where there was no exchange. In some cases people moved, taking artefacts with them. More commonly, people collected local materials themselves. This is thought to be the case with the movement of obsidian from Melos, which has been found in nearby settlements.

STUDYING MATERIALS

Many of the methods used in studying materials have been discussed in Chapter 3 and they should be referred to for further detail. This section provides some additional pointers for various stages in the use of material. You need to be familiar with a range of materials, particularly metals, ceramics and stone, and how they were used for the periods you are studying. This should include at least one

example of **diachronic change** and the development of technology. For example, the production of bronze axes from initial flat types to later socketed axes or the gradual improvement in the efficiency of stone tools from Oldowan pebble tools through Acheulean and Mousterian types to the 'creative explosion' of the Upper Palaeolithic.

Acquisition of materials

Extraction of clay, stone and metal ores up to the point where the material is ready to be used are most frequently studied. Aside from sourcing materials the remains of extraction sites such as mines and quarries provide insights into technology and scale of production. Waste material also provides a signature for particular processes whether it is chippings from roughly dressed stone or slag from smelting iron. Waste can be subject to microscopic and analytical procedures similar to those for artefacts. The distance materials

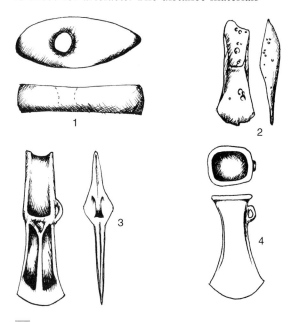

Figure 10.15 The development of axes. 1 is stone, 2–4 are bronze.

KEY SITES

Three Mediterranean shipwrecks

Three wrecks excavated in one region of the Mediterranean over the last forty years provide a glimpse not only of trade patterns of the ancient world but of how shipbuilding techniques changed over time in response to social and environmental factors.

Kyrenia, Cyprus *c.* 300 BC

This wreck was a small merchant vessel with a cargo of amphorae from the island of Rhodes, identifiable by their seal stamps, and millstones. There were very few personal possessions, only a few bone eyelets from a sandal and some fig seeds. Underneath the hull a collection of concretions were recovered. When opened and used to produce resin casts they proved to be iron javelins, some of them bent from impact on the hull. Since there are no natural hazards in the area, this evidence led the excavators to believe that pirates may have sunk the *Kyrenia*. The

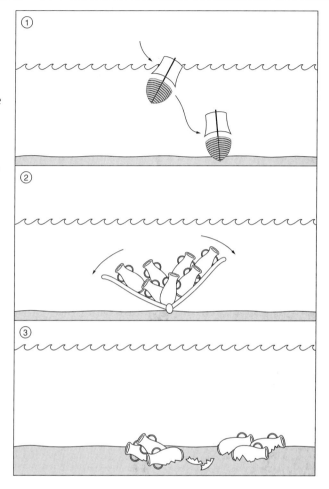

Figure 10.16 *The decay of the Kyrenia wreck*

vessel had settled down onto the ocean bed, and gradually became covered in silt. As its mast and rigging rotted away, the lower part of the hull was forced outwards by the weight of the cargo and broke apart.

Protected by the silt, which choked off oxygen and killed the marine worms that infested it, the remains of the hull were preserved. The ship was built in the traditional way of the classical Greeks, which is 'hull first'. Planks are carved by eye to fit along a keel, with timber selected for its natural curvature as appropriate to different parts of the vessel. The sculpted planks were held together along their edges by thousands of mortise and tenon joints which gave a very strong hull braced only with frames at a later stage. This process wasted 70–80 per cent

 **KEY SITES** *cont.*

of the wood used and required a high standard of craftsmanship from the shipwright. It would only be possible in a society which valued craftsmanship, where raw materials were abundant and where time was no problem. The man who built the *Kyrenia* was probably a slave and his time was his master's.

Yassi Ada, Turkey *c.* AD 625

This wreck was dated by coins recovered from the wreck to the reign of the Byzantine Emperor Heraclius. An elaborate 'steelyard' with the head of a boar at one end and a sliding bust of Athena at the other declared itself to be the property of 'George senior, sea-captain'. Historical documents suggest he was one of a growing class of merchants who financed their own ventures and often captained their own ship. The vessel itself was partly constructed in the old classical 'hull-first' style, with logs sculpted to fit. However, this time the mortise and tenon joints were less carefully executed. They were fewer in number and often nails were driven through them once the plank was located. The upper section of the hull was built by the new 'frame-first' method. Many flat planks were cut from a log and twisted against internal frames as they moved forward along the hull. This more economical use of materials and time suggests that social conditions had changed from the time that the *Kyrenia* was built. The Byzantine shipwright was a free man contracted to do the job. His employer would have been concerned to save time and timber and therefore money. Byzantine society still used slaves but only in the household and not in an industrial context.

Serce Limani, Turkey

This medieval Arab merchant vessel was found to contain a cargo of glass. Eighty intact pieces from the ends of the ship possibly represented personal possessions or items of merchandise but the centre of the ship held several tonnes of raw and broken glass. The raw glass or 'cullet' would have been added to new batches to improve quality and the broken glass seems to represent the sweepings from a glass factory. Many of the pieces were twisted or malformed in the process of blowing or moulding and had been discarded. The excavators classified the millions of pieces of glass by sorting them according to attributes such as colour, pattern and location on original vessels, for example rim sherds. By following this process meticulously a large number of pieces were eventually re-assembled. The cargo demonstrates craft specialisation and the technology of production, but the fabric of the ship itself is equally rewarding. The Serce Limani ship was built entirely by the 'frame-first' technique. First the keel was laid down. Frames were attached to it and planks bent around the frame to form the hull. The technique is still used in shipyards around the Mediterranean and gives a strong hull while being economical in use of wood. Many hull planks can be cut from a single log. This development clearly happened between the building of the Yassi Ada and the Serce Limani

KEY SITES *cont.*

wrecks in the early medieval period when historical scholars tell us that there was considerable conflict between the expanding Arab world and the Byzantine Empire. Historical records describe massive losses of ships through warfare. It is easy to visualise a cycle of forest clearance to feed an ever-increasing demand for ships creating a situation where there was pressure to budget-build new ships. The Serce Limani vessel shows signs of compromise on quality and it was also 'armed to the teeth'. In addition to the glass, large numbers of spears and a cache of fine swords were discovered. These three wrecks demonstrate diachronic change in technology over a thousand-year period and a range of economic specialisation (▶see p. 227).

http://www.diveturkey.com/ inaturkey/projects.htm

http://www.diveturkey.com/ inaturkey/serce.htm

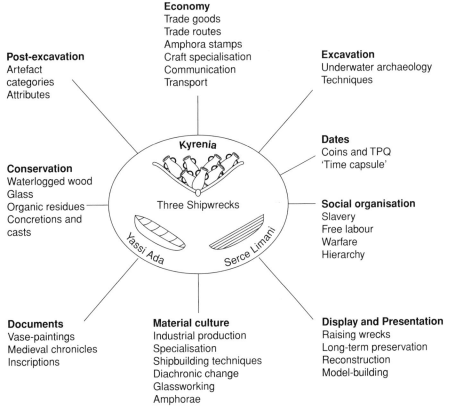

Economy
Trade goods
Trade routes
Amphora stamps
Craft specialisation
Communication
Transport

Post-excavation
Artefact
categories
Attributes

Excavation
Underwater archaeology
Techniques

Conservation
Waterlogged wood
Glass
Organic residues
Concretions and
casts

Kyrenia

Three Shipwrecks

Yassi Ada

Serce Limani

Dates
Coins and TPQ
'Time capsule'

Social organisation
Slavery
Free labour
Warfare
Hierarchy

Documents
Vase-paintings
Medieval chronicles
Inscriptions

Material culture
Industrial production
Specialisation
Shipbuilding techniques
Diachronic change
Glassworking
Amphorae

Display and Presentation
Raising wrecks
Long-term preservation
Reconstruction
Model-building

***Figure 10.17** Three shipwrecks: the key aspects and links*

KEY SITE

Boxgrove

Boxgrove was occupied by hominids of the type Homo heidelbergensis around 500,000 years ago. It was a beach backed by sea-cliffs. Microwear studies of tools and animals bones produced interesting results. In one case fragments of flint were visible in a 'knife-cut' where they had broken off a tool during butchery. In another case, the bone of a rhinoceros, it was clear that human butchery marks lay under the tooth marks of a scavenging carnivore. In other words, the human had got there first. Hunting evidence came in the form of a horse scapula with a very neat circular perforation on the outside and a splintered 'exit wound'. This suggested a high velocity projectile, perhaps a fire-hardened wooden spear such as the ones discovered at Lehringen. The find of an 'antler hammer' potentially provides a new perspective on human mental capacity and behaviour for this period. It suggests a degree of planning, forethought and 'curation' that was believed to be beyond the capacity of hominids at this stage in evolution. The hammer also provided corroborative faunal dating evidence. The antler came from a giant elk which became extinct around 500,000 years ago.

http://www.ucl.ac.uk/boxgrove/   Pitts and Roberts 1997

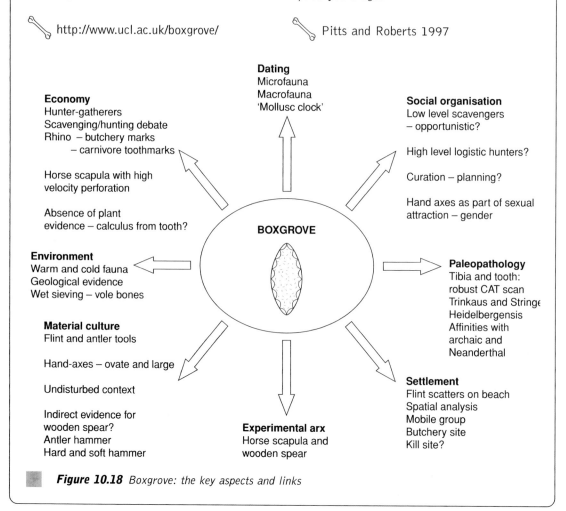

Dating
Microfauna
Macrofauna
'Mollusc clock'

Economy
Hunter-gatherers
Scavenging/hunting debate
Rhino – butchery marks
        – carnivore toothmarks

Horse scapula with high
velocity perforation

Absence of plant
evidence – calculus from tooth?

Social organisation
Low level scavengers
– opportunistic?

High level logistic hunters?

Curation – planning?

Hand axes as part of sexual
attraction – gender

BOXGROVE

Environment
Warm and cold fauna
Geological evidence
Wet sieving – vole bones

Material culture
Flint and antler tools

Hand-axes – ovate and large

Undisturbed context

Indirect evidence for
wooden spear?
Antler hammer
Hard and soft hammer

Paleopathology
Tibia and tooth:
robust CAT scan
Trinkaus and Stringe
Heidelbergensis
Affinities with
archaic and
Neanderthal

Settlement
Flint scatters on beach
Spatial analysis
Mobile group
Butchery site
Kill site?

Experimental arx
Horse scapula and
wooden spear

Figure 10.18 *Boxgrove: the key aspects and links*

have travelled can be significant. Materials which have travelled far from their source and which are relatively rare in the context they are found in are often referred to as exotics. This term also often implies a high 'value' for the material in the eyes of the people using it and consequently its possession may suggest high status. Such materials include gold in burials, for example Bush Barrow, Roman amphorae in Late Iron Age burials. Exotic materials often have their own inherent symbolism.

Manufacture

Analysis of materials and finds of tools and processing features such as kilns are vital in understanding production. Our understanding of Bronze Age metallurgy combines chemical and physical analysis of ores, interpretation of moulds and finished artefacts, and analogies drawn from ethnography and experimental archaeology. Similar approaches have been applied to stone tool manufacture and ceramics production.

It is not only finished artefacts that provide interesting sources of information about raw materials. A wide range of techniques may be applied to sites as different as the scatter of stone fragments discarded by a prehistoric hunter-gatherer making tools in a temporary camp in East Africa (for example refitting), or the ruins of a nineteenth-century lead mining complex in northern England. Many details of the very recent industrial past either went unrecorded or the relevant documents have not survived. Scientific excavation and the recovery of carefully chosen samples for analysis will help to clarify both types of site. Our understanding of these processes has to be balanced by awareness of the differential survival of materials. Our knowledge of ancient woodworking, for instance, largely comes from exceptional wet sites (►see p. 51).

 KEY STUDY

Late Ice Age hunting technology

Knecht's (1994) study of the evolution of Upper Palaeolithic projectile points has shown in detail how people adapted to the ice age environment and to the animals available for hunting. It has also demonstrated advanced conceptual abilities among these people and an acute awareness of the physical properties of the raw materials that were available. Knecht was able to illustrate technological progress towards more efficient, flexible spears. Another major consideration in the gradual changes in material and design was the ease of repair whilst away from camp. She also carried out experiments using a goat carcass to test the velocity and efficiency of the spearpoints as hunting weapons. Her findings corroborate those from Stellmoor. Flint points propelled by bow, spearthrower or unaided human muscles were formidable weapons, capable of penetrating animal tissue and bone. The hunting of large, dangerous prey could be carried out effectively and more safely from a distance.

KEY SITE

The Sweet Track

The only areas of higher ground on the area of peat wetland known as the Somerset Levels are slight sandy knolls. These have been used for settlement since the Neolithic. Prehistoric people faced the problem of ensuring effective communication between settlements and they solved it by constructing sophisticated trackways. They invested considerable communal effort into ventures that in some cases lasted only a few years. The 'Sweet Track' has been dated to the Neolithic period around 4000 BC, which makes it earlier than most of the megalithic monuments. Its construction reveals considerable woodworking skill and woodland management. The planks of the walkway were split from tree trunks using wedges, and other components were made from coppiced wood from oak, hazel and alder. This implies sustainable management strategies and forward planning. Items found alongside the track, such as jadeite axes from Europe, suggest far-reaching exchange contacts. Environmental evidence such as spiders and rodent-gnawed hazelnuts provided much detail about the surrounding wetland. Dendrochronological dating of the timbers suggest that the Sweet Track was built fairly quickly and only lasted some eleven years before going out of use.

 Coles and Coles 1976

Figure 10.19 *A replica of part of the Sweet Track at the Peat Moors Visitor Centre. The various construction methods are clearly visible*

KEY SKILL

Improve your style!

A comment frequently seen on student reports and returned work is 'your style could be improved'. It is often difficult to work out what this means and harder still to do something in response. Sometimes the comment actually refers to structure and sometimes to written English. Generally speaking it is about how you knit the essay together. Here are three mechanical things you can do to help yourself in your next piece of work:

1   Use words and phrases which lead you to consider several pieces of evidence and reach judgements

Include all of the following at least once:

for example   however   therefore   an alternative

potentially   extent   on the other hand   nevertheless

2   Gobbets and gambits

One way of looking at your notes is that they represent lots of chunks of knowledge. These are your gobbets. In writing a response to a question you need to join these together as seamlessly as possible. The linking phrases which join up explanations or examples are gambits. (▶see p. 164.)

3   Vary your sentence length

At secondary school you may have been encouraged to use longer words and more complex sentences. Sometimes this can lead to rather turgid writing. To make your work more 'punchy', experiment with alternating sentence length. Short sentences can give your work more impact and are often clearer. Never use a complex word if a simpler one does the job just as well.

SPECIALISATION

Specialisation is often used as an indicator of social complexity. It demonstrates a degree of interdependence within a society and often between that society and others. The more complex a society becomes the more interdependent its members become. If the production of artefacts is concentrated in the hands of a few people it also implies skills are not available to all members of society. It may indicate age and gender differentiation. There are two main types of specialisation:

■ *Attached specialists* are craftsmen who live in close proximity to a high status person. They may be part of their extended family and related by birth or marriage.

■ *Independent specialists* produce goods to market for their own profit. They are not controlled by anyone else but may still be interdependent. For example, the hundreds of specialists working in the leather trade in Fez, Morocco. Each worker specialises in one of the many stages involved in turning raw, uncured skin into finished products, selling them and transporting them. All of these people are craftsmen in their own right. All depend on others in the chain for their business to survive.

IDENTIFYING SPECIALISTS IN THE ARCHAEOLOGICAL RECORD

Very often archaeology concentrates on the finished products as evidence of craftwork, for example mosaics, figurines, swords or ships (▶see p. 221). However, manufacturing debris can also be important, as can the very names of locations where craft workers concentrated, which may have survived, albeit in altered form, over time. Both of these sources are illustrated in Viking York where there is much waste material from leather working and trial

Economics
Roman shops – London
Fez market and shops
Craft guilds
Sutton Hoo – trade and exotic material
Basse-Yutz – coral
Wine trade
Shipwrecks – trade and communication

Settlement
Craft areas in towns

Coppergate – Jorvik

House of the Bacabs
Oaxacan patio in barrio at Teotihuacan

Deir-El – Medina workers' village in Egypt

Social organisation
Complexity and interdependence
Attached specialists
Patron and kinsman
Hierarchy and royal craftsmen
Wine – novelty effects on society
Social and political role of iconography in Copan and Egypt

SPECIALISATION

Ethnography
Inka
Hawaii
Fez

Material culture
Leather working and dyeing
Cloisonné technique
Maya painting and codex
Teotihuacan mass production
Bronze flagons – Basse Yutz
Enamel inlay
Copan – stoneworking

Religion and ritual
Scribe tomb
Copan
Sutton Hoo
'Temple' as patron
Amphorae in burials
Sculptors of Akhenaten

Figure 10.20 (above) *Specialisation: the key aspects and links*

Figure 10.21 *The interconnections between specialists in the Fez leather trade*

pieces for carving in bone, together with the name of the most famous excavation site in York – 'Coppergate' – which comes from the Old Norse for 'Street of the Barrel-Makers'. Burial evidence has often been interpreted as evidence of specialisation, where particular tools are found in graves. The Sutton Hoo burial contains several examples of crafts-manship from all over the Anglo-Saxon world, in particular a tiny pyramidal jewel that had been originally attached to a sword hilt. Each face is a plate of gold with tiny 'cells' built up on it with gold wire in the technique known as *cloisonné*. Each cell is fitted with its own individually cut prisms of garnet and some are provided with chequered metal foil underneath to enhance the glitter of the stones. The precision and exquisite craftsmanship of the

worker at such a small scale is breathtaking. That so much time and effort was lavished on what is really a tiny detail of the king's burial goods is also a testament to his status.

ART

This term is applied to images and objects (often produced for non-utilitarian purposes) which show appreciation of aesthetic qualities. It may include decoration on functional objects or decoration that forms part of a system of **iconography**. The *meaning* of art is culturally embedded and may prove difficult to access. It is most relevant to the themes in Chapters 8 and 11. Studies of art under material culture should concentrate on the technology of their execution rather than on interpretation. Thus if

KEY STUDY

Copan

A fortuitous earthquake buried a craft workshop in this Maya town very quickly. Tools of the trade were left on the workman's stone bench in a ceramic bucket. The craftsman had worked precious stone such as jade into items of jewellery and inlays for teeth. There were no metals in this society so his tools included antler drills, sand paste and bladelets of obsidian, probably mounted into a wooden haft to act as a saw. Such painstaking and time-consuming work was largely directed towards producing prestige items for a wealthy lord. This was an attached specialist who was not working for himself and was not part of any market system. His time was his lord's, a man to whom he was almost certainly related and in whose patio he lived.

Also in Copan, a burial demonstrates that craft specialisation was not restricted to the lower ranking members of a complex society. The body lay in an elaborately decorated chamber at the heart of the acropolis. The floor of the tomb was littered with decomposed pieces of bark codices – the books of the Maya. Rich grave goods and the sacrificed body of a young slave had also been provided. It was clearly a royal burial but whose was it? The ages at death of the kings of the appropriate era did not match the skeleton. Ceramics in the tomb provided clues. Some of them were clearly associated with painting. Indeed one carried a human portrait of a man wearing a special monkey headdress and with scribes' brushes in his mouth. He represented the patron god of scribes. The body was probably a son of King Smoke-Imix , a royal scribe whose duty was to paint the books containing the history and mythology of his dynasty, and who performed a vital role in sustaining his family's power and status.

 Schele and Miller 1986

KEY STUDY

The Basse-Yutz flagons

A pair of bronze flagons, now in the British Museum but originally from Alsace, can be used to make a number of points about the nature and role of craft specialists. They are from the Iron Age and yet they are made of bronze in common with most decorative objects from that period. They were decorated with inlaid enamel and coral that must have come from the Red Sea. The artist linked Celtic mythology with classical ideas in the iconography of the pieces, combined with a sense of humour. Ducks appear to swim down the stream of liquid as it is poured from the spout. These jugs were almost certainly used to serve wine, a novel drink in central Europe at this period, which was imported from the classical world to the south. The mixture of native and classical ideas in the art shows clearly that classical culture was having a great impact on the Celtic world long before the Roman conquests. The Celtic craftsman exploited exotic materials and iconography to enhance a vessel used to serve an exotic drink at an institution which classical writers tell us was central to Celtic society – the feast. We have to imagine the gleam of polished bronze, lifted high to pour the dark red wine in a glittering stream into the goblets of rival chieftains. The ability to procure the fashionable wine and outface others who still relied on the old beer or honey mead was a powerful way to mark status.

In Celtic society craftsmen were regarded as part of the elite. They were on a par with bards and druids, in view of the 'magical' processes that they controlled, turning dull ores into functional objects like chariot fittings or superb works of art like these flagons. They had a much wider social role than the purely functional at a time when kings began to advertise themselves through coinage and the iconography it carried.

 http://www.thebritishmuseum.ac.uk/
world/europe/western/before.html

the context of study is Palaeolithic cave art, the focus should be on skills of draughtsmanship, paints used and the techniques of painting.

Higher levels of study will require you to grapple with definitions of art and material culture. Pottery provides a good example of the sort of issues you might want to consider. Ethnographic studies suggest that both the production and the form of pottery are often determined by cultural rather than purely material considerations. A pot can be functional in terms of its ability to hold its contents and withstand heat but other aspects are more to do with its social use than its functionality, in particular decoration and colour. Beliefs and values determine the 'right way' for things to look even when that way is not the most functional. In Middle Saxon Southampton, imported pitchers became popular. They were more functional for pouring liquids than existing pots, yet local potters did not copy them. Instead they continued to turn out traditional vessels. Another instance where symbolism may have outweighed practicality was the use of flint as temper in some prehistoric pottery. There are usually alternative tempers available and flint would be painful to work in.

 KEY STUDIES

Palaeolithic cave art

A common misconception is that Upper Palaeolithic cave art in Europe consists of 'hunting scenes' which we can interpret through our imagination. Nothing could be further from the truth. In most cases we cannot be sure which images on a particular wall were painted at the same time, never mind whether they 'go together' in any meaningful way. Images of animals predominate but not usually in proportion to their importance as a food source. For example, reindeer were one of the most common prey species but they were not the most frequently painted. Images of human beings tend to vary hugely between schematic at one end of the scale, as at Cougnac and Lascaux, or intensely realistic, as at La Marche. In addition to the main images there are also many 'signs', which have been interpreted literally as spears, nets, traps and houses. A different approach, pioneered by Lewis-Williams and Dowson (1988), sees these 'signs' as **entoptic** or geometric shapes that are 'hard-wired' into our central nervous system as humans. We project them over the top of images from everyday life when in an altered state of consciousness such as a trance. These geometric shapes are shared by all modern peoples and therefore by the people of the Upper Palaeolithic. Similar analysis has been carried out on the Neolithic rock art of Britain and Ireland.

A second example of the range of interpretation concerns an image from a lesser-known area of Lascaux cave. It consists of a bison on one side, which may or may not be related to the rest of the image. The bison appears to have its entrails hanging out and to be pierced by several feathery 'spears'. Both of these features could be interpreted in other ways. Opposite is a figure of a man with a staff below him topped with the image of a bird. On closer inspection the man is seen to have an erection. His hands and feet are rather like those of a bird with four toes, his face is elongated, ending in a beak and on top of his head is a crest. A recent interpretation of these images has suggested that the human figure is a shaman in a trance state. Shamans in Bushman groups often describe themselves as feeling weightless and elongated. The shaman is being transformed into his animal spirit companion, in this case a grouse as suggested by the crest on the figure's head. We are invited to imagine the man dancing and imitating the movements and sounds of the bird as part of his performance, probably dressed in a bird costume and carrying magical artefacts such as the staff below him. Ethnographic rituals such as this were described among the native Americans of the north-west coast in the nineteenth century and some of their elaborate masks and ritual equipment can be seen in the British Museum and Pitt-Rivers Museum. On the other hand, the staff may be a spearthrower.

As a result of the many interpretations of meaning, there are almost as many interpretations of the function of these images. Several writers have suggested a religious aspect to the work, such as totemism (▶see p. 148), or magic related to hunting or fertility. Others have suggested that their function may have been educational, transmitting knowledge about animals or belief and culture, perhaps as part of rites of

Figure 10.22 *Drawing of images which may be of a shaman transforming*

passage. Many of the paintings are not in easily accessible areas. Of course they may have had several functions, perhaps changing over time including art for art's sake.

We can be more certain about the techniques of cave art. Research has discovered the use of ferrous and manganese oxide for paint, chewed twigs and fingers as brushes and stone lamps

KEY STUDIES *cont.*

with animal grease or pine torches for light. Recent work at Pech Merle has shown how paint can be blown through stencils of leather to produce handprints. Cave art can be viewed at the following websites:

 http://www.culture.fr/culture/ arcnat/chauvet/en/gvpda-d.htm

 http://www.culture.fr/culture/ arcnat/lascaux/fr/

 KEY SKILL

Writing evaluative essays on concepts

These are often the types of essay which students find hardest. Questions on this theme often take the form 'To what extent can archaeologists recognise X?' X could be status, gender, chiefdoms or war. Whichever it is, you need to deploy several relevant case studies to explore the concept and its archaeological visibility. The nature of the topic means you need to be very aware of bias in interpretation and of the strengths and weaknesses of models, particularly ethnographic ones, which archaeologists have employed. You need to be comfortable with the terminology and to construct a complex argument.

The following exercise includes examples from different periods. To produce your own version, replace these with your own examples.

Q: To what extent can archaeologists recognise territoriality?

1 Discuss what territory is. Is it the same as site catchment or the hunting ranges of Mesolithic foragers?

2 Discuss modern notions of territory, which is static and rooted in ideas of the sovereignty of nation states. This is marked with physical borders, coinage distribution, flags and other symbols.

3 Discuss some possible archaeological examples of territory:

- *Bronze Age:* land divisions on Dartmoor or Fengate – territories, ranches or a bit of both?

KEY SKILL *cont.*

- ■ *Iron Age:* hill forts and Thiessen polygons, coin distribution, Roman accounts of tribal areas

- ■ *Roman period:* coinage, public buildings, Hadrian's Wall (a border?)

- ■ *Medieval period:* boundaries (for example Wansdyke), coinage, charters, siting of castles

4 Discussion: does territory mean the same thing in all periods? Is it a dynamic or static concept? What types of evidence are the most/least persuasive? What are their strengths and limitations?

5 Conclusion: in which of your examples is there the strongest evidence and why? For example, is this because there is more likely to have been territory in those examples or is it to do with survival of evidence? Use these points to explicitly address the 'how far' element in the question.

Chapter 11

Social Archaeology

YOUR GOALS

You need to

- ■ understand the main concepts used
- ■ use case studies to apply and test the key concepts
- ■ grasp the strengths and weaknesses of the techniques used by archaeologists to reconstruct society from physical evidence
- ■ develop your ability to write evaluative essays.

Hawkes (▶p. 138) identified the archaeology of past social systems like that of ritual as a difficult topic for archaeologists. Despite this, most archaeologists have written with confidence on the societies they have studied and used a wide range of models (particularly from ethnography) to help interpret their sources.

WHAT IS SOCIAL ARCHAEOLOGY?

Social archaeology can usefully be divided into three main subsections. How societies organise themselves ranges from the basic units of family, **kin** and **bands** to the political organisation of states. Divisions within society include different treatment based on age or gender and also stratification according to wealth, power or status. Finally there is social action and change. This can include phenomena like warfare or how and why societies changed in the past.

When studying this topic, an anthropological or sociological textbook (for example Giddens 1989) is a useful source of help with terms. Since this is the last thematic chapter of this coursebook there is danger of repetition. Where possible, we have cross-referenced issues here to studies in earlier chapters. We have also tried to include critical points in each subsection to help you write evaluative essays.

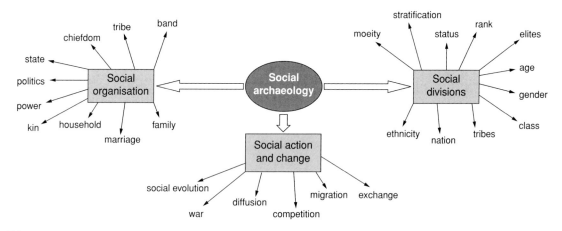

Figure 11.1 *Terms used in social archaeology*

For non-literate societies, archaeologists have relied heavily on evidence from burials to understand social organisation. Burial evidence has also supplemented historical records for the classical period. In addition, information has been drawn from settlement patterns, artefacts and art. Since the strengths and weaknesses of these sources are similar for each topic, we have tackled them more fully for status and gender and avoided repetition on the other topics. Where you are writing evaluative pieces you should ensure that you refer to status and gender in your reading.

FORMS OF SOCIAL AND POLITICAL ORGANISATION

Archaeology developed in the earlier part of the twentieth century when evolutionary ideas were being applied in the social sciences and when much of the world was directly ruled by colonial powers. It is understandable then that evolutionary models of social development were applied to the past. As societies became increasingly 'advanced' and 'civilised' they were expected to develop along similar paths. Much

archaeological research sought to trace this development and identify reasons for particular regions being more advanced than others. Although western ideas of superiority have been challenged in recent decades, what are now termed neo-evolutionary models of social development are still commonplace.

All of the terms used to classify social organi-sation conceal considerable variation. However, we do need to use such concepts as the starting point for comparing and contrasting social groups and talking about them.

Bands are self-sufficient groups of a few families. Leaders are likely to have emerged because of experience or personal qualities and to have been temporary. Bands may have been fluid, with families or individuals moving to join other groups. They may also have only lived together during particular seasons. The term is most frequently used in archaeology for the Upper Palaeolithic and Mesolithic. To some writers bands looked like an egalitarian society although ethnographic research has shown that inequalities exist in many modern bands.

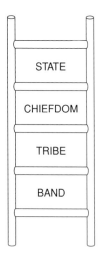

Figure 11.2 *A social-evolutionary ladder of the development of societies (after Service 1971)*

Tribes are larger than bands with kinship linking the group together. Leadership may be fluid. Tribes often have activity leaders who are recognised as having skill and authority in particular areas such as hunting or ritual. Potentially most adults may be leaders in some areas and therefore none may stand out overall. Of the models of political organisation and leadership that have been borrowed from anthropology for tribes, the most influential has been the **Bigmen** of New Guinea. These are individuals who rise to prominence through their skill in key areas of economic and social life such as herding or hunting. Their position as Bigmen allows them to conduct trade and alliances on behalf of their group of several hundred people. Their position is cemented by their ability to provide generously for their followers. They accumulate wealth, usually pigs or another food source, and redistribute it at

major feasts. The position is not hereditary and others who are better placed to dispense generously often replace Bigmen.

Both bands and tribes are sometimes referred to as **segmentary societies**. This is where society is made up of lots of similarly sized groups with little difference in wealth, status or power between them. This contrasts with the more ranked and unequal chiefdoms and states.

Chiefdoms are more formally organised and ranked than tribes. Within ethnographic literature there is a huge range of different forms of chiefdom with numbers of followers ranging from around 1,000 to 10,000, so we must assume the same is true of the past. Chiefdoms are usually hereditary, although the role may alternate between a group of families rather than remain in just one. As a result in most cases chiefs are viewed as different from the rest of the social group. They usually have an important ritual role as well as redistribution, law giving and leadership roles. Their permanent position and high status may result in other differences including more marriage partners and more or different possessions. Social ranking in chiefdoms can be very elaborate.

In some instances kings differ from chiefs in terms of scale. Kings will usually preside over several social groups, each with their own subking or chief. The term was used for nineteenth-century Africa as well as for the classical and medieval worlds so variation is considerable. The position is hereditary with some, although not all, being seen as divine.

| Households | Bands | Kinship | Clans | Age Sets | Gender | Moiety |

Figure 11.3 *Horizontal forms of social divisions which might be the basis of segmentary societies*

They are likely to have a larger than usual household and may have permanent social and economic organisations based close to them, for example a permanent guard. Their need to display their position through exotic goods and provide gifts to supporters may mean that their household includes attached specialists.

States are political systems where permanent institutions develop independent of individual leaders. There are likely to be formal laws, weights and measures and specialists associated with justice, warfare and taxation. Many kingships will also be states, although not all. All modern societies are nation states. Key features are likely to include permanent borders, uniform currencies and centralised authority. Developed states tend to be very complex with a tendency to increasing specialisation.

Figure 11.4 *Egyptian hieroglyphics from Esna. The translation of such scripts was a triumph of early archaeology. However, this has tended to reinforce the idea that we can only understand those societies from the past which have a written culture. Writing systems have also been used as a marker of advanced civilisations. This too has been used in a negative sense since by extension societies without writing have been seen as 'uncivilised'. Archaeology has done much to correct this view*

> **KEY TERM**
>
> **Moiety**
>
> A division of society into two halves (or moieties) which was common in North America. People are born or are inducted into one or the other. Depending upon the society rules they must either marry within the moiety or marry someone from the opposite moiety.

There are also many ways of organising society which don't fit neatly into a hierarchy. The most basic unit is the family or household, which exists in all societies. Kinship is another. The significance of blood or marriage ties varies considerably. In the past they may have been the most important form of social organisation, for example the Scottish **clan** system. Although their relevance in modern western society has declined there are still exceptions, notably the Mafia. Other divisions, which may cut across simple group definitions, are age or moiety-based groups. Their existence means that individuals may have several different affiliations. It is worth noting that bands, tribes and chiefdoms still exist in different parts of the world.

Identifying social and political organisation in the archaeological record

It is likely that the forms of organisation that have ranking and permanent institutions will be most strongly represented in the archaeological record. Chiefdoms and kingships where status is ascribed (▶see p. 241) may have permanent high status buildings as well as symbolic artefacts. Bigmen are less likely to be visible in the archaeological record. The role is associated with adult males in their prime. By old age they may have redistributed their wealth so it may not even appear in their graves. The affiliations of individuals may not all be recorded on material the archaeologists recover. While pottery that carries emblems of particular groups may survive, clothing, tattoos or tribal scars will not. In life the latter group may have been more important.

Settlement size provides a clue to social organisation. In general, societies composed of lots of

small settlements are associated with bands and tribes. The development of henges and hill forts in Wessex during the Bronze and Iron Ages has been used by some archaeologists to trace the emergence of chiefdoms and kingships. Evidence of specialisation in terms

KEY STUDY

The Omaha

O'Shea (1981) was able to compare eighteenth- and nineteenth-century ethnographic descriptions of the Omaha by European explorers with burial evidence to test the visibility of status and social grouping in mortuary data. Where social divisions were vertical or ranked, there tended to be evidence in the grave goods. In addition, while rank may be concentrated in particular age and sex groups in the population it is more archaeologically visible than horizontal divisions which are more equally distributed. Horizontal social divisions based on clan, moiety and age tended to be archaeologically invisible. From the historic accounts it was clear that some of these identities had been celebrated during the funerary rituals while a person's ranking had not been emphasised. This may indicate that the horizontal divisions were more significant in life. It also tells us that we cannot hope to read all status from burials.

KEY STUDIES

Later Bronze Age Britain and Ireland

A succession of writers have examined landscapes and the settlement patterns within them for evidence of increasingly hierarchical societies. The extension of food production has been linked with evidence of exchange in exotic goods over very long distances. The implication is that powerful individuals were amassing surpluses to trade on behalf of their communities. Contemporary evidence from Greece, which was at one end of the European 'prestige goods chain', provides a model for this. The heroes of Homer's epics often derived their wealth from agriculture and spent it on war and on gifts for their kin, followers and allies, including fine weapons and feasts. Many studies have pointed to increasing control over the land during the Bronze Age through the building of boundaries, for example Fleming 1988. There is also evidence for increased craft specialisation and intensification of production, particularly of weapons as at Runnymede. Grogan's (1999) regional study of Irish hilltop enclosures showed that these very visible, but not always defensive, settlements were established at regular intervals across the landscape. Artefacts suggest that these might have been the bases of local chiefs.

of crafts or bureaucracy has also been used in this respect. Models from Egyptian tombs show many specialists at work and there is a fine collection of them in the British Museum.

POWER AND SOCIAL CONTROL

Power, the ability to make others do what you want, can be approached via status or via evidence of social control. This can be inferred, but not proved, from the apparent organisation of labour for large communal monuments such as the henges of Neolithic Wessex. In some cases such as Egypt or the Maya the religious control exerted by the Pharaohs or Maya shaman-kings is illustrated in art on artefacts and temple walls.

Typically the more powerful figures are larger and wear more elaborate costumes. Their subjects, or those they have defeated, are smaller and sometimes depicted naked and

Figure 11.6 *A smiting scene from Edfu which has similar characteristics to the Palette of Narmer*

bowed or lying face down. For example, most Egyptian temples have 'smiting scenes' on their walls. These show the pharaoh holding a mace in his upraised right arm with which he is about to dash out the brains of captives held by their hair in his left hand. The captives are shown in submissive poses and are usually clearly identified as racially distinct from their Egyptian captors. At Edfu the pharaoh Ptolemy XII Neos Dionysos is shown grasping his prisoners by their topknots about to slay them. However, he is not known to have actually waged any wars. The subject matter of the relief is purely conventional.

THE ARCHAEOLOGY OF RANK AND STATUS

These terms are often used interchangeably but do have slightly different meanings. Status is associated with social prestige; rank implies a position within a hierarchy. Both status and rank may be inherited or acquired during life by an individual. **Ascribed status** is where an individual inherits social position, usually at birth, for example being born into royalty. **Achieved status** is where the individual earns or obtains position due to efforts during their

Figure 11.5 *Communal labour, whether voluntary or forced, was required to build the great monuments of the ancient world such as these temples at Tikal. Exploration of the extraction and carving of the materials and planning, organisation and logistics of transport and constructions gives us insights into social organisation in the past*

life, for example qualifying as a doctor. Rich burials of children are often interpreted as evidence of ascribed status.

Archaeologists employ a number of sources of evidence in their attempts to recognise status in past societies. In a few cases such studies are text-aided but in general they have to rely on material culture to provide answers. All of the main approaches try to isolate particular variables that will allow differentiation between sectors of a society and between individuals:

 KEY STUDY

The Palette of Narmer

This cosmetic artefact excavated at the Egyptian city of Hierakonpolis dates from 3000 BC, the period just before the First Dynasty when the rules and icons of kingship were being established. It is considered a classic example of the manipulation of iconography in support of an individual's status.

The king's name is written in hieroglyphs at the top, surrounded by a frame which is reminiscent of the architecture of the royal palace. The catfish (Nar) and chisel (mer) spell out the Horus name of the king, Narmer. He is depicted below in a standard pose. The king stands, left hand clasping the topknot of a kneeling captive, with a mace in his right hand. The hieroglyphs tell us that the prisoner's name is 'Wash'. The design immediately above him shows a falcon on papyrus plants pulling back the head of a figure who looks remarkably like Wash and is to be identified with the Nile delta. The main figure is wearing the white crown of Upper Egypt and a flywhisk, early symbols of kingship. Below are defeated enemies and a sign that represents a fortified town. We are clearly being told that the king has won a victory over an enemy in the north, the delta.

On the right-hand side of the palette the king, carrying the mace and flail, and this time wearing the red crown of Lower Egypt, is explicitly labelled and accompanied by standard bearers called 'The Followers of Horus'. They march within a panel that represents the gate of the royal palace, towards two rows of bound and decapitated prisoners. The dead prisoners are now powerless and reduced to order, compared with the figures on the other side who have spread-eagled limbs. This may be symbolic of the Egyptian concept of order. In the central panel are two mythological beasts with their long necks entwined to symbolise harmony and perhaps the unification of the two lands of Egypt. This is echoed by the two crowns, which would later be incorporated into the 'Double Crown', indicating that the pharaoh was 'The Lord of the Two Lands'. At the bottom right is a raging bull, representing the king's anger, trampling a man and a walled city. There is a balance in the composition, with harmony offsetting the violence, but the message is abundantly clear. The enemies of Narmer can have been in no doubt as to what lay in store for those who defied him.

 Kemp 1993

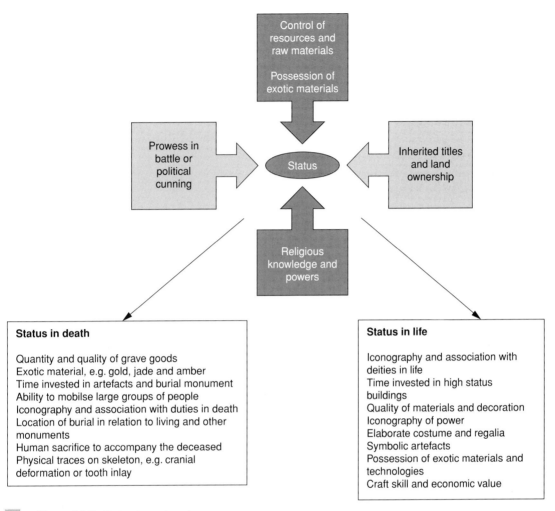

Figure 11.7 *Status in archaeology*

Burial evidence

Personal status is often suggested on the basis of grave goods. Rich burials of individuals such as those at Sutton Hoo, Varna and Bush Barrow are usually interpreted as being the graves of high status individuals. Sometimes there is additional evidence to confirm this, as in the cases of Tutankhamun and the royal scribe burial at Copan (▶see p. 230). The latter was identified from its central location, rich grave goods and human sacrifices and from the 'health' of the skeleton, which had little sign of wear. This burial, on a balance of probabilities, represented the royal scribe and son of Copan's greatest king, Smoke Imix.

In the Royal Cemetery at Ur, mortuary practice involved the sacrifice of attendants with royalty. The grave of Pu-abi included a 40-year-old woman who is identified as a queen on a sealstone buried with her. She was accompanied by exotic objects, including a lyre with a golden bull's head decoration, gold and silver vessels, a magnificent headdress of golden leaves and rosettes and twenty-three of her courtiers. These 'victims' seem to have gone to their deaths willingly as there was no sign of coercion. Human sacrifice to accompany the dead may be aimed at establishing the power and status of an individual. Equally there are many instances where such behaviour is a ritual full of meaning for the whole community in terms of the fertility of the earth or the continuity of cyclical events.

However, we need to take care that we don't impose our values and assume that certain materials held the same value and prestige in past societies as in our own. In some cases symbolic associations may be an equally important factor in the choice of raw material, such as jade in Mesoamerica. Even the gold at Varna (see cover) may not be what it seems. Some of the richest graves there are empty 'cenotaphs'. It may be that the gold represents offerings from the living rather than the belongings of the deceased. A further complication occurs with vessels such as beakers. Their contents may have been the material of greatest value rather than the pottery. Other organic materials such as textiles, food or wood may have been placed in what to us appear to have been 'poor' graves, but these rarely survive.

 Parker-Pearson 1999

Status is only likely to be represented *in* death where the person held that status *at* death. In cases where status or rank did not stay with the individual for their whole life it may not be visible. Similarly, where beliefs dictate that people should appear equal in death (as in Christian burial), indicators of status may be absent. In general, ascribed status is more likely to be visible than achieved status. The position

 KEY STUDY

Branc

Shennan's (1975) study examined a major cemetery and tried to assign values to types of grave good in order to establish social differentiation in terms of gender and age. Instead of assuming that what we might value, for example gold, was of most value in the past he used other measures. The key one was energy expenditure. In other words, artefacts that required more skill, effort and resources from long distances were likely to have been most prized.

of burials, their orientation and any funerary monument associated with them can also be used to examine status.

Settlement evidence

Status can also be inferred from settlement evidence. Settlements that in themselves are viewed as high status due to size or quality of artefacts are generally expected to be the homes of high status individuals. The palaces at Knossos and the hill fort at Danebury (▶see p. 180) have both been interpreted in this way. High status individuals might be expected to have different houses from other people. The energy expenditure model can be applied here too. Houses may simply be bigger because the inhabitants have more to store or may have larger household units. They may also occupy a prominent position. Eighteenth-century landowners chose to build in prominent positions in the landscape to emphasise control over land. Rich merchants in earlier periods clustered in central positions in towns. In many

KEY TASK

Investigating status and rank in your settlement

Identify some useful criteria for identifying status and rank in your community. House prices may be one guide; local information on occupation and earnings by electoral ward may also be available. Focusing on the built environment (houses, gardens, enclosures, not cars), use observation to compare different areas. Identify whether there are visible indicators of rank and status and what they are. Present this in diagrammatic form.

cases the houses will be larger, more elaborate and built of better quality materials – part of a general display of wealth and status, which might also include dress and visible forms of consumption. Romano-British villas, for example Chedworth, and palaces, for example Fishbourne, can be compared to see the relative differences in status between them. The layout of a site may reveal individual status through the control of space and therefore the way people relate to each other. Higher status people are also more likely to enclose their property in a more visible way than are others. These aspects and the control of space and access can clearly be traced in medieval castles and monasteries and in earlier sites such as brochs (►see p. 185).

Artefactual evidence

Concentrations of valuable finds can be used to suggest locations used by important individuals. Evidence of long-distance trade in exotic or prestige goods or of the craft workshops of attached specialists can also be important. Value in these cases is usually assigned in terms of the effort or energy which went into their construction. Particular types of artefact may also be significant. Fine weapons, ornaments and feasting equipment are all associated with chiefs and kings. Sherratt's (1997) analysis of bell beakers suggests that these were part of a wider chiefly assemblage which included battle axes, horses and, ultimately, individual burials in barrows. He interpreted the beakers as part of a drinking culture, perhaps in imitation of the metal drinking and feasting vessels of classical Greece. The association of elite warriors and feasting has echoes in the archaeological record of the Iron Age, in the Saxon and Viking period and until well into the Middle Ages.

THE ARCHAEOLOGY OF GENDER

Archaeologists usually distinguish between sex, which is biologically determined, and gender, which is regarded as a social construct. Gender is the identity assigned to different sexes. In any human society there is at the very least some difference between the roles of men and women. This stems from the fact that women give birth and that there are obvious anatomical differences between male and female. Gender explains these differences and specifies what is to be done about them. There is tremendous variation from one society to another. In the early stages of hominid development, males were up to twice the size of females but this distinction had largely disappeared by the time modern humans emerged. Paradoxically, gender differences were far more extreme in late nineteenth- and early twentieth-century West European societies, than they were among historically known food-foraging peoples.

Assumptions about 'natural' roles and their significance profoundly influenced the development of archaeology up to the 1970s. In particular, males were portrayed as the active sex in human evolution. For example, hunting was seen as the key humanising activity in evolution. Since then the importance of scavenging and the likely role of women in the transition from gathering to horticulture has been recognised. Even among the !Kung bushmen, often seen as archetypal hunters, women actually contributed much more protein to the daily intake of the group than did the men. Hunting was very hit and miss, while gathering of wild plant foods made up 60–80 per cent of the !Kung diet.

As with most areas of archaeology, ethnographic study has been employed to gain insights into task differentiation between males and females. One weakness in this approach has been that most anthropologists have been male. This has led to criticism that they are more interested in male activities and have failed to observe female tasks and behaviour. If this is true then we need to be particularly cautious in transferring such observations to archaeological material. A further point to be borne in mind is that gender is rarely just two opposite identities, and if we are to avoid stereotypical responses we should treat gender as a continuum – a curve along which individuals are placed from female to male, according to the norms of particular societies.

Studies of gender have relied heavily on burial evidence including human remains and grave goods. Settlement and architectural analysis and artistic sources, where they survive, have supplemented this.

Human remains

Differential evidence of disease can be used to identify gendered patterns of activity or consumption. Canadian Inuit hunter-gatherers from the 1890s show osteoarthritis in the right hand and jaw of women, combined with tooth loss. These women spent considerable time preparing skins and sewing. They made the thread by rolling sinews against their cheeks. Areas most pressured by this activity reveal damage. The men hunted with harpoons, which sometimes caused disease of the right shoulder and elbow, while kayak paddling also resulted in distinctive wear of the bones. Other studies of damage and wear have identified gender-specific activities as diverse as basket-making, fighting and grinding corn.

The quantity and quality of food consumed may relate to status. Chemical analysis of prehistoric Native American skeletons show that women have a higher strontium:calcium ratio than men in the same community. This may indicate that they ate a smaller share of the available meat. However, strontium levels also alter when a woman is pregnant or breast-feeding. Differential care and nutrition of female and male children might also show up in X-ray analysis of bones. Lines of increased bone density, known as Harris lines, reflect periods of malnutrition during growth.

Graves and grave goods

The association of male and female burials with different ranges of grave goods has been noted in many cultures. From the Neolithic onwards arrowheads, daggers and other weapons are frequently found in male and not female burials, which seems to confirm that these activities were male-dominated even by the prehistoric period. From the Bronze Age

KEY STUDY

Tell Abu Hureyra

Having sexed and aged the skeletons at this Neolithic site, Molleson found distinct differences between the sexes in terms of patterns of wear on their bones and of associated degenerative diseases such as arthritis. The male skeletons showed lesions and strain in the arms such as might be associated with throwing spears. This fitted well with the faunal evidence for hunting gazelle (►see p. 206). Female skeletons show heavy wear of the big toe, knee, thigh, pelvis and lower back. Today this might be termed 'repetitive strain injury' and was clearly caused by regular motion backwards and forwards of some duration. The querns, which were used for plant processing on the site, would have to be used for several hours a day by each family to obtain enough ground wheatflour to satisfy their needs. Using a quern necessitated kneeling down using the big toe curled under as a lever and pushing the top stone of the quern to and fro, sometimes hyper-extending the muscles of thigh and back if the stone was pushed too hard or too far. Over a lifetime this task would have caused the sort of damage and arthritis that we see in the female skeletons at Tell Abu Hureyra. Molleson suggested that women and their daughters would have shared this laborious work.

Another distinctive pattern were grooves in the sides of some of the female teeth on each side of the jaw. Ethnographic parallels suggested that this resulted from drawing fibres through the teeth to work and soften them as a preliminary stage in making baskets. This hints at the beginnings of craft production on a household level, a factor also indicated by the survival to a good old age of some individuals without teeth (the empty sockets had closed over during life). This would not have been possible without the ability to prepare soft foods, probably initially using sieves of basketwork and later of ceramics. A final indicator of gender roles lies in the discovery that women were most often buried under the floor of the house, suggesting strongly that this was their area of activity and their domain in life.

 Fagin 1995

women were regularly buried with a variety of ornaments and jewellery such as pins, necklaces and bracelets. While this may indicate different roles in life there are problems with this analysis. Until recently, sexing of burials often relied on the grave goods. Jewellery without weapons were expected to be female graves so these finds were used to define female burials. Today there is less confidence in this interpre-tation. DNA analysis at West Heslerton (►see p. 187) showed that some females were buried with weapons and some men with jewellery. Many museums are currently reviewing their labelling of burials. Whether beautiful objects are just jewellery and whether daggers are always indicative of fighting has also been questioned. Spear-throwers have been found in some female burials of the mid-western Indian

KEY STUDY

The Birdlip princess

This rich Iron Age burial from the middle of three barrows contained a mirror, a range of jewellery including amber and shale objects, and some bronze bowls. It was interpreted as a rich woman's grave and some speculated that it might even be that of Boudicca. However, recent examination of the skull has shown that it has masculine traits. The assemblage is also notable in that the artefacts have all been broken and one of the vessels was placed over the face of the skeleton. Could it be the burial of a male shaman rather than a princess? Another burial was discovered in 1999 in the Scilly Isles with similar characteristics.

Knoll culture of the third millennium BC. Were they just ceremonial or to do with inheritance, or did women as well as men hunt?

Rich male graves are often interpreted in terms of what *he* earned or won, whereas when a woman is found with elaborate grave goods they are often attributed to her husband or father. For example, if women over a certain age have certain grave goods and younger ones do not, it may be argued that these represent goods transferred at marriage. The possibility that women have achieved their own wealth is rarely considered. Examples of high status Iron Age female burials include those at Wetwang Slack, which features a 'chariot' burial surrounded by rich grave goods, and the Vix Burial at Saone, which has a gold torc, huge Greek bronze krater (wine-mixing vessel) and

decorated metal bowls. A different kind of status may be visible in the female graves at Khok Phanom Di where craft specialisation seems to have played a role in achieving higher social ranking. The Pazyryk 'Ice Maiden' also suggests high status based on a particular talent.

 http://www.pbs.org/wgbh/nova/icemummies/remains.html

Differential survival can be an issue when studying gender differences. In the Mesolithic period men, and especially older men, appeared to receive special treatment, being buried with ochre, antlers or stone artefacts. However, if women had grave goods of organic materials, perhaps offerings of plant foods and medicinal herbs rather than joints of meat, and tools or ornaments of wood, these would not have survived.

Settlement evidence

Studies which have used differential distribution of artefacts to identify male and female activity areas, such as Clarke (1972) at Glastonbury or Flannery and Marcus at Guila Naquitz, could be criticised for making assumptions about gendered tasks. For example, the complete absence of large men's fingerprints on pottery at Khok Phanom Di might argue against the involvement of adult men in potting. However, while small fingerprints could have belonged to women potters they could also be those of young assistants. More recently, studies of architecture have been used to explore the way in which societies structured gender in the past. Gilchrist's (1995) study of the relationship between ideas of chivalry and gender roles and the different zones of medieval castles is a good example.

Artistic sources

Depictions of males and females in scenes on pottery, reliefs, wall paintings and metal artefacts have been quarried for information about gender roles. Some appear fairly straightforward and provide evidence for a division of labour. Pottery from Sopron, Hungary, from the sixth century BC shows figures which seem to be women engaged in weaving and spinning: one is dancing or praying while another figure, which may also be female, is playing a lyre. Men in comparison are riding horses, herding animals and leading horse-drawn wagons. Other material is more ambivalent. A depiction of a person gathering wild honey from a tree at Bicorp, in Spain, from 7000–4000 BC has been interpreted as both male and female by different commentators. The majority have assumed it is a woman due to the size of the buttocks and the flowing hair.

Figure 11.8 *Drawing of a classical vase. Artistic sources have been used to provide information not only on what people looked like but also on social organisation and values*

Even where artistic images are clearly of females or males, they cannot always be taken at face value. At Knossos (▶see p. 212) a series of figurines of bare-breasted women with full-length skirts has been found. They frequently have snakes twined round their arms. There are also frescoes which show women and men involved in various activities. They are easily distinguished as the Minoans adopted the convention of painting the skins of women white while those of men are painted brown. Women are depicted more commonly than men. Taken at face value it seems that elite women may have had more status and the right to participate in a wider range of activities than women in many other societies. Some writers have gone further and suggested this is evidence of a matriarchal (headed by women) society. However, representation cannot in itself be taken as evidence of high status, nor can we assume that the women depicted are typical. A similar debate has raged over Palaeolithic 'Venus figurines'. These images of pregnant female figures have been found across Europe and are remarkably uniform in character and style. Most appear to be associated with hearths and home bases. They are made of a variety of materials including baked clay (Dolni Vestonice), mammoth ivory (Lespugue) and limestone (Willendorf). Interpretations have ranged from mother goddesses through fertility symbols to primitive pornography.

Until recently, sexuality in the past was rarely considered by archaeologists. Indeed, in several countries collections of artefacts with sexual imagery are often kept from public view. In 1999 the British Museum faced a dilemma over whether to display a rare Roman vase that depicted homosexual sex. A recent survey of knowledge about sexuality in the archaeological record appears in Taylor (1997).

POPULATION AND ETHNICITY

Demographic information about past populations is largely obtained from human remains. Where there are large collections from cemeteries they can reveal information about the age and sex structure of the population, average height and life expectancy of adults as well as common illnesses and injuries. DNA offers the opportunity to explore relationships between people and to determine how homogenous any population was. It has also been critical in tracing the evolution of humans. Artistic sources and preserved bodies can fill in details of appearance.

Ethnicity and race have the same relationship as sex and gender. One of each pair is in our DNA, the other is in our heads. Racially we are all Homo sapiens but ethnicity consists of cultural norms and values that differentiate one social group from another. Physical differences are sometimes, but not always, used to distinguish different ethnic groups.

Until the later twentieth century cultural approaches to archaeology tended to dominate interpretations. In some cases they were used to support racist political ideas, such as Nazi archaeology identifying particular ceramic styles with the territory of ancient (Germanic) tribes (▶see p. 121). Such approaches also led to a diffusionist 'invasions model' of social change in Britain with successive waves of invaders bringing developments and their own special pottery, for example, Windmill Hill Folk or Beaker People. This idea fitted with colonial experience of worldwide progress flowing from more 'civilised' to 'backward'

peoples, but it has been shown to be deeply flawed by the application of scientific techniques. Stonehenge is the most famous case. A generation of classically trained archaeologists had shown how the people of Bronze Age Wessex built monuments in imitation and with help from advanced Mediterranean civilisations. Yet radiocarbon dating has shown that Stonehenge pre-dated the Mediterranean monuments it was supposed to have been influenced by. This cultural model of social change tends to undervalue the achievements of indigenous people as in the case of Iron Age brochs (▶see p. 185). In Neolithic studies the current orthodoxy has shifted away from seeing all change as due to migration. For example, while the spread of farming in central Europe is largely interpreted as colonisation, its eventual adoption after the Neolithic standstill (▶see p. 208) in north-western Europe is increasingly seen as the result of choices made by local foraging groups.

Even where we know invasions took place, the archaeological record is not always helpful. For example, there is little evidence for the Norman Conquest in sequences of medieval ceramics. Some evidence is ambivalent. Belgic coins found in South East England from the late Iron Age have been used to support Caesar's description of immigration into the area from Gaul. However, there are other mechanisms by which the coins could have got there. As with other forms of identity, where ethnic allegiances are expressed in organic material such as textiles, evidence may not always survive.

KEY SITES

Pompeii and Herculaneum

Recent developments at these two Roman towns, destroyed by Mount Vesuvius in AD 79, provide an insight into the way archaeology has developed. The first excavations in 1748 were a search for treasure to adorn royal palaces. Today the material evidence is painstakingly studied to try and bring an ancient culture to life.

Classical accounts, particularly Pliny's letters, led to a view of a cosmopolitan population being entombed in ash at Pompeii or engulfed in mud at Herculaneum by the sudden eruption. The ghoulish plaster casts of victims have been used in conjunction with the range of good-looking people on the wall paintings to illustrate this view. Vulcanologists have now shown that the eruption did not happen without warning. Evidence for grand villas being taken over by squatters who hung agricultural implements over grand wall paintings suggests that many of those who could had left. Statistical analysis of the piles of disarticulated bones in the basements of Pompeii has yielded a picture of the 'average Pompeian'. Skull deformities suggest a group of closely related people and a high proportion of older women. This suggests that ideas about Roman lifespans may be wrong. If women survived childbirth then they had a strong chance of surviving to a good age, even approximating modern levels. The high number of older people also suggests a grim scenario – that they were the ones left behind!

Figure 11.9 *Drawing of the huddled remains of people killed at Herculaneum*

Conversely, early excavations at Herculaneum suggested that the town was abandoned long before the final eruption since so few bodies had been found. That idea changed dramatically in 1982 when excavations on the waterfront of Herculaneum uncovered hundreds of skeletons in the arches facing onto the beach. These may reveal more details of population structure.

 http://www.brad.ac.uk/acad/archsci/ field_proj/anampomp/links.htm

 http://www.cs.berkeley.edu/~jhauser/ pictures/history/Rome/Pompeii/

KEY STUDY

Saxons and Britons

Historical sources suggest that Anglo-Saxon invaders slaughtered or displaced native Romano-British people from much of England in the fifth and sixth centuries AD. On the assumption that 'Germanic type' artefacts equalled Saxon invaders, archaeological material was used to trace the arrival and spread of migrants across the country. Similarly, areas where Saxon pottery or metalwork was absent were identified as places still held by Britons. There are a series of problems with this version of events. First, the material itself. In some areas such as East Anglia or Oxfordshire it can be difficult to differentiate Saxon from Romano-British Greyware or Iron Age pottery, unless it is decorated. Where it can be identified, it sometimes turns up well before historical sources say the Saxons arrived, for example at Eynsham Abbey. This may illustrate the point that ethnically distinctive material may be used by other groups. Exchange, trade, small-scale migration or adoption and copying by indigenous people would also spread material.

Harke's (1990) study of Anglo-Saxon cemeteries suggested that they included Romano-Britons, thus indicating co-existence. Male burials with swords were on average 1–2 inches taller than those without. This was not due to different diets and suggested two distinct ethnic groups. By the seventh century this distinction had disappeared, probably through intermarriage. DNA analysis of several cemeteries revealed two models of Anglo-Saxon immigration. In some, complete kin groups were represented, which points to separate communities, while in others, males with weapons existed alongside female skeletons, showing continuity with the Romano-British period. Harke terms this the 'warband' model. Over time, DNA evidence supports a mingling of the two populations into 'the English' while the dominant culture remained 'Anglo-Saxon'. Analysis of the feet from burials at Lechlade cemetery by Jackson (1995) also pointed to great local population continuity. Settlement data, for example West Heslerton (▶see p. 187), supports this view. Some recent studies have noted that swords found with burials were not always robust models and were also found with women. This may suggest that they had a symbolic value rather than identifying male warriors.

For detail and links on Anglo-Saxon cemeteries see the website below.

 http://www.gla.ac.uk/archaeology/
staff/

SOCIAL CHANGE

Most periods will have examples of social changes to which you will be directed. The kind of evidence discussed in this chapter and those on economics and settlement will provide the focus for work on this area. Studying social change is likely to require you to discuss a range of different models to account for

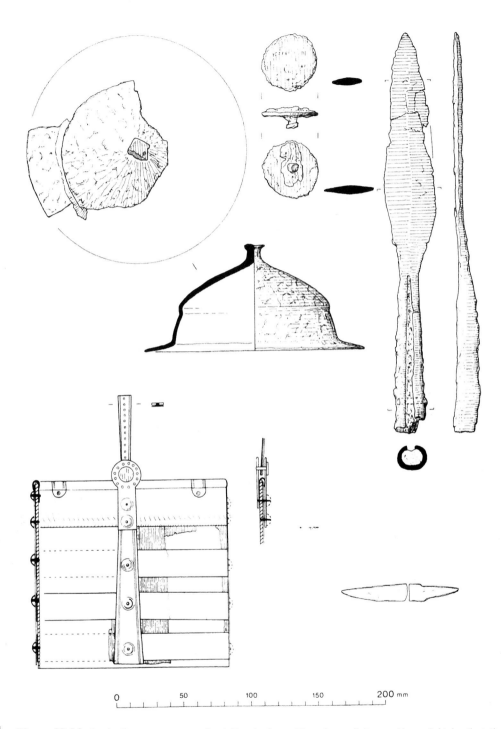

Figure 11.10 *Anglo-Saxon grave goods at Empingham. Your immediate reaction might be that the deceased was a warrior. However, there is some evidence that such grave goods were a mark of ethnic identity in the early medieval period rather than a direct link with what a person did. Compare with burial plan (Figure 2.3) p. 30.*

change. Essentially these will fall into two groups. External factors include immigration, diffusion, conquest and environmental change. Internal factors include evolution, competition and innovation. You need to ensure you examine and appraise an appropriate range of these. The adoption of agriculture provides a good model of this and the Pizza exercise (▶see p. 258) is a useful way of ranking your theories. In examining change don't forget the opposite: stasis. For much of the time things remain as they are, and that needs explaining too. A useful tool for examining forces for change or stasis is the force field diagram (▶see p. 210).

SOCIAL CONFLICT

Not all social conflict is violent. Probably its most common form is competition in either display or consumption. Our society is no different in this respect. Various attempts have been made to trace this sort of competition from the Neolithic onwards. Tilley (1996) suggested that developments in the design of Swedish passage graves might have been the product of local competitive emulation. Other writers have come to similar conclusions about the henges of Wessex, an idea that was taken up by Cornwell in his 1999 blockbuster novel, *Stonehenge*.

Warfare

In literate societies, warfare is one of the first things to be documented. It seems likely that in societies with oral traditions it forms a major part of their history too. From Homer we know something of the wars of Bronze Age Greece while medieval recording of Irish and Icelandic sagas may provide insights into Iron Age warfare in north-western Europe. Tomb

■ *Figure 11.11* *The massive bastions of the Hanoverian base at Fort George near Inverness. Its state-of-the-art defences were probably impregnable in the late eighteenth century. However, this monument rarely saw any fighting and has continued to be used by the military up to the present. Was its symbolic importance, as a massive statement of royal power in the Highlands, more crucial?*

KEY STUDY

Trajan's Column

This monumental pillar in Rome commemorates the conquests of the Emperor Trajan in his campaigns against the Dacians. Scenes show in tremendous detail the equipment and organisation involved in the campaign. The battle scenes depict the tactics used by the legions and their effectiveness. The key events of the campaign are included and its effects, allowing for some bias, are also illustrated.

Figure 11.12 *Artistic sources on warfare tend to tell the victor's version of events. Consequently, we approach them with some care as exact records of evidence. However, their unwitting evidence of equipment and organisation can be valuable. Trajan's Column provides a superb example*

paintings and inscriptions in most of the classical civilisations of Eurasia and Mesoamerica provide graphic depiction of the nature of battles. However, all these accounts tend to be very stylised and to focus on key individuals or heroes. There is much that archaeology can add to help understand both fighting and strategy.

Apart from historic and artistic accounts, the physical evidence of weapons and fortification usually provide the main sources for

identifying warfare. In some cases actual battles become visible. For instance, the 'war grave' at Maiden Castle with its famous iron arrowhead embedded in a defender's spine, or the mass grave at Towcester which was recently subjected to detailed analysis in terms of the sequence of events and the injuries visible on each individual.

Of course, not everything that looks military may have been. Both weapons and fortifications can be symbolic. Early metal daggers and 'rapiers' were relatively fragile. While they could have been used to kill, they would have been less effective than flint-tipped spears or stone axes. The swords that emerge in the Bronze Age are quite a different matter. Their shape and balance suggest that they were ideal for slashing at opponents in fighting at close quarters. Analysis of their edges has shown that many have damage associated with metal-on-metal contact. Fortifications can also mislead us about the nature of warfare. 'Hill forts' with their massive circuits of ramparts suggest sieges. There is evidence of attack at a few, such as flint arrowheads around the entrance at Crickley Hill, but these are exceptions. Warfare in the Iron Age is more likely to have looked like a cattle raid than pitched battles between rival armies, at least until the Romans arrived. A similar bias would occur if we looked at the major physical evidence of warfare between France and Germany in 1940. The Maginot Line, bypassed by the Germans, is still visible while traces of mobile tank and infantry formations are harder to discern.

Figure 11.13 *It looks like a turret but were brochs, such as this example from Strathnaver, military buildings? Recent evidence (*▶*see p. 185) suggests that they were more important symbolically and for reinforcing status and local control*

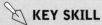 **KEY SKILL**

Evaluation exercises

Scales of justice

The ability to reach supported conclusions is expected at A Level and above. Learning how to reach judgements takes time and requires confidence building. One way of doing this is through short exercises where you get used to quickly summing up strengths and weaknesses. A simple task is to take three or four methods and list their advantages and disadvantages for particular tasks or in general. If you present the information in graphical form you are more likely to remember it. Adapting the scales of justice is a popular version. Try this as preparation for the next piece of work you have on methods.

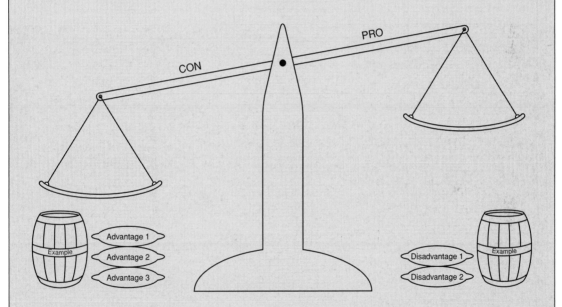

Figure 11.14 A scales of justice diagram

KEY SKILL *cont.*

Evaluation exercises

Archaeological pizza

This is a more sophisticated exercise. You can do this by yourself or it can be a team or whole class exercise. It will help you get used to using supporting evidence and prioritising points to reach a judgement.

1 Draw a large pizza shape with a circle of 'topping' in the middle.

2 Take an issue you have been studying where there is considerable debate and at least five different theories. For example, 'What happened to towns in Britain in the fifth century?' or 'What sort of social change were the Anglo-Saxon invasions?'

3 Put each theory into one of the inner sections of the pizza.

4 Research supporting evidence and enter it in the 'spalshes' (tomato or mushroom) in the outer sections of the relevant slice.

5 Adjust the size of the slices so that the most convincing argument is the largest slice and so on.

6 If you have done this as a team exercise, each team has to argue for their version.

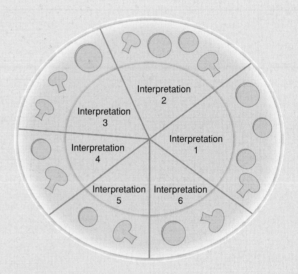

Figure 11.15
An archaeological pizza diagram

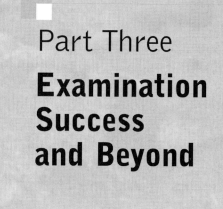

Part Three
Examination Success and Beyond

Chapter 12

Doing an Archaeological Project

YOUR GOALS

You need to understand

■ how to choose an appropriate topic

■ where to obtain help and evidence

■ how to plan and manage your time

■ how to record sites and materials

■ what to include and how to present your study.

Most courses, including A Level, require students to undertake a piece of personal research and submit their findings for assessment. This may be called coursework, a personal study or simply an archaeological investigation. Whatever its title it will have a set of written instructions as to the precise nature of your task. This will include guidance on what you must eventually produce and in which format. While this chapter cannot address these particular requirements, it covers issues which are common to most students' experiences and needs. You should keep your specific research brief to hand as you read through this section. The real examples included in the section are all based on good A Level projects.

HOW TO CHOOSE A TOPIC

Study the assignment brief issued to you. It may include constraints such as the word 'local' or you may need to undertake some 'first-hand' observation. It is essential that you choose a subject that fits the requirements of your course, is based on evidence which is accessible to you and, most importantly, is something on which you will enjoy working.

It must be archaeological

Archaeology embraces many other academic disciplines and sources in attempting to understand past cultures. These range from biology through geology to architecture. It is common to find overlap emerging in a project. Graveyard surveys, for example, link strongly to social and economic history while studies of hedgerows will require some botanical knowledge. While links to other disciplines are clearly valid you must consider balance. Archaeological content should dominate the final work. For example, analysis of the structural evidence for different phases of building within a medieval castle is archaeo-logical whereas exploring events and personalities linked to its use are usually of a historical nature. A general rule of thumb is that archaeology deals directly with the physical remains of the past whilst history is more concerned with analysing events using documentary sources.

You must be able to access your sources

Being able to visit your chosen sites or monuments, or conduct research within a museum or archaeological unit should be high on your agenda. Research benefits from a first-hand approach and it is more than likely that you will need to make more than a single visit to your source(s) of evidence. A first visit – probably following initial research in the library – will be to familiarise yourself with the object of your study. You need to get a feel for the extent of the site(s) under review or the range of artefacts available. Follow-up visits will be required for more detailed research. This might include surveying earthworks or sorting and drawing artefacts. Often students find that there are points they missed on previous visits which can be checked on later ones. If you have chosen sites at too great a distance such opportunities to revisit may be impractical. This is particularly true when students are tempted to select sites overseas. Your holiday visit to Pompeii may have fired your archaeological imagination but is unlikely to have resulted in meaningful research and the cost of a later visit to check measurements makes this a rather expensive option. Sites within range of home, school or college are your best bet.

Access does not just mean closeness. There are other people such as landowners involved. Public rights of way can be found in OS maps while better known sites are listed in gazetteers, often with directions for access. But in many cases there is no easy or direct footpath. Regardless of the pending 'right to roam' legislation, if the site is on somebody's land you will need their permission to visit it. This is even more important if you want to survey it. In 1999 a gamekeeper chased a student away from a stone circle in Derbyshire. His project was delayed for months while he then tried to get written permission from the landowner. It would have been better to have done this first. It is sometimes difficult to discover who owns particular fields so build in time to find out and consider fallback projects in case permission is refused or you don't receive a reply. If you hope to use an artefact collection, you need to check with the keeper that this is possible and determine when you can have access to it. To give yourself the best opportunity in all cases, write early in your research programme, explain briefly your reasons for wanting access to the land or collection and offer a range of suitable times when you could visit. A stamped self-addressed envelope may add a degree of success to the response rate. Permission should be obtained from the site manager if you are studying an excavation and want to record more than a few cursory notes or photographs.

It is easy to get caught out with access issues. A common excuse for shortfall in studies is that sites or museums were closed at the time

Figure 12.1 *Not a good time of year to survey Badbea. Summer vegetation obscures most of the stone and earthwork remains of this settlement built by refugees from the Highland Clearances*

the student tried to pay a visit. A phone call in advance would have found this out. A more difficult situation is where the site is accessible but it is overgrown with vegetation. Summer grass or bracken growth can easily mask relatively minor features such as hut circles or medieval village remains. Winter is often the best time to visit earthworks but the enthusiastic student can still be caught out: one keen fieldworker had to wait several weeks for snow to melt on Bodmin Moor before his barrow survey could be undertaken.

Supporting literature will vary in quantity according to the topic selected. Key texts to establish a context for your research are usually essential as most studies benefit from an understanding of the relevant background.

If you find too many books on your subject it will run the risk of lacking originality and it might be better to reconsider your focus. On the other hand, it is possible, as the case studies show, to identify an aspect of our material past where there is little direct written material on which to draw. This should not dissuade you from continuing, as there are many untapped areas of archaeological potential. It is easier to say something new about the pattern of round barrows or pillboxes near your home than it would be to say something original about Hadrian's Wall. You should seek advice from your tutor on background reading and sources whatever your topic. Access to this material is also easier if it is a local site or collection. If your school or college does not have much, local museums and libraries probably will.

You also need to find the correct balance of available evidence to study. Too much and you run the risk of superficiality, too little and the problem will be achieving a meaningful outcome. The curator of your local museum might welcome an apparently sensible and enthusiastic student who offers to catalogue their Romano-British pottery collection; a concentration on just the Samian ware might in reality be more feasible and appropriate for your study. If you do work with a third party such as a local archaeologist be sure to seek their professional advice but always refer back to your tutor who will best understand the requirements of your study.

So the first stage in your research is to ensure adequate and appropriate sources and access to them. Often at this stage some change may be needed to the original title in the light of your findings.

BASIC RESEARCH OPPORTUNITIES

The archaeological evidence to underpin any study usually comes from field evidence within the landscape, whether urban or rural, or artefactual evidence. The range within both these sources is vast and offers many possibilities for work at different levels.

GCSE students
- Two short pieces of work. A whole group is likely to work on the same questions.
- One piece describes sites, features or field studies and interprets them at a general level in the context of its period. The second piece identifies and interprets a collection of material, usually artefacts. Recovery, conservation and preservation may also be considered.
- High level responses show consistent and detailed accuracy in observation, recording

and interpretation and include some analytical outcomes. Full details are available from the AQA syllabus.

 http://www.aqa.org.uk/qual/gcse/arc.html

A Level students
- At A2 level the personal investigation is one of the three assessed modules. Each student selects an individual choice of topic and question. Access to HE assignments are likely to be similar.
- Students must develop an investigation of a question, issue or problem in an archaeological context. It has to be based on named sites, monuments or museums and must consider how archaeologists might approach such an investigation.
- Pass level responses must go beyond a straightforward factual account of evidence they have identified. Evaluation and analysis feature strongly in high level responses. Full details from AQA.

 http://www.aqa.org.uk/qual/gceasa/arc.html

Undergraduate or HND students
- No standard practice. Some courses require research diaries on summer excavation work, others set investigations similar to those at A level in year 1 or 2.
- Students may undertake research for their extended essay or dissertation. Requirements vary from one university to another but the focus of such work tends to be sharper the higher one proceeds up the academic ladder.

Sites and monuments

All sites can be studied in terms of spatial distribution and layout and their chronological

EXAMPLE 1

What evidence is there to suggest an Irish influence on the portal tombs of Wales?

'Kate' began with a comparative study of some portal tombs of south and north Wales and Ireland – leaving Cornish and Scottish examples outside the scope of the study. She combined a desktop survey of excavation reports with fieldwork. She hoped to discuss distribution, construction, orientation, typography, material culture, mortuary practices and chronology. However, few sites had 'comprehensive' excavation reports and therefore she reduced her commentary on finds and mortuary practice and placed greater emphasis on evidence from recording surviving remains in the field.

Sources

- SMRs
- Archaeological trusts
- Key sites: Pembrokeshire (4), Merioneth (3), Ireland (13)
- Museums: National Museum of Wales, National Museum and Library, Dublin
- Wide bibliography including prehistory texts and excavation reports
- Contacts: three practising archaeologists were contacted and all responded

Methodology

Kate established a background context from literature and produced distribution maps and commentary for the sites in Wales and Ireland. She reviewed academic arguments and established a hypothesis that there was an Irish origin/influence for Welsh sites. Her recording of sites included details of location, height above sea level, siting, orientation, style and material of construction. Where possible details of internal structure and reports on burial rites were also included.

Content/discussion

Figure 12.2 Pentre Ifan, an example of a portal tomb

Kate began by considering definitions of portal tombs as types of megalithic structure and acknowledging the limitations of the evidence for burial rites. She then made a range of detailed comparisons and contrasts including statistical tables. She examined different theories in depth and commented on each against the evidence she had gathered. She went on to reflect on other Irish/Welsh influences of the time in terms of 'passage' graves and axe trade. Her conclusion noted that evidence is open to interpretation but having weighed the evidence she outlined a sustainable argument.

Additional illustrations included photographs of twenty-three sites, two site plans and drawings of typical Neolithic artefacts. She acknowledged help and included an extensive bibliography. Her field notes were placed in an appendix.

development. Most can also be examined for typological development. Investigations can centre on any one, two or all of these factors to facilitate the depth of research needed. Whatever your choice of sites or monuments you should never go alone when doing fieldwork. Apart from the personal safety aspect, which cannot be over-stressed, a companion can hold tapes or discuss your observations with you.

The extent of the task should have a strong bearing on the selection of sites or monuments. Single sites may not always be sufficient. An Iron Age hill fort allows for both desktop research and field survey within the context of its landscape; a single pillbox would be too restrictive but a collection of coastal defences a sounder proposition. Studying a local group allows comparison and contrast to be developed which enables you to reveal your true archaeological investigative skills. Neolithic tombs provide such an opportunity. These monuments are widely distributed across western Europe particularly on the Atlantic coasts. They are chronologically distributed throughout the Neolithic period. Distinct regional typologies have been identified with styles ranging from long barrows to stalled cairns. For many students in the British Isles they are accessible and can be adapted to suit almost any purpose in terms of projects. A popular approach is to look at their distribution in terms of the Neolithic landscape, to establish original groupings or clusters, or to compare orientation. Islands such as Guernsey or Arran present obvious opportunities. Other approaches include comparing inter-visibility or to report on the condition and current threats to the monuments.

Of course visible monuments, which include those you can find on OS maps, are rather like the tip of an iceberg. By far the greater proportion of evidence of past activity is hidden below ground. Those studies that only reflect on visible evidence may well fail to deal with the larger picture. Reference to aerial photographs and SMR documentation is useful in establishing evidence that cannot be recorded or accessed in other ways.

You may be also be able to consult the results – usually published – of previous excavations on the sites. You need to decide how much of your evidence will be derived from such sources and how much from your study of unexcavated sites. Few personal studies achieve high grades by simply paraphrasing the work of others. Excavation reports are also a particularly difficult medium to summarise effectively. However, if sites have been excavated then you have no option but to investigate via the site report or archive.

Including a well-known site in a group study of several sites such as Chedworth and other Cotswold villas can lead to a loss of balance. The data on one site far outweighs that easily obtainable on the others. This imbalance can be countered by a title which lays the stress on the better known site or which focuses on conservation and preservation issues. Sites with guidebooks should carry a health warning for students. They can seem a bonus when you are hard-pressed for time but the availability of such material can tempt you into producing a study which owes too much to others' work. At worst this can turn into an archaeological version of I-spy.

Artefacts

The potential for studying artefacts is vast. These range from Palaeolithic stone tools to relatively recent objects like clay pipes or horseshoes. Materials could include ceramics, stone, bone, metal, organic remains and glass.

EXAMPLE 2

A survey of ground and polished stone and flint axes from East Kent

'Hamid' set out to examine finds from a small area in some detail and to catalogue quantity, type and distribution. He hoped this might shed some light on Neolithic settlement in the region.

Sources

- Kent SMR
- Canterbury Archaeological Trust
- Kent Archaeological Review
- Archaeologia Cantiana

- Museums: British Museum, Canterbury, Dartford, Dover, Folkestone, Herne Bay, Maidstone, Powell-Cotton
- Wide bibliography including general prehistory texts and articles in archaeological journals

Methodology

Much previous research has been related to the petrological analysis (via thin sectioning) of axes to establish their source and the

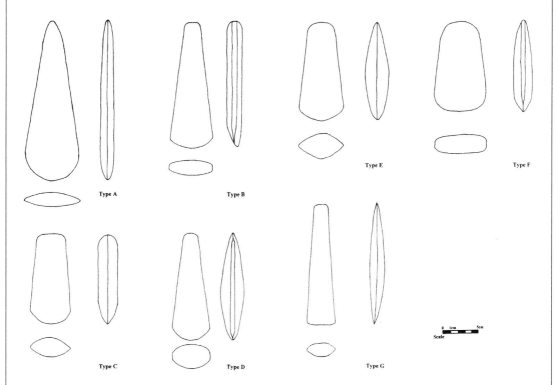

Figure 12.3 *A type series of stone axes: the seven profiles against which the axes were matched for typological analysis*

EXAMPLE 2 *cont.*

distribution patterns of products. Records on 125 axes were compiled from published data and museum records. Hamid used a self-devised sheet to list museum accession number; find spot; stone type; dimensions; completeness; condition; presence of cortex; other comments. The most complete were sketched in outline for shape comparison. Using typology and analysis of size and weight Hamid established a seven-type classification with description and illustration of one axe in each type. Charts were produced to show number of axes per group.

Having produced his catalogue, Hamid evaluated it and discussed its implications for understanding the archaeology of Neolithic Kent.

Content/discussion

Hamid acknowledged the difficulty in establishing an accurate number of axes. He observed that some are held outside Kent while others in Kentish museums were unprovenanced. More were likely to be in private collections and unpublished. Most were chance finds but others could be linked to archaeological sites or other Neolithic material. The section on raw materials acknowledged the work of others. Most axes were made from local flint but petrological analysis linked others to axe factories. He was able to construct distribution maps with links to known Neolithic sites and natural features. Further discussion centred on possible implications of the findings for exchange and identifying settlement and the function of the axes themselves.

Accompanying illustrations included location maps, six tables of data and typological drawings. No photographs were used; the project was acceptable without them. The project listed acknowledgements and had a comprehensive bibliography. The axe record sheets were placed in an appendix.

However, artefacts are less frequently used as source material for projects than sites and monuments. This may reflect the pull of the outdoors and landscape archaeology but probably also stems from the greater barriers that exist between the researcher and the guardians of material culture. Artefacts are most likely to be in museums or with archaeological units. Individual excavators or collectors are less easy to identify as resources for students.

Most museum material is in storage. Some of it will be fully catalogued. Curators tend to display their better items so these objects are often unusual rather than representative. To fully explore a museum's holding of any particular aspect of material culture will require museum staff to locate and get out appropriate evidence. Many will do this but will want sufficient notice and a clear idea of what it is you wish to study. Arrangements will have to be made for frequent visits to work on the material as cataloguing and drawing are time-consuming activities. These can only be done during opening times which may mean Saturday or holiday appointments.

Archaeological units hold most recently excavated material and their time is even more limited than that of museum staff. Their role is not curatorial and it will need personal introduction to access a part of their store of artefacts. Some students obtain work experience placements with units and may be able to develop links through such activity. Other sources include local societies who may do some excavation or, more rarely, local excavators. Some metal detectorists might allow a study of their findings – such a recording and analysis could well prove fruitful.

Fieldwalking

Some students use their links with museums, units, universities or landowners to identify sites under the plough and arrange their own fieldwalking exercise. If it is well researched and planned this can lead to excellent, original studies. Farmers need to be approached sensitively for permission and in good time. Their schedule of activity needs to be known so that you can organise the fieldwalk at a convenient time both to them and yourself. You also need an initial visit to check that archaeological material is visible in the topsoil. Try not to be overambitious and do get some help. It takes longer to set up and walk an area of a field systematically and gather the evidence than you might think. Two students fieldwalking a 200 metre square would walk approximately 10 kilometres each. On ploughed land that represents a considerable expenditure of energy! Washing, identifying and analysing the finds will also take much time.

Archaeology from the modern period

Most archaeological texts focus on later prehistory to the medieval period. However,

this should not limit you and particularly if you live in a built-up area, you may find it easier to focus on standing buildings or more recent structures. Students have studied buildings ranging from docks to petrol stations. The remains of the industrial age and also of the Second World War are particularly rich sources for studies.

Industrial archaeology including agricultural evidence

Early transport systems such as canals and railways often leave linear traces, now often fading, of their routes. A keen eye for landscape and interpretation backed by older Ordnance Survey maps can be just what a student researcher needs. Both wind and water mills survive in a range of conditions and often have constructional sequences that can be ascribed to different phases of development. Where they have been converted into homes you may find the owners rather proud to show off original elements of the building. Mines are often landscaped after their closure and the danger of hidden shafts should discourage their use as a source for study. However, harbours, their associated buildings and tramways may survive in sufficient state to warrant investigation. Despite urban regeneration it is quite possible to identify buildings whose original purpose has now given way to new uses. Breweries, maltings, cinemas and mills all fall in this category. They lend themselves to questions asking, 'To what extent can the development and function of the remains at X be identified by archaeological survey?'

There is a vast range of vernacular farm buildings in the countryside. Even on modern farms you may not have to look far to find some older features. Records of this diminishing archaeological resource are needed and your study could add to them. One rural

EXAMPLE 3

'To what extent can a correlation be established between air photographic evidence and that revealed by fieldwalking?'

The Trent Valley in Nottinghamshire has featured as a case study in two major publications on aerial photography: *A Matter of Time* by the Royal Commission on Historical Monuments (1960) and their subsequent study, written by Whimster, *The Emerging Past* (1989). 'Cara' chose to fieldwalk two fields that had produced cropmarks to establish whether the pattern of finds reflected the location of the features in the air photographs. In other words to see how closely these two methods of site identification matched.

Sources

■ Notts SMR
■ Trent and Peak Archaeological Trust – air photographs
■ Practical fieldwalking guides
■ Texts on regional air photography and site identification
■ Teacher and SMR staff assistance with artefact identification

Methodology

Preliminary research at the Trent and Peak Unit showed Cara that most fields in the target area had revealed cropmarks. She gaining access permission and dates of ploughing from local farmers then selected fields that were due to be ploughed. Next she created a collage of cropmarks from the collection of photographs of all angles and heights that she had located by grid reference at the local archaeological unit. The cropmarks within the target fields were scaled and drawn onto plans.

Local volunteers comprising family, friends and fellow students systematically fieldwalked each field. Finds were cleaned, sorted, weighed, counted and identified. This process took two months. Patterns from the plots of fieldwalked finds and cropmarks were then compared.

Content/discussion

The cropmarks could be described as either enclosures or circles. Based on her reading she hypothesised that they were land boundaries of Iron Age or Romano-British date. She anticipated that they would have been the site of huts or barrows and expected to find concentrations of artefacts from those periods on the surface.

The evidence proved inconclusive. Sufficient material was recovered to argue for activity in the Roman period but when plotted against the cropmark features no direct correlation could be established. The validity of the exercise as a piece of research and fieldwork is not prejudiced by the results. It provided a local topic with both desktop and practical aspects.

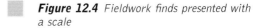

EXAMPLE 3 *cont.*

In addition to acknowledgements and a bibliography Cara presented location maps, aerial photographs and plans of fields plotting cropmarks, fieldwalking pattern and finds distribution. She drew selected finds and included photographs of fieldwalking.

Figure 12.4 *Fieldwork finds presented with a scale*

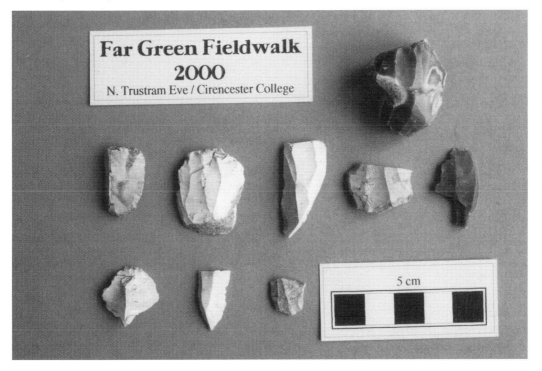

structure which makes an ideal vehicle for manageable research to identify, record, illustrate, compare and produce distribution maps of is the dovecote. While there are some classic examples of free-standing structures (how many visitors to Avebury have noticed the circular dovecote belonging to Avebury Manor just opposite the entrance to the museum?), many are located in the end of barns or stables. Another disappearing feature are churn stands. Milk used to be collected from farms in churns placed at the roadside by farmers. They were put on stands so they could be easily lifted across to the lorries. Many stands still exist, though now redundant, and can be found, often rather overgrown, in hedgerows near to a farm's access onto a road. Styles vary (typology) and different materials were used. Very few are recorded.

✎ EXAMPLE 4

Industrial archaeology: the Dudley (No. 2) Canal from Selly Oak to Halesowen, Birmingham

'Tom' attempted to evaluate the archaeological significance of the surviving surface evidence for 8 km of a canal abandoned nearly fifty years ago. The line of the canal passed through a park and housing and industrial estates. A significant feature was the Lappal tunnel which had collapsed in 1917. At nearly 4 km it was one of the longest canal tunnels ever built.

Sources

- Background texts and pamphlets on canals and industrial archaeology
- Maps: Birmingham Canal Navigations; 1:25,000 OS for modern information; 1" OS (1967) for canal route shortly after closure; 1:2500 OS (25" to mile 1881–2) showing sites of spoil heaps from the tunnel
- Contacts: college library, Birmingham Central library archives, Country Park Ranger, local inhabitants with local knowledge/memories

Methodology

Tom began with maps to establish the line of canal and accessibility. He planned to walk the length of the earthwork, observing and recording key features by note-taking, drawings (including profiles) and photography. He paid particular attention to bridges, wharves, overflows and tunnel spoil heaps, which had the appearance and the same fieldwork requirements as barrows.

Figure 12.5 *Students using tapes, ranging rods and clinometers to measure Painswick Beacon Hill Fort in order to construct profiles of the earthworks*

Content/discussion

The first part of the line from the Worcester and Birmingham canal was easily identified in Selly Oak Park but the junction was obliterated in 1953 so Tom used local oral evidence and a dismantled towpath bridge to establish its position. Landscape interpretation

EXAMPLE 4 *cont.*

revealed where the line of the old canal survived infilled between house gardens, which had been laid out when it was still a landscape feature.

Photographic evidence showed tunnel portals at the end of cuttings but like much of the canal these cuttings had been infilled. Locating boggy ground in the current landscape helped to reveal their original locations.

The tunnel had been constructed by digging several shafts down to the proposed level of the canal and then cutting a bore on either side. The resulting spoil – red clay in this case – was brought to the surface. Once the tunnel had been cut and lined with brick the shafts were back-filled, but the bulk of the excavated material remained in heaps on the surface.

Tom attempted to identify these 200-year-old spoil heaps from remains in a housing estate and adjacent Country Park by using an 1881 map. Erosion enabled him to determine the constituent material of the mounds and even retrieve reject bricks from the tunnel lining.

Towards Halesowen the canal ran on a huge earthwork embankment which was larger than the bank and ditch system at Maiden Castle. Tom was able to record profiles and compare them with eighteenth-century illustrations.

Tom's project included acknowledgements and a bibliography reflecting the Birmingham Canal Navigations and industrial archaeology. He produced plans, photographs and profiles of features, and map extracts were placed in an appendix.

The Defence of Britain

This area of archaeological research has been given a boost recently by the Defence of Britain project which is recording some of the monuments slowly eroding away in the coastal and inland landscape. About 450 airfields were built during the Second World War particularly in the east. Coastal defences survive in many places simply because no one has bothered to remove them, for example the concrete blocks designed to slow a seaborne invasion at Fairbourne, Gwynedd. Running in lines across the countryside are numerous pillboxes designed to hold up an invading army. These could be studied for typology or distribution. In towns, metal was collected during the war to 'help the war effort'. Careful examination of the tops of garden walls reveals the extent of

such activity and provides fresh and original archaeological evidence literally on the doorstep.

 British Archaeology August 2000

 http://www.britarch.ac.uk/projects/dob/index.html

Experimental archaeology

Planning, conducting and evaluating an archaeological experiment or reconstruction can seem an attractive option. It can make a worthwhile study but there are pitfalls to avoid. In many cases it is an advantage if you have some familiarity with the craft involved in the experiment. Prehistoric flint knappers or

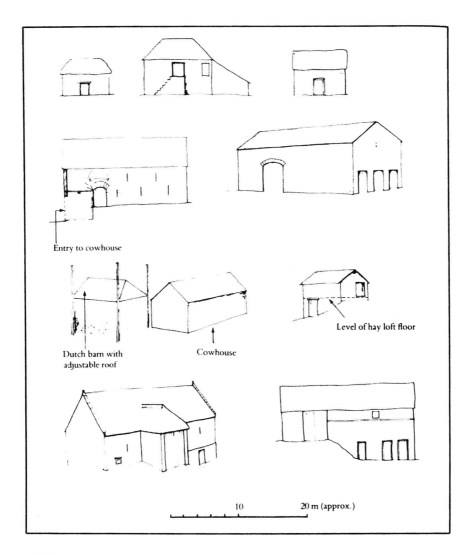

Entry to cowhouse

Dutch barn with
adjustable roof

Cowhouse

Level of hay loft floor

10   20 m (approx.)

Figure 12.6 *Diagram of types of barn. The range and typology of such structures offer opportunities for fieldwork in most parts of the UK. Identification of examples, establishment of distribution patterns and recording techniques are all valid exercises, which might form the basis of local studies (after Lake 1989)*

Romano-British potters had practice and experience on their side when they were making the artefacts we recover from excavations. Therefore if you don't have skills in knapping or wheel-made ceramics, you might be advised to avoid this type of project. Home-made hand-built pots, which do not resemble any archaeological material, 'fired' in a bonfire in the back garden do little to explain or extend understanding of ceramics, their manufacture or firing techniques.

However, a student adept at woodworking might reconstruct and fire a bow, testing draw

Figure 12.7 *This pill box at Kilnsea dramatically illustrates the need for the recording of Second World War monuments. Such examples can be combined to form the basis of an archaeological study*

strength and range with different arrows and arrowheads. The groove and splinter technique of bone working for slender items such as pins can be reproduced with animal bone from the butcher and some sharp flint flakes. If you are able to visit experimental centres such as the Peat Moors Centre near Glastonbury you may be able to get advice on opportunities for developing these skills.

WHERE TO GET HELP AND ADVICE

During the topic selection process you will have identified an accessible range of resources. Where this involves the services of others, for example museum staff or SMR personnel, any request needs to be as clear and succinct as possible. The best practice is to make it clear that you have already done some background research and focused on several questions to which you feel your contact might be able to offer answers. Don't pick a topic and send it to various possible sources of help expecting a completed project by return! Timing is also crucial. While you need to do exploratory work before making contact with requests for assistance or publications, you cannot afford to delay your approach for too long as agencies have their priorities and ordering material from them will involve a built-in time delay.

National resources

Whatever project you select there will inevitably be something of use on the Web. If nothing else, it can make access to sources of information faster. Start with one of the archaeological gateway sites (▶see p. 303). Of particular use for projects in England is the National Monuments Record (NMR) site. It is comprehensive and self-explanatory. It offers a search service, which is free 'subject to limitations', and free information packs. Topics available include 'Archaeology of England' and 'Aerial photographs of England'. A valuable link from NMR is to an alphabetical list of SMR addresses. These are your local sources of detail on known sites and their staff offer advice and printouts of information on their database.

If you want to find out if any excavations have taken place at your site, visit the Excavation Index:

✎ http://www.ads.ahds.ac.uk/

This site offers a search option via <catalogue> <accept/enter> and putting the place name (the parish) in the box offered. It lists what it

EXAMPLE 5

Sites and settlement patterns before 1900 in an Oxfordshire parish

'Marc' aimed to establish what continuity of occupation/settlement could be discovered by a survey of extant features and recorded sites. His fieldwork centred on an earthwork adjacent to Grims' Ditch, which had apparently not been studied or recorded previously.

Sources

- Oxfordshire SMR
- Centre for Oxfordshire Studies
- Texts on landscape archaeology and fieldwork
- 1841 Tithe map
- Ordnance Survey maps 1877–1914
- NMR in Swindon

Methodology

Marc used the SMR to create a comprehensive list of sites. He gained permission and visited them all before deciding to focus on two particular features for fieldwork survey. These were an earthwork and a surviving ridge and furrow near the village. After researching fieldwork techniques he recorded these features. He was able to use combinations of maps, documents, aerial photographs and hedgerow dating to establish the oldest boundaries in the area.

Content/discussion

Marc's summary of evidence was set against the geology and topography of the parish. He described a section of Grims' Ditch and other earthworks and discussed their possible age. He found documentary evidence for a Norman church but could find no physical evidence to support this. Similarly, there was an excavation report on an Anglo-Saxon cemetery but no evidence for contemporary settlement. He was able to use maps to suggest the possible development of the parish and suggest further possible study opportunities including excavation sites.

In addition to acknowledgements and a bibliography of landscape archaeology and fieldwork techniques, Marc included profiles and field plans, annotated maps and photographs and a distribution map of sites. Larger map extracts were placed in an appendix.

calls 'archaeological interventions', which covers more than just excavations, and notes where the record of that 'intervention' is maintained. The result may send you back to the NMR but at least it indicates archaeological activity has occurred at your chosen site location.

Museums

Museums often list 'supporting research', as part of their mission and many will have education officers who may be able to help. However, they are usually busy and their main focus is primary education so you need to book visits and be clear in advance about the help you want.

 http://www.mda.org.uk/vlmp/

Units

Archaeological units are less easy to discover as they are professional organisations in the business of offering archaeological services to those who need, and will pay for, them. Although their focus is not curation or education their staff may assist if approached sensibly. Local units can be found from the link below or by typing 'archaeological units' into a search engine.

 www.dur.ac.uk/Archaeology/BritArch/ Units.html

Libraries

Libraries vary hugely in the archaeology stock they hold. Local libraries may hold local collections including an archaeological journal but are most used for background texts or the (rather slow) inter-library loan service. University libraries (where archaeology is studied) or national organisations such as the NMR are the best option and will hold excavation reports and journals. However, you will need special permission to enter some university libraries and they do not usually let you borrow. It is worth persevering partic-ularly with excavation reports, which are as near as you may get to the evidence for some sites. Some older reports may be difficult to find. One last resort is to look for them at second-hand archaeological booksellers (▶see p. 302).

PLANNING AND MANAGING TIME AND WORD LIMITS

Your research will be guided by instructions from your tutor or syllabus, which specify presentational style, length and deadlines. You must take note of these 'rules'. If the stipulated length of a study is 3,500–4,000 words (as at A level) you should plan to produce a study that fits within these parameters. This may influence your choice of title as examiners are looking for depth of research and argument rather than the superficial treatment of a large number of sites or artefacts. Sometimes the required length in thousands of words may seem daunting. If you divide it up into sections and then subdivide each again you will find you have a framework on which to construct your study. A sensible model includes introduction, background information, research methods, research results, analysis and evaluation, and conclusions. You need to ensure the emphasis falls on your research and analysis rather than providing masses of background scene-setting.

Fight the tendency to put off starting! Every May, A Level projects are handed in with letters enclosed as appendices revealing that key information was still being sought only a few weeks earlier. There are many sources of information on time management and their advice is equally applicable in the context of archaeological coursework. The specific issues for archaeology students revolve around the frequent mix of indoor and outdoor activity where planning and sequencing of work is crucial. The 'desktop' research may involve libraries, museums, the Sites and Monuments Record and the National Monuments Record, all of which have their own time constraints. Outdoors you may be able to access your sites at will but you may require permission and have to work round the farmer's calendar (fieldwalking needs ploughed fields) and the weather. You need to plan and start early.

Word processors have made preparing studies much easier. You can collate information and notes as you go along, integrate visual images and perfect drafts more effectively. Try to ensure that you also record all sources used so that your references and bibliography are complete. Incidentally, nobody will believe that your hard disc crashed (and you forgot to make a back up) the night you were printing the final copy. That excuse sounds like 'my dog ate it' to this generation of lecturers and examiners.

RECORDING EVIDENCE

How much of any site or range of artefacts you record will depend on the nature of the investigation and to what extent the site in question is central or more peripheral to the discussion. There is also the question as to the state of the site when you come into contact with it. While photographs and sketches will usually suffice for GCSE, A Level and university projects will require more detailed recording to support your analysis and interpretation. Wass (1999) is an excellent basic guide while Drewett (1999) provides a greater range of techniques.

Your record is likely to comprise four major types: drawn, written, photographic and diagrammatic. Drawings include location maps, plans of features or buildings, profiles of earthworks and elevations of structures. You may be able to illustrate relationships or phases through the medium of such illustrations. You will certainly need to make notes so that you can describe key features in your report. Assume that your reader has a sound archaeological understanding, but not necessarily knowledge of your site, and address your work

to them on that basis. Photographs are useful in illustrating things you have identified and showing developments in the case of excavations. Tables and diagrams should be created where you have large amounts of data such as with fieldwork projects. They are also valuable for making comparisons and showing processes. A quick library search of archaeological texts will provide a wealth of examples.

Recording sites or features

Planning sites

You will probably wish to produce field drawings of earthwork sites. While drawing skills and surveying equipment obviously help, much can be achieved with simple gear: 20 or 30 metre tapes, ranging poles, a compass and marker arrows (try tent pegs with coloured ribbon) form a handy 'starter kit'. The simplest plans are likely to be made up from measuring or pacing the main features and roughly drawing hachures to indicate slopes.

For more accurate diagrams you will need to lay down a grid over the features to be recorded. A base line should be established and then a second main grid line should be fixed at right angles to the first. Parallel lines to each of these then form a total grid. It is advisable to fix reference points so that you can return to the same grid, but you will need to do this sensitively and with permission from a landowner. You cannot leave obtrusive markers on public land or where grazing animals might damage themselves. Ideally this grid should be linked to reference points on OS maps. Once a grid is established you can plot it onto graph paper and by taking measurements from two fixed points to the feature, plot it by the process of triangulation.

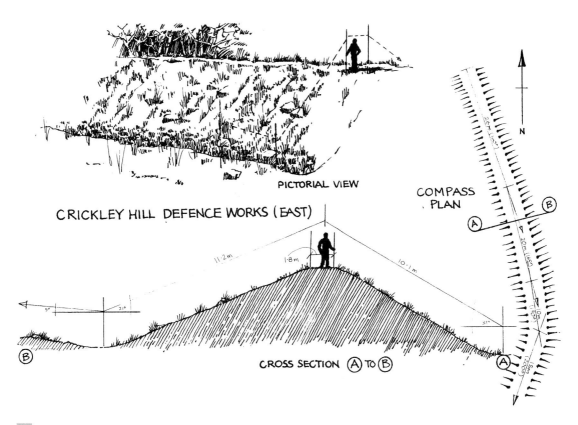

PICTORIAL VIEW

COMPASS PLAN

CRICKLEY HILL DEFENCE WORKS (EAST)

CROSS SECTION Ⓐ TO Ⓑ

Figure 12.8 *A student drawing of the profile of earthworks at Crickley Hill including an example of the use of hachures*

When recording slopes, place marker arrows (one colour) along the upper edge and others (a different colour) at the lower extent of the slope. This enables the lines of the feature to be plotted and the arrows can be reused. Conventional hachures, where the head of the hachure represents the top of the slope and it gets thinner as the slope goes down, should be used. They indicate the direction and length of the slope. Steepness is indicated by heavier infill of the hachure, head shape or the closeness of the hachures.

Profiling features

If you want to draw a scale profile of an earthwork you may need more equipment. However, there are some simple methods which are effective. A horizontal line fixed across the earthwork at 90 degrees to its main alignment and kept level provides a baseline. Measurements are taken from it to the ground at fixed intervals that will establish the profile of your site. A series of shorter lengths may make maintenance of a level easier and can offer a solution for longer slopes as long as adjustments are calculated accurately. Ensure you record this. It is essential that you employ the same scale for both horizontal and vertical scales or your drawings will suffer from distortion. If you have access to more equipment, such as a level and measuring staff, your task will be quicker. Alternatively, your geography department may have clinometers or gradiometers which you could borrow and use to construct profiles in a series of angles and lengths.

If you follow the basic rules of setting out, measuring, plotting to scale and drawing up your field results it is possible for enthusiastic archaeology students to produce a decent original plan.

Recording excavations

Recording part of a current excavation site is similar to what the real excavation team will be doing. You need to consider how much detail you require in terms of plans, sections and photographs. You may need to ask about evidence relating to the various phases of occupation and to see particular finds, but it is unlikely that the specialist reports will be ready in time for you to see. A tape recorder might be a useful aid for when you have the chance to make enquiries.

Recording buildings

Photography and sketches of the lower levels and key external features are needed to illustrate building materials and phases. If you have internal access then room plans and details of construction and decoration can be added. You are unlikely to be able to get precise measurements for elevation drawings but using tapes, clinometers and some basic trigonometry can help produce a reasonable approximation.

Recording artefacts

There are archaeological conventions for the illustration of many finds and these can be studied in archaeological reports. Producing quality drawings is neither quick nor easy. You should consider the extent of your artistic skills and try them out against the recognised

formulae for archaeological illustration so that you can judge your aptitude for this exercise. A reasonable alternative for those objects you may have collected yourself in fieldwalking is to scan them and trace the printout.

Often when there is a quantity of pottery to review attention is paid to what are called 'diagnostic' sherds, for example rims and decorated pieces. The less significant sherds can then be grouped and described as collections. Such sherds may be counted and weighed and the information about them given in tabular form rather than by illustration.

Smaller objects like bronze brooches or flint tools require careful treatment by the illustrator and will always need to be drawn

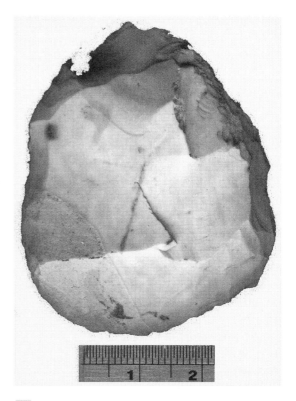

Figure 12.9 *A scan of an artefact recovered by fieldwork*

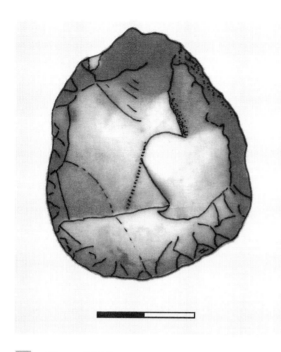

	Quantity	Weight	Average Weight
Black Burnished Ware	77	676 gms	8.8 gms
Grey ware	70	457 gms	6.5 gms
White Ware	2	50 gms	25.0 gms
Severn Valley Ware	18	117 gms	6.5 gms
Samian Ware	5	19 gms	3.8 gms
Other	13	126 gms	9.7 gms
Totals	185	1445 gms	7.8 gms

Figure 12.11 *Bar and pie charts are ideal for displaying the results of fieldwalking*

WRITING UP

There are two considerations here: what does the reader of your study really need to know about your site? How can you best present the evidence? Assume that your reader has a sound archaeological understanding, but not necessarily knowledge of your site, and address your work to them on that basis.

Refer again to the assignment brief. There may be specific advice on structure and presentation. This may include instructions, title pages, abstracts and appendices. It will probably mention plagiarism and referencing.

Plagiarism

This means using other people's work unchanged or without acknowledgement. Avoid it at all costs. It is particularly easy to slip into accidently where you are heavily reliant on one guidebook or report, or where you download material as notes from the internet. Be on your guard and if necessary adjust your question to avoid repeating somebody else's enquiry.

Presentation

Your original plan, probably somewhat adapted in the light of research, will form the basis for the work you submit. You will have sifted and

Figure 12.10 *A tracing made from the scan in Figure 12.9 with key features highlighted. This technique provides a good example of how those of us without good drawing skills can present illustrations*

from at least two perspectives – front-on and side-on – to give a clear indication of their design. Sometimes in the case of objects, for example flint axes, it is the profile shape that is relevant in the report rather than a detailed drawing showing the flaking process. Each artefact should be drawn to a scale, shown in the drawing. Some description needs to be written to make clear to the reader matters relating to the object that the drawing does not necessarily convey, for example colour or texture.

A range of details should be used when cataloguing objects (see p. 267). These will include provenance, dimensions and description of key features.

✎ KEY SKILL

Referencing

Referencing is an important part of a quality study and is insisted on at degree level. Get into the habit not only of listing your sources, both books and journals, but also of putting the page references into your draft notes as you select interesting comments or information. There are several referencing systems but the Harvard (author–date) version is becoming standard. Wherever you write something which is based on another's work you should reference that original work in a bracket immediately after your statement, giving the author's surname and the date of publication. In the bibliography you should list all your sources alphabetically by author. You also include date of publication, title, publisher and place of publication as shown below.

An example from case study X:

'The discovery of eight flint axes from Creteway Down at Folkestone can be associated with finds of Neolithic date from the same area. (Clarke 1982)'.

The study's bibliography contained the following entry:

Clarke, A. F. (1982) *The Neolithic of Kent – A Review. Archaeology in Kent to AD 1500*, CBA Research Report No 48, pp. 25–30.

There are some variations on the Harvard system in use in different universities, so check with your supervisors exactly which format they want. At A level, the version above is acceptable.

Websites must also be referenced. No standard has yet emerged. You should list full web addresses and what they are in the bibliography. You could number them and use (web1) etc. in the body of the text although some universities may want the full address in the text.

sorted a range of materials and evidence and need a clear idea of the layout and balance of your work before you start writing. A flow diagram is useful.

Your illustrations should add to and explain points raised in your commentary. Avoid the temptation to put your photographs in just because you paid for them! Illustrations are probably best within or close to the text that refers to them. The ability to use a scanner is useful here. Always ensure that there is some annotation of any illustration. Transparent overlays are useful for illustrating distribution and your interpretation of phases. Maps can be traced as the base for these.

Preparing for your Archaeology Examination

YOUR GOALS

You need to

- find out what you will be required to know and do
- organise your notes in order to revise
- ensure that you understand and have examples for all key areas
- train yourself to respond in a way that will be successful.

The key to successful revision is to be proactive. Start early and take charge, don't wait until the last moment. However, it is also possible to spend a long time revising ineffectively. You need to focus from the start on what you actually need to do and to revise actively. The key is to ensure that you understand your subject and can communicate that understanding in the format required by the examiners.

CATALOGUING YOUR PORTFOLIO

Ideally you will have been cataloguing and cross-referencing your notes as you went through your course. If you are like 90 per cent of other students you won't have even thought about this. This should therefore be your first task.

- Start by putting your notes into an order. You may have a course content list supplied. If not, then you could organise your notes chronologically or by theme. The key is to get them organised.
- Now see what you have got. One way of doing this is to write out lists or grids. The latter are preferable because they will enable you to make connections and use the same material in several ways.
- Compare your lists with course or syllabus details. Are there gaps? If there are then your next task will be to copy up notes from a friend or make some from a key text.
- Cross-reference your notes. You may be examined on methods, sources or topics so you need to have flexibility about how you use material. There are several ways of

What do examiners

want to see?   **not want to see?**

| Paragraphs
Clear structure
Argument
Detailed supporting evidence
A range of relevant case studies
Conclusions | Poor spelling
Long descriptions
Irrelevance
Few examples
Woolly sentences, e.g. 'the first
chapter of the human story'. |

Figure 13.1 *What examiners want to see*

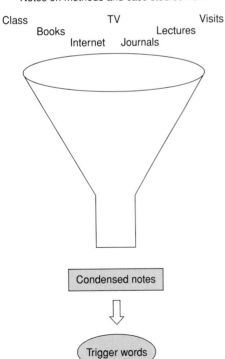

Figure 13.2 (left) *Condense your notes*

doing this such as colour coding, using Post-its or producing grids. A particularly useful way is to use index cards.

Reducing information onto cards

Many student find index cards useful for learning and condensing essential knowledge and to help them apply their understanding. To produce good cards you have to decide what is the essence of each topic, case or method you need to learn. This is a useful discipline in itself as it forces you to consider relevance to exam questions and to be selective. How much you write on each card will depend on your confidence in your ability to remember. Some students go through a process of reducing notes in this way several times until they are left with keywords or phrases. This process in itself helps with revision of knowledge. Because

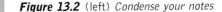

Geophysics *Survey*	**Ancient Monuments and** *Ethics*
	Archaeological Areas Act 1979
Resistivity: Deviation of electrical conduction due to resistivity of ground. Generally due to dampness.	• Consent of Secretary of State is required prior to changes to scheduling
Magnetometers: Deviations in the magnetic field, caused by heating of hearths, kilns, filling in of pits, and solid features.	• RCHME tasked to record, assess, and monitor monuments
Metal Dectectors	• Areas of Archaeological Importance can be designated to delay development pending proper assessment and exc.
Radar and Sonar	
Remote Sensing: Radar, infrared	
Dowsing	

Head-Smashed-in *Kill Site*	**Sweet Track** *Trackway*
Bronze Age >5,500 BP	**Neolithic** 3807/3808 BC
	John and Bryony Coles
• Southern Alberta, Canada	• 1800m to Westhay Island in Somerset Levels
• Blackfoot Indians	• Dendrochronology dating = Europe's oldest road
• 50 hectare animal processing area	• Planning and org. Prefab units. Laid in 1 day by 12
• Plains bison	• Temp track of ash and lime. ST of high quality oak
• Cairns to channel animals	• Maintained 10 years then disuse (warmer climate?)
• Skin-lined boiling pits, drying, fires,	• Jadeite polished axe placed beside track
• Seasonal kill site, feasting and storage	• Pottery vessels, stirring spoon, arrow heads, 2 axe heads

Black Patch *Settlement*	**Star Carr** *Settlement*
Mesolithic 1,300 BC	**Mesolithic**
	JGD Clark (1949–51)
• Sussex Downs (East Sussex)	
• 5 small round house platforms, 7 enclosures	• Platform on swampy lake side. Birch and moss
• Largest: 8m diameter, entrances to SE	• 3–4 families, 20 people
• Storage pits, racks, looms, internal furnishings	• Flint and antler tool making
• Differential functions: Head of family (storage and craft), wife (food preparation), relative 2× animal shelter	• Faunal remains indicate summer occupation
	• People probably based on the coast
• Ethnographic comparisons	• Dogs kept for herding?
• Loom weights, burn flint, flint	
• Hulled barley, emmer, cattle, sheet, pig, deer	

Boxgrove *Kill Site*	**Trade and Exchange** *Economics*
Palaeolithic 470,000 BP	
Michael Pitts and Mark Roberts (1982–)	**Gift Exchange and Reciprocity**
	• *Kula network of Melanasia (Solomon Sea)*
• Tibia and 2 teeth – Britain's earliest hominid	**Redistribution**
• Boxgrove man: Robust, heavily muscled, active, 'cold adapted', 6 foot tall, and right handed.	• Tribute or appropriation
	• Central organisation
• 'Kill' = Horse in GTP17 with neat hole in shoulder blade	• *Knossos, Danebury*
• Butchery marks around eyes and tongue	**Market Exchange**
• Hide curing: Flint scrapers and bone needles	• Internal or port-of-trade
• No evidence of fire or camps and monuments	• *Ancient Greek Agora*

Figure 13.3 *Examples of revision cards. The process of selection involved in making these will help you remember the detail*

you have had to process the information it lodges in your memory much better than if you had just read or underlined notes. The words or phrases themselves will work as prompts and suggest additional material to you.

REVISION ACTIVITIES

Mix and match

This is one of several ways in which you can use the cards you have just made. It can be done individually or turned into a game with other students. Divide case study cards and themes or aspects of themes into two separate piles. Turn over one card from each pile and then try to make a connection, for example Boxgrove and Technology. This can be done with both sites and methods.

Make up mnemonics

Mnemonics are usually made by taking a number of linked words and then trying to make a new word from the first letter of each, for example Trench, Area and Box makes 'Tab'. This can work as a prompt when you need to remember a list of detailed points. It is probably best for methods or 'what can be learned from . . .?' type questions. Use it sparingly. There is a limit to the number you will recall and exams are increasingly about applying understanding rather than remembering lists.

Mindmaps

A creative way to remember connections is to create a visual map of a subject in our minds. This works on the principle that we remember key images better than keywords. Start by placing a major concept, theme, site or method

on a page. Identify four or five main aspects you wish to learn and mark them in bold on lines radiating out from the original word. Next draw something which each word suggests to you at the other end of the line. The more personal your choice of image, the more likely you are to remember. (It doesn't have to be sensible.) From here other connections can radiate out much like a spider diagram. cSee examples on pp. 182 and 237.

Visual reminders

For archaeological methods, visual cues can be useful in revising and checking your understanding. One method is to produce your own sketches such as the examples in Figure 13.4.

Playing games

Many students find that games help them to remember and also encourage them to make links between areas of knowledge. They also break up the revision process. Many popular games can be adapted. These are just two you could try.

Archaeological dominos.
Two archaeological words are put on each domino (card). Deal them out and play in the normal way with the following addition. Each time a player lays down a domino they have to make a connection between the two words.

Blockbusters.
If you draw a hexagonal grid on a piece of acetate (OHT) the task of setting up this game becomes straightforward. The question setter inserts a letter into each hexagon and teams compete to make lines across the 'board', as in the popular television programme. All the clues should come from the syllabus.

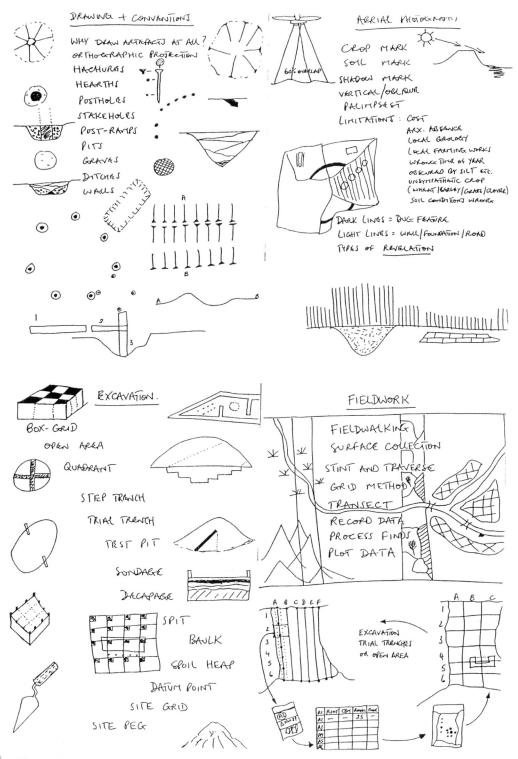

Figure 13.4 *Example of visual cue notes. If you are a visual learner, this may work for you*

TACKLING EXAM PAPERS

Ideally you should have become thoroughly familiar with the format and type of questions used in the exam during your course. Examiners do not try to catch students out and are highly unlikely to change their types of question without warning. The specific questions and any sources used are likely to be new to you but their format and what you are asked to do will be largely familiar. You need to work out what each paper or section wants you to do. To do this you need to look at the command words and the type of markscheme used.

Command words

The way your essays are organised will reflect the command words in the question. For example, for the question, 'Compare the evidence for complex settlement from two areas that you have studied' the command words provide you with a ready-made structure:

> Introduction: define keywords (complex settlement). Identify the two areas and say why you have selected them.

> Region 1 Case study of Oaxcaca Valley Explicit links to command words
>
> Region 2 Case study of Valley of Mexico Explicit links to command words

> Discussion tries to identify common ground and major differences by reference to clearly established criteria such as size, specialisation, planning, etc. Aim for breadth in consideration of similarities and differences. Consider strengths and weaknesses in the evidence base for each region.

> Conclusion: to what extent are there general patterns?

Mark schemes

Mark schemes are increasingly published, so there is little excuse for not looking at them. Short questions which ask you to explain or describe usually reward you with one mark for each point drawn from a source that is linked to the question or for each occasion where you deploy your own knowledge in a relevant way. Most questions worth more than a couple of marks and essays are usually marked to 'levels of response' markschemes where the levels are defined by set criteria. If there are five levels in a 25-mark essay you will not score high marks unless you write to suit the criteria for levels 4 and 5. Shorter structured questions are typical of schemes of assessment for AS level and larger structured questions and essays for A2. Both use levels. The examples of 'levels' markschemes in the Appendix (p. 305) provide the answers to the exercises on pp. 24 and 57. The lower levels are usually for responses that include some relevant material, but do little with it, or a comment with little or no support.

Looking at markschemes and doing practice assignments are obviously essential and you will do this as part of your course. One way of helping yourself is to play the role of examiner. Try setting questions in the style of the exam. Produce a markscheme, write responses and then mark your work. An alternative is to swap questions with a friend. Either way, by putting yourself into this role you will gain insights into what you need to do.

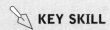 **KEY SKILL**

Understanding command words

All questions contain words or phrases which let you know what the examiner expects of you. It is important that you become familiar with the words and phrases used by archaeology examiners. The list below is roughly ranked in order of difficulty. Words in the top half of the list are usually used only for short or structured questions. Those in the lower half are also used for essays. The marks allocated will provide you with further clues. For example, for two marks the examiners will want a couple of words or sentences, for ten marks at least a paragraph.

Command words	What they mean	Examples
List	Simply write down names or examples.	List three methods of dating.
Describe	Say what something looks like using scales	Describe the feature shown at A.
Define	Give a precise meaning. (An example helps too.)	Define taphonomy.
Illustrate	Provide examples to support a definition or point.	Illustrate your argument.
Explain	Show how something works or give reasons.	Explain how the source of artefact A could be identified.
Outline	Describe with reasons.	Outline how an archaeologist might survey the field at X.
Account for	Explain clearly with supporting reasons.	Account for the lack of surviving evidence of X.
Compare (or Compare and contrast)	Identify similarities and differences.	Compare the sections of pits 23 and 46.
Synthesise (or summarise)	Reorganise materials to create a new version.	Synthesise the data in tables A to D
Analyse	Break down into parts, find patterns and links. Order the factors identified.	Analyse the data provided in tables B and C.
Justify	Give reasons for and provide supporting examples.	Justify your selection of method in question 2a.
What can archaeologists learn from . . .	This is a list type essay but it is not just a list. You have to provide examples and assess	What can be learned about societies in the past from the way they disposed of their dead?
Assess (or discuss)	Identify strengths and weaknesses to reach a judgement.	• Assess the reconstruction drawing in source A. • 'Nucleated villages were a medieval development from the eleventh century onwards.' Discuss.
Evaluate	Assess and reach judgements about the relative value of some items.	Evaluate the evidence for industrial use of the site in source C.
How far (or to what extent)	Present both views, assess and reach a judgement.	• How far can archaeologists be sure about when hominids began hunting animals? • To what extent does archaeology support historial views of the Vikings?

Essay mark schemes

This shows in table form the hierarchy of levels for A Level and the undergraduate essays of two major university departments. Keywords and phrases have been extracted from the whole documents. Where statements sound similar they are shown at the same level.

Grade 25	A Level	Degree Level	Grade /16
		Critical thought and flair. Sound and relevant factual knowledge. Evidence of extensive reading, properly referenced. Logical, balanced and well supported arguments. Written without significant grammatical errors	15 or 73–9% Sound 1st
Level 5 **21–25**	Consistently analytical. Consistent corroboration with relevant detail from a range of contexts. Clear and consistent attempts to reach judgements. Strong communication skills. Strong conceptual understanding. Some evidence of independent thinking	Sound, competent, methodical and comprehensive. Lacking critical flair. Evidence of some reading beyond obvious texts which are referenced. Examples cited where relevant. Well written, without major grammatical errors	12 or 63–65% Solid 2:1
Level 4 **16–20**	Sustained analysis. Range of accurage and relevant supporting material. Covers main issues but may be unbalanced. Attempts to reach a judgement. Little narrative. Effective communication skills		
		Unoriginal and occasionally flawed. Where they are original they lack supporting evidence. Reading has been shallow. May be brief. Argument may be biased and not all may be relevant. May have significant grammatical or structural flaws. If several flaws are present it should be in a lower band	9 or 53–55% sound 2:2
Level 3 **11–15**	Understanding of relevant issues. Generally analytical with some narrative. Focused on the question but unbalanced treatment of it. Argued, but not consistently. Some relevant supporting material. Effective use of language	Not really satisfactory but shows just enough grasp of the subject. May be muddled and poorly argued. Weak and limited evidence with no sign of reading. Sections may be irrelevant. Arguments may be biased or simplistic. May be poorly written and structured	7 or 48–49% Solid 3rd
		Barely acceptable. Weak and shallow arguments. Lack of critical thought. Limited evidence. No reading. Poor English. Often confused or irrelevant although basic facts should be correct	5 or 45–47% Basic 3rd
Level 2 **6–10**	Some understanding of relevant issues. Lacking weight or balance. Relevant descriptions. Some irrelevance or inaccuracy. Some effective use of language		
Level 1 **1–5**	Largely narrative. Outline description. Very generalised. Lacking direction or links to the question. Limited communication skills	Unacceptably brief or muddled and flawed. Often irrelevant, difficult to understand and lacking basic understanding	3 or 30–39% Clear fail

Figure 13.5 *A level and undergraduate mark schemes and how they might relate to each other*

Examination essays

The advice on ▶pp. 190–1 is as relevant to the examination as it is to essays written outside the examination. For essays in any subject the same essential rules apply:

- Accurate factual statements
- well linked to the question
- supported by detailed and relevant case study data
- lead to success.

The examples shown in Figure 13.5 are drawn from A level and undergraduate levels markschemes for essays.

In the exam

Most of you will have taken many exams already. As always the same golden rules apply. In addition, don't forget your ruler and magnifying glass!

Take a watch in and use it. Divide the number of marks into the time available. Allocate time per question and try to stick to it.

Use your time effectively. Read the question paper before you start. Where you have a choice, make sure that you have understood all the questions before you make your choice. Often the longest questions, particularly those with quotations, look harder than they actually are. Try to avoid doing a question just because it contains a keyword you know about, you need to address the whole question.

On essay papers rough out a number of plans at once and add points later in case you forget them. They can save you time but don't spend too long doing this at the expense of the actual essay.

If you finish early there is bound to be something you can improve on. Examiners are looking for:

- *Breadth*: have you considered all the ideas which might be appropriate to the question?
- *Relevance*: have you linked all your points to the command words in the question?
- *Support*: have you produced enough detailed specific evidence to illustrate the points you have made?

And finally . . .

You may have a battery of fluffy toys ready to bring you luck in the exam but sound preparation is a surer way to success. If you have absorbed the lessons in this book you should be able to cope with whatever you are asked. Don't forget that all examination essays will have flaws. No examiner expects perfection and if you have worked throughout your course you should succeed. The following examples give you an idea of the standard at A Level.

EXAMPLES OF MARKED RESPONSES TO EXAM QUESTIONS

These two essays were produced by students who attempted NEAB 1997 A Level Paper 2 under exam conditions. They illustrate common strengths and weaknesses and illustrate the difference between a weak and a reasonably strong answer. In reading them, bear in mind that the students were under pressure and had to write four essays in 3 hours. The examiner's comments are italicised.

What is the evidence for the organisation of production for *one* type of artefact?

This is a 'list type' essay. The question offers the opportunity to bring in all the methods and sources used by archaeologists in investigating one type of artefact you are familiar with from your course of study. Note the word 'one'. Detailed knowledge will be required to do well and a high level answer would compare evidence for different aspects of production.

Pottery has been used to date and research past societies. It provides evidence of social development with specialisation by art and decoration. It is often found in burials which provides clues to its function.

This is not a good start. 'Axel' has not really addressed the question and has interpreted artefact as a type of material, which is not specific enough. It would have been better if he had selected Neolithic bowls or Samian tableware.

Through analysis of the inclusions in the clay, petrology can show the origin of the natural resources and suggest the location of pottery production.

This would be relevant to any ceramic material. A specific example should have been included.

Pottery was first produced in the Neolithic around 4000 BC. Early pottery was very heavy and coarse with round bottoms for example Grimston ware. Its basic shape was probably because there would have been no flat surfaces or tables so the rounded bottom would have prevented tipping on an uneven earth. [Diagram]

Excavations at windmill hill produced finds of Gabroic ware, which had lugs for holding or suspension. Inclusions included basalt which could be sourced to the lizard area of Cornwall. This suggests trade and distribution in the Neolithic. Windmill hill pottery was another tradition of pottery making.

Axel has produced two relevant examples here and linked them to a method and hinted at how distribution might be studied. His diagram (not included here) also had some relevance.

Hearths and deposits of fired clay provides evidence of pottery production. Because it is so durable large quantities are often found on archaeological sites. Even though it is ususally damage, archaeologists can learn a lot from it.

Improvements in technology were accompanied by improved style and methods of decoration. The southern tradition of Peterborough wares included carination. It has been suggested that pots were not just functional items but also decorative. String was knotted and used to decorate pottery. This was called maggotting. Quills or reeds were also used to pierce and inscribe pottery. They may have been used as high prestige items to show a persons status or given as gifts in alliance making.

Much of this is relevant but it is not well focused. Axel should have discussed how archaeologists know how the pots were decorated. He is starting to narrate the development of pottery rather than address the question.

Black burnished ware is distinct and easily recognisable. It was produced in the Poole Harbour area of Dorset. Iron age settlements in Hamworthy have evidence of kiln sites and also at the Roman site at Lake Gales in Wimborne.

Again this is descriptive. It would have been better to discuss what can be learnt about production levels in those settlements.

Pottery continued to be produced and developed as a status item. Samian ware was decorated with a lion's head. It was very fine and produced for decorative use and for people to demonstrate their status. Beaker ware was also very fine. It is usually found often in burial sites which suggests it had a very specific purpose. Beaker ware may have been brought be immigrants or the idea imported from Europe. By the late Bronze Age British 'Beaker' pottery was produced. Both types being identified by thin section analysis of the original material and its inclusions.

This is largely descriptive and not made relevant. It could have been used earlier to illustrate petrology. It is not a conclusion. Overall, Axel has provided some material that is relevant to the question, and some limited examples. There is an attempt to organise the material into paragraphs, but it is not sustained. There is no direction to the essay aside from a loose chronological order. There are also some inaccuracies. While a specific artefact was not identified, much of the material could have been used. However, there was insufficient focus on methods. It is a high level 2 answer and scored a borderline 10/25.

'A sedentary way of life is necessary for storage practices' Discuss.

This is a discursive type essay on a settlement and economic topic. It is more demanding conceptually than the previous question and so a lesser depth of knowledge might be required.

It also requires you to reach a judgement in response to the statement in the question. It offers the opportunity to draw on examples across your course.

There is great variation in both storage methods and the substances which are stored. Food, wealth and other resources can all be stored to extend their availability and thus help in time of hardship or shortage. Storage is also an economic strategy. A sedentary way of life in fact makes storage practices necessary because people can no longer follow the seasons and forage for wild foods.

Even in the Palaeolithic and Mesolithic periods when a mobile, hunter-gatherer society is generally regarded as having existed there is evidence of storage. At the cave at Pontnewydd in Gwynedd animal bones have been discovered in recesses contemporary with occupation layers which suggests the cave had been used to deposit animal 'joints'.

'Zia' has not begun her response by defining the terms but it is clear that she has understood them. She has confidently provided an example that challenges the statement in the question.

Star Carr, which was excavated by Graham Clarke in 1949, was dated to the Mesolithic around 7000 BC. Like a number of other sites it seems to have been used as a seasonal base during the winter months. People seem to have used locations on estuaries, rivers and the coasts. At some there is evidence of tree clearing to provide grazing for red deer and to make hunting easier. This manipulation Of nature suggests a move towards storage. These mobile groups could not take much with them as they moved. Their choice of tools, personal jewellery, their dogs and possibly tent frames represents a storing of potentially useful material or curation. They may have used perishable forms of storage such as wicker or birch bark containers to carry or store thins such as honeycomb.

Not all relevant. More could have been made of the nature of evidence for this type of storage and whether absence of evidence means absence.

Palaeolithic people may have benefited from natural storage of mammoths in glaciers but the first type of storage the used was probably smoking. Stakeholes on some sites have been interpreted and drying or smoking racks. Salt may have also been used, but the early hard evidence usually comes from settled communities. Briquetage found in the Iron Age provides evidence of widespread use.

Zia is making up for a lack of specific knowledge with some generalised examples here. They are all relevant.

At Danbury and other hill forts from the Iron Age storage is seen in the large pits and the 'four poster' structures. Pits up to 20 feet deep and 7 feet across were dug down into the bedrock. Apparently they were used for grain although ritual purposes have also been suggested. Some pits provided enough grain to keep a large population fed for a year. In the pits the outer layers of grain decay giving off carbon dioxide which preserves the remaining grain by inhibiting bacteria. 'Four posters' are identified by four postholes in a square pattern. They are generally interpreted as granaries but may have had some other use such as chicken coops. This storage was only appropriate because of the agricultural surplus produced by large numbers of sedentary farmers. It provided them with insurance against the vagaries of the weather meant that time spent in travelling

from one site to another could be used in production of foodstuffs.

A very relevant example with some depth of knowledge. There is a clear attempt to relate it to the question although not all the paragraph is relevant or accurate. She will not be penalised for this, but she has wasted a little time in writing it.

Earliest agricultural people in the early Neolithic also began to 'store' their dead. 'The mixed up remains in tombs and long barrows represent a form of macabre storage. Again this is linked to sedentism. A further type of storage is evident in individual burials during the Bronze Age. Personal ornamentation was a reflection of wealth and being kept on the person meant it could be safeguarded. People in earlier mobile societies did not seem to accumulate such wealth.

Zia raises two good points here. While she could be criticised for not knowing about alternative theories and evidence she will not be penalised. Many centres lack recent texts and this would not be fair. She is thinking laterally about storage and would gain credit even though points are underdeveloped.

Today coinage is the most recognisable form of storage of wealth. Coins appeared late in prehistory and like jewellery are easily transportable and concealed. They are not an encumbrance to mobility in the same way that herds of cattle might be.

This relevant, general point represents a lost opportunity. She could have discussed social storage and the contradictory idea of very mobile forms of storage developed in sedentary societies.

Mobile populations require small-scale storage of light and easily transportable products. Larger scale storage of bulky items are more appropriate to sedentary populations. 'Sedentary' and 'storage' are usually linked because if a group stores a high percentage of the wealth or resources in one place and then leaves them unattended for long periods the stored items are very likely to be exploited or damaged by other third parties be they animals or human. If you store a great deal you need to be sedentary.

The conclusion addressed the question and attempted to reach a judgement, which qualifies the initial statement.

Virtually all the essay was relevant, analytical and well focused. Zia demonstrated the ability to think widely about the concepts involved and structured her paragraphs in a logical way. She was low on examples and some sections were flawed, but there was still enough here to reach the bottom of band 4 and a mark of 16/25.

Chapter 14

Where to Next?

Studying Archaeology in the UK

BELOW UNIVERSITY LEVEL

There are plenty of opportunities to study archaeology although the range of qualifications is relatively small. To get further information on any of them either contact your local institution or the Council for British Archaeology (CBA) Education service.

 http://www.britarch.ac.uk/educate/ed1.html

Short courses are offered by Colleges of Further Education (FE) and the Workers Educational Association (WEA). Typically these will be 2 hours a week for ten weeks and are generally aimed at adults. Increasingly, colleges will offer an Open College Network (OCN) certificate for these courses.

Day schools or conferences are offered by university departments, FE colleges, local and national archaeological organisations and museums. Many of these involve lectures at university level although some are practically based. The two key sources on these are *Current Archaeology* (*CA*) and *British Archaeology* (*BA*) magazines.

Field schools, or training digs, are offered by universities and some local organisations in the summer. Details are advertised in *CA* and *BA* magazines.

GCSE Archaeology

This is offered by AQA.

 www.aqa.org.uk/

Students study archaeological methods and one period of British archaeology from prehistory to post-medieval. There is an exam on each section which follows a standard format. Paper 1 involves interpretation of a map and aerial photograph followed by a series of short questions on a range of methods. Paper 2 has a choice of several illustrations of sites or artefacts, each with a number of short questions. There is also a short piece of coursework. GCSE is largely offered by FE colleges and a few schools.

AS and A Level Archaeology

These are also offered by AQA. The AS can be taken separately or as the first stage of an A Level. Each exam is broken down into three sections or modules. Five of these sections are examinations which each last between one and one and a half hours.

AS Level (first half of A Level)

> *AS1*
> Finding and excavating archaeological sites
>
> *AS2*
> Post-excavation analysis, dating, interpretation and presentation
>
> *AS3*
> Religion and ritual
> One from: Later British and Irish Prehistory, Roman Britain, Ancient Egypt, The Maya

AS level examinations consist of short questions focused on a series of sources. For AS1 and 2 you will have to interpret the sources, for AS3 the sources are largely there as a stimulus.

A2 (second half of A Level)

> *A4*
> Settlement and society
> A thematic approach with no prescribed content
>
> *A5*
> Material culture and economics
> A thematic approach with no prescribed content
>
> *A6*
> Coursework. A personal investigation. ▶See Chapter 12

A4 and A5 each have a stimulus-based question and a choice of essays. They can be approached through the study of any period.

AS and A Level are offered in some FE colleges and schools. To find your nearest centre, contact the AQA or CBA.

There are also some elements of archaeology in the Classical Civilisation A Level offered by OCR and in the Advanced Vocational Level Travel and Tourism Course.

Access to higher education

These are general courses aimed at adults returning to education and offered in FE colleges. A few of these offer archaeology as an option in their courses.

AT UNIVERSITY

Most courses are offered at degree level although there has been an increase in the number of sub-degree programmes on offer such as HNC and HND. Some of these are focused on practical archaeology. While degrees almost always involve study at university, some universities, notably Bournemouth, have franchised sub-degree programmes to FE colleges.

At degree level there is considerable variety. You can study archaeology as a BA or a BSc, or in Scotland for four years for an MA. Detailed information can be obtained from the CBA or from the 45 institutions offering elements of archaeology in various degrees. Archaeology can be studied on its own, in combination or as part of other subjects. The information here largely applies to where it can be studied as a single subject. All courses will include elements on the development of archaeology, its methods and techniques, as well as the theory used to make sense of archaeological evidence. Beyond that they will vary considerably in their choice of topics.

In considering university courses you may want to give thought to the following:

- Is the course thematic or period based?
- Which periods can I study?
- Does the assessment pattern suit me? Is it continuous assessment or final exam based?
- What is the department strong in (for example science at Bradford, prehistory at Sheffield)?
- Does it have a practical or heritage element (for example Bournemouth)?
- What kinds of placements and excavation opportunities are on offer?

- How is it rated?
- Am I likely to get the qualifications to get an offer?
- Do I need previous experience? (You should try and get some practical experience)

Market forces

Some courses have more applicants than others. They normally deal with this by asking higher grades from prospective students. If you are a standard A level student you simply have to get the grades. If you have any other educational background it is worth contacting the department directly for advice before making your application. Many are particularly keen on mature students, even if they haven't got A levels.

League tables

Universities are ranked on research and teaching. A good research record may tell you that the university has published good research or that it has a lot of researchers. You may not actually be taught by the key researchers. There also appears to be a bias towards larger departments in the way the tables are calculated. Bournemouth University in particular seems to have suffered in this respect despite producing important national research such as the MARS report. Teaching tables may reflect the quality of lecturing. One has to be a little careful interpreting these. Unlike GCSE and A Level there is no systematic comparison of the quality of degrees from different universities. A 2:1 from one institution may or may not be as good as a 2:1 from another.

Figure 14.1 *Although it is sometimes difficult to arrange, you should try to get some practical experience of archaeology prior to applying or going to university*

Figure 14.2 summarises recent government assessments and information on A Level grades asked for. It also lists some of the specialisms

University	Main degrees	Major specialist areas	Teaching grade	Research grade	Entry points
Queens, Belfast	Arch. Archaeology—Palaeoecology BA or BSc	Science, Prehistory		5	20
Birmingham	Ancient Hist and Arch.	Forensic		4	24
Bournemouth	Arch. BSc	Heritage Management		3b	14—16
Bradford	Arch. BSc	Science		5	20
Bristol	Arch	Classical		5	22
Cambridge	Arch and Anthropology	Theoretical, Early Medieval		5*	30
Kent, Canterbury	Classical and Arch Studies				
Wales, Cardiff	Arch	European Prehistory, Conserv	E	4	20
Trinity Coll, Carmarthen	Arch Heritage Conservation			3b	10
Durham	Arch BA and BSc	Prehistoric, Roman, Early Medieval		5	20—22
Edinburgh	Arch Environmental Arch MA	Prehistory and classical		4	22
Exeter	Arch	Wetlands, Western Europe		3a	22
Glasgow	Arch MA and BSc			4	22
Wales, Lampeter	Arch	Landscape	E	3a	16—18
Leicester	Arch BA and BSc	Urban, Museum, Local		5	20
Liverpool	Arch BA and BSc Egyptology			4	20
London, SOAS	History of Art and Arch	World archaeology			22
London, University Coll.	Arch BA and BSc Egyptology	World archaeology		5	22
Manchester	Arch	Classical			24
Nottingham	Arch	Prehistory, Roman or Medieval		3a	20
Newcastle	Arch	Practical		3b	20
Wales, Newport	Arch Prehistory and Arch	Prehistory		3b	
Oxford	Arch and Anthropology			5*	28
Reading	Arch	Prehistory and Roman		5	22
Sheffield	Arch and Prehistory, Arch Science	Prehistory, World		5*	22
Southampton	Arch	Prehistory, Maritime		5	20
King Alfred s Coll., Winchester	Arch BA and BSc	Heritage Management		2	14
York	Arch BA and BSc	Medieval		4	22

Ranking is based on the teaching quality then research column according to government inspection in 1998.
On research, Archaeology departments as a whole were ranked very highly (5th of all subjects).

The grades indicate the following standards:
5* = International excellence in most areas
4 = National excellence in virtually all areas
3a = National excellence in a majority of areas

5 = International excellence in some areas
3b = National excellence in the large majority of area
2 = National excellence in up to half areas

Quality of teaching is rated as follows:
E = excellent. S= Satisfactory, U = unsatisfactory

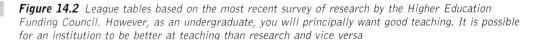

Figure 14.2 *League tables based on the most recent survey of research by the Higher Education Funding Council. However, as an undergraduate, you will principally want good teaching. It is possible for an institution to be better at teaching than research and vice versa*

on offer but is not intended to be comprehensive. With over 100 different possibilities for joint or part honours courses in archaeology, there are many other opportunities to study archaeology in other university departments. Examples include Pre-Columbian Art and Architecture at Essex, Maritime Studies at St Andrews or Wetland Archaeology at Hull.

STEPPING UP TO DEGREE LEVEL

If you have studied A Level Archaeology, you may find that there is not much of an initial step up. You may even find that you have less to do at first. As with most subjects there is considerable overlap between A Levels and many first year undergraduate programmes. It is worth considering this in your choice of programme. It may be a good idea to select new topics or periods from those you did at A Level to broaden your knowledge and maintain your interest. If you have chosen a course with a practical scientific or statistical element you may find this new. Although you will generally get support at the university, these are areas you should prepare for if you haven't done them for a while.

University lecturers and undergraduates have identified the following areas as different from A Level or where students sometimes struggle:

- Working more independently or in groups
- Making oral presentations (including papers) in an interesting way
- Coping with theoretical concepts
- Adjusting to the idea that knowledge is always the product of interpretation
- Coping with maths and science elements
- Coping with wide chronological and geographical ranges
- Adjusting to the precision required in excavation
- Using academic libraries, journals and texts
- Writing essays in an academic style (▶see pp. 190–1)
- Using academic referencing from books, journals and web pages in assignments (▶see p. 282)

Chapter 15

Finding the Best Information

There are so many excellent sites, museums and written and electronic resources available to archaeology students that we can only list a fraction of those available. Since selection has to be subjective we have included those resources that we have found most useful and which our students have made most use of. Although we have tried to provide a good range within it, our choice is clearly biased towards our own interests. Another person's list would undoubtedly look very different. Other sources, which provide additional depth on topics contained in the text, are listed in the bibliography.

TWENTY VERY USEFUL BOOKS

We have divided this section into four. The focus is largely on Britain and Europe and full details of each text are in the bibliography. Make sure your school or college buys a copy of these books.

General texts

■ Ashmore, W. and Sharer, R. (1995) *Discovering our Past*. A good text for the visual reader, with diagrams well used to illustrate methods and thinking.

■ Fagin, B. (1994) *In the Beginning*. A detailed introduction to archaeology from an American perspective.
■ Greene, K. (1995) *Archaeology: An introduction*. This has good coverage of reconnaissance, excavation and post-excavation techniques. There is a very useful web link to case studies at http://www.staff.ncl.ac.uk/kevin.greene/wintro/
■ Orme, B. (1981) *Anthropology for Archaeologists*. A great little text for getting you to think outside European assumptions.
■ Renfrew, C. and Bahn, P. (1991) *Archaeology: Theories, methods and practice*. This has become *the* encyclopadia of cases studies for a generation of archaeology students.

Archaeological sources and methods

■ Coles, J. and Lawson, A. (eds) (1987) *European Wetlands in Prehistory*. Provides an excellent insight into differential preservation and the value of wet sites.
■ Drewett, P. (1999) *Field Archaeology*. For detailed coverage and clear explanations of methods.

- Muir, R. (1981) *Reading the Landscape*. A book to open your eyes to evidence of past activity embedded in the countryside.
- Schick, K. and Toth, N. (1993) *Making Silent Stones Speak*. Good on the use of experimental archaeology in investigating early hominid activity in Africa.
- Wass, S. (1999) *The Amateur Archaeologist*. A good aid for project work.

Period studies

- Cunliffe, B. (ed.) (1994) *The Oxford Illustrated Prehistory of Europe*. Well illustrated and authoritative.
- Hunter, J. and Ralston, I. (eds) (1999) *The Archaeology of Britain*. Contains an excellent introduction to each period of British archaeology since the Upper Palaeolithic.
- Parker-Pearson, M. (1993) *Bronze Age Britain*. A very accessible and well-illustrated introduction to the Neolithic and Bronze Age.
- Welch, M. (1992) *Anglo-Saxon England*. A good introduction to the post-Roman period with good sections on buildings and burials.
- Wenke, R. (1999) *Patterns in Prehistory*. An overview of the majority of human history from a world perspective.

Archaeological themes

- Binford, L. (1983) *In Pursuit of the Past*. The introduction to understanding the formation of the archaeological record.
- Bradley, R. (1984) *The Social Foundations of Prehistoric Britain*. A ground-breaking book which looks at how patterns in the archaeological record can be used to reveal the social and ritual nature of past societies.

- Fagin, B. (1995) *Time Detectives*. A very readable series of case studies including several mentioned in this text.
- Parker-Pearson, M. (1999) *The Archaeology of Death and Burial*. Wide-ranging and drawing on ethnography to examine past beliefs and practices.
- Sherrett, A. (1997) *Economy and Society in Prehistoric Europe*. A stimulating series of essays on topics as diverse as horses and alcohol.

To look at reviews of archaeological texts, try the Time Team guide at http://www.btinternet.com/~johnandsandy.colby/ttbook/index.html

ARCHAEOLOGY BOOKSELLERS

There are often only limited ranges of archaeological texts in general bookshops. If you know what you want but can't get it, try these two specialist companies:

- Castle Books: http://dspace.dial.pipex.com/town/square/fe63/index.htm
- Oxbow Books: http://www.oxbowbooks.com/

JOURNALS

In most subjects you would be unlikely to look at journals before university level. However, in archaeology it should be different. The first in this list are all very accessible and are often beautifully illustrated. The remainder are useful sources of case studies. Many good case studies only appear in journals.

British Archaeology (BA): http://www.britarch.ac.uk
Current Archaeology (CA): http://www.archaeology.co.uk/

Scientific American:
http://www.amsci.org/amsci/amsci.html

Antiquity: http://intarch.ac.uk/antiquity/
Assemblage: http://www.shef.ac.uk/~assem/
Internet Archaeology:
http://www.intarch.ac.uk/
Proceedings of the Prehistoric Society:
http://www.britarch.ac.uk/prehist/

GATEWAY WEBSITES

We have listed websites throughout the book where they provide more information on methods and case studies. To find other information you should head for one of the many archaeology gateway sites. Each of these will provide you with a huge number of links. You should be able to find something on almost everything you are looking for. We usually do.

World Archaeology:
http://archnet.uconn.edu/
http://www.discoveringarchaeology.com/
http://www.staff.ncl.ac.uk/kevin.greene/
wintro/

Europe: http://odur.let.rug.nl/arge/
http://www.discoveryprogramme.ie/

Britain: http://www.archaeology.co.uk/
http://www.britarch.ac.uk/info/uklinks.html
http://www.bbc.co.uk/history/ancient/
archaeology/

Key national sites

Cadw: http://www.cadw.wales.gov.uk/
Council for British Archaeology: http://www.
britarch.ac.uk/
English Heritage: http://www.english-heritage.
org.uk/

Historic Scotland: http://www.historic-
scotland.gov.uk/
Rescue: http://www.rescue-archaeology.
freeserve.co.uk/

PLACES TO VISIT

We have tried to ensure some regional coverage with our suggestions although there is inevitably a bias towards those which we have used and found useful.

Twenty museums to visit

There are two good websites which list many of Britain's museums although some of the smaller ones do not seem to be online yet:

- ■ http://www.mda.org.uk/vlmp/
- ■ http://www.museums.co.uk/

1 Ashmolean Museum, Oxford
2 British Museum, London:
   http://www.thebritishmuseum.ac.uk/
3 Devizes Museum (Neolithic-Bronze
   Age)
4 Ipswich Museum (Anglo-Saxon)
5 Keiller Museum, Avebury (Neolithic-
   Bronze Age)
6 Museum of the Iron Age (Danebury),
   Andover
7 Museum of Archaeology and
   Anthropology, Cambridge
8 Museum of London
9 Museum of Wales, Cardiff:
   http://www.nmgw.ac.uk/
10 National Museum of Scotland, Edinburgh
11 Newcastle University Museum (Roman)
12 Petrie Museum, London (Egypt):
   http://www.petrie.ucl.ac.uk/intro.html
13 Pitt Rivers Museum, Oxford
   (anthropology): http://units.ox.ac.uk/
   departments/prm/

14 Salisbury Museum (Neolithic-Bronze Age)
15 Jewry Wall, Leicester
16 Lincoln Museum
17 Corinium, Cirencester (Roman)
18 St Albans (Roman)
19 Manchester (Egyptian)
20 Tullie House, Carlisle

Recreations and experimental sites

- Butser Ancient Farm, nr Petersfield
- Peat Moors Visitor Centre, nr Glastonbury
- West Stow Anglo-Saxon village, nr Bury St Edmunds
- Flag Fen, Peterborough
- Jorvik Centre, York
- St Fagins, Newport
- Weald and Downland Museum: http://www.wealddown.co.uk/
- Ironbridge Gorge, Telford

Visits to archaeological monuments

Where possible, several are grouped together to make a useful day out.

- Avebury–Keiller Museum–West Kennet–Windmill Hill
- Stonehenge–Durrington–Winterborne Stoke
- Arbor Low–Stanton Moor–Cresswell Crags, Derbyshire
- Grimes Graves, Brandon–West Stow
- Hadrian's Wall–Vindolanda–Housesteads
- Chedworth–Corinium Museum–Great Witcombe
- Fishbourne Palace–Butser
- Maes Howe–Ring of Brodgar–Stones of Stenness
- Maiden Castle–Dorchester Museum–Cerne Abbas Giant
- Mary Rose, Portsmouth: http://www. maryrose.org/
- Wharram Percy–Fountains Abbey

Answers and Mark Schemes

Key task: test your understanding of physics (p. 18)

Resistivity area survey best for 2, 3, 4, 6, 8; also useful for 5, 9, 10.

Magnetometry area survey best for 1, 9, 5, 6, 10; also useful for 3, 4, 8.

Neither useful for 7.

Key skill: short questions test (p. 24)

1a Cropmarks (1 mk) circular enclosures or barrows (1 mk).

1b L1   Differential colour or tone due to buried features (1–2 mks).
L2   L1 plus explanation of effect of differential access to water by crops (3–4 mks).
L3   L2 plus comment on possible type of crops and season (4–5 mk).

1c L1   Answers in list form or descriptive account of limited relevance (1–2 mks).
L2   At least one relevant method described. Top end for relation to this site (3–5 mks).
L3   Several relevant methods considered with consideration of appropriateness at top end (6–7 mks).

Key task: test your understanding of methods (p. 57)

1a Cropmarks (1mk), reason for cropmarks (1 mk).

1b L1   Answers that describe the differences or provide a brief list (1–2 mks).
L2   One or two points of contrast explained (3–4 mks).
L3   Several points of contrast explained. For example, greater definition from the excavation, only partially excavated, some marks may not be archaeological (5–6 mks).

1c L1   Generalised comments about excavation or evidence. Descriptions (1–2 mks).
L2   Focus on phasing with some mention of dating or stratigraphy (3–4 mks).
L3   Both stratigraphy and dating discussed (5–6 mks).
L4   L3 in detail, for example how exactly might a layer be identified and relatively dated (7–8 mks).

Key task: test your grasp of dating methods (p. 92)

Spear (C14), shells (ESR, AAR, C14), seeds (C14), burnt flint (TL), mudbricks (archaeo-magnetism, TL), Saxon bones (C14), kiln (archaeomagnetism), cave bones (uranium series or ESR for the calcite deposits), figurine (typology, TL, archaeomagnetism), boat timber (dendro, C14).

Glossary of Terms and Abbreviations

This list does not pretend to be precise in an academic sense. It is intended to give you a simple definition of words that may be new to you so that you can comprehend the sources you come into contact with. For greater sophistication you should use an archaeological dictionary. Every subject has a lexicon of acronyms and abbreviations. Archaeology (arx) is no different. The glossary contains those, which you are most likely to come across, and with which you should familiarise yourself.

Absolute dating: Giving the age of something according to a calendar or historic scale, e.g. BC, AD, BP. This is also referred to a chronometric dating

Accelerator mass spectrometry (AMS): An advanced radiocarbon dating method which can work for tiny samples

Achieved status: Position or prestige in society earned through one's own efforts or qualities

Aerial survey: Locating and defining archaeological sites from the air. Photographing cropmarks and parchmarks during drought conditions usually produces the best results

Anaerobic conditions: Where there is insufficient oxygen for the bacteria, which normally break down organic matierals to thrive, for example waterlogged sites

Analogy: Interpreting something with reference to something else. For example, 'it is similar to X'

Animism: Belief in spirits

Anthropology: The study of humans. It has many subdivisions including Archaeology and Ethnography

Arable: Growing crops

Archaeological record: What survives in the ground before excavation or the records produced by archaeologists after the whole excavation and analysis process

Archaeology: The study of physical remains to help understand the behaviour of people in the past

Archaeometry: The application of scientific analysis to archaeological materials.

Artefacts: Can refer to anything made or modified by humans. Tends to be used most frequently for tools.

Ascribed status: Position or prestige in society due to inheritance

Assemblage: Artefacts from a particular period which typically appear together. Also used to describe a collection of materials, for example animal bones from a particular site

Atomic absorption spectrometry (AMS): Measuring light energy emitted by different elements. Different combinations provide different spectra

Attribute: A quality of an artefact which allows it to be grouped with others, for example colour, texture

Attritional bone profile: A table plotting the age and sex of animal bones which suggests that younger and old members of herds were killed. It suggests scavenging or selective hunting by humans or other predators

Augering: Using a drill to take a core through deposits in the ground

Band: A hunting and gathering based society with groups of under 100 people

Bigman: A non-hereditary position of status in some small-scale parties gained through the ability to amass and distribute resources – often through feasts.

BP: Before present (actually 1950). Absolute dating used for periods in the past where historical dates (BC and AD) are irrelevant, for example the Palaeolithic.

Cache: A store of food or artefacts

Calibration: Using one method to correct inaccuracies in another, for example using

calendar dates from tree ring sequeces to calibrate raw radiocarbon dates

Catastrophic profile: A table plotting the age and sex of animal bones which shows the natural distribution of animals in a herd. It suggests a natural disaster or unselective slaughter

Central place theory: A geographic model developed by Christaller, which predicts that central places would develop at regular spaced in an ideal landscape

Characterisation: Identifying the origins of materials from their physical characteristics

Chiefdom: A ranked society with the inherited or elected role of chief at the top. Likely to have some specialisation in crafts and types of building

Clan: A system of social organisation based on blood and marriage ties

Context: The position of an artefact, the layer of soil it was found in and other artefacts found with it

Coppicing: Repeatedly cutting trees back to a stump in order to encourage them to grow long straight poles which can then be harvested

Coprolites: Preserved faeces

Core: A prepared lump of stone from which tools can be made

Coring: Driving a hollow tube into the ground to get a stratigraphic sample of the subsoil

Cropmarks: Variations in the tone or colour of crops due to underlying archaeological features

Curation: Deliberatrely preserving artefacts, for example jewellery or weapons. This can result in artefacts from an early period being discovered 'out of sequence' on a later site

Cursus: Linear monuments, sometimes several kilometres long, constructed in the Neolithic period

Debitage: Waste from the manufacture of stone tools

Dendrochronology: Tree ring dating

Depositional processes: The various means by which archaeological material becomes buried

Desktop study: An office based search of historical and existing archaeological records about a site

DHA: Direct historical approach. Using oral evidence and studies of a modern population to form hypotheses about an earlier culture in the same region

Diachronic change: Gradual change over a period of time

Disarticulated: Bones that are mixed up, no longer in the right places

Distribution patterns: Plots of archaeological finds either on a site or across a region which are analysed to determine the behaviour that caused them

DNA: Deoxyribonucleic acid. The material that makes up genes and determines the nature of living things

Earthworks: Literally a series of 'humps and bumps' on the surface that indicate the buried remains of buildings, boundaries and field systems

Ecofacts: Natural material that is of archaeological interest. It could include human remains, food waste or environmental material such as pollen or snails. Not artefacts

Entoptic: Internally produced. For example, entoptic images are generated by the brain itself rather than reflecting what has been seen

Ethnicity: Identity of different groups based on their distinctive cultures

Ethnoarchaeology: Studying modern groups of people to understand the behaviour that leads to particular patterns of deposition

Ethnography: Observation based study of modern social groups

Excarnation: Defleshing a corpse in some way as part of mortuary ritual

Exchange: Not just trade, but any interaction where something passes between people. It could include information, gifts or money

Fall-off analysis: measuring the rate at which the number of particular artefacts decline as the distance from their source increases. It is used to diagnose particular modes of exchange

Faunal dating: Relative dating based on the evolutionary sequence in which mammals have developed

Feature: Non-portable archaeological remain such as aspects of a site for example posthole, hearth

Fieldwalking: Systematically searching ploughed fields for the remains of artefacts and buildings to detect likely settlement areas

Foragers: Groups subsisting on wild foods. Plant foods are usually the most important

Formation processes: How archaeological material came to be created, buried and transformed to create the archaeological record

Funerary rites: Events to mark the final rite of passage of a person. Overlaps with, but is not the same as, *mortuary practice*

Glyphs: Reliefs of figures or signs carved on stoen. Usually Mesoamerican

Geochemical survey: Using techniques derived from chemistry to detect traces of past activity from soil samples. See phosphate analysis

Geophysical survey: Using techniques derived from physics to detect remains under the ground. See resistivity and magnetometry.

GIS: Geographical Information Systems: linked maps and databases

GPS: Global Positioning System. A handheld device for locating your position using satellites

Hoards: Deliberately buried artefacts. May have been placed in earth or water for security, as offerings etc.

Horticulture: Encouraging particular plants to grow, for example by weeding round them. Used to identify a stage in food production before agriculture

Horticulturalist: Groups subsisting largely on plant foods, some of which they may plant. May be mobile and not using permanent fields

Hunter-gatherers: Groups subsisting on a mixture of wild animal and plant foods. May be mobile

Iconography: Art that may have a religious meaning

Inclusions: Material added to clay to provide strength and improve the firing process. Also known as temper

Inhumation: Burial

Intensification: Increasing production. Usually applied to food production but can apply to extraction or manufacture

Isotopic analysis: Studying bone to identify the signature of different types of food for example seafood

Kin: Relatives through blood and marriage

Liminal: Something on the edge of normal society. May be a boundary or a group of people. May be seen as dangerous and likely to require ritual to deal with it

Lineage: A group sharing the same ancestor

Lithics: Stone tools

Magnetometry: Detecting buried remains through magnetic variations between them and the surrounding soil

Market exchange: A system of exchange where producers compete in terms of prices. It is often associated with money or bartering and particular exchange sites, for example shops or markets

Material culture: The total physical remains of a former society including artefacts, buildings, etc.

Matrix: The type of soil or other material in which an artefact is found

Mesolithic: A label given to the period from the end of the last Ice Age until the development of farming. Sometimes used to refer to groups living by hunting and gathering. In Britain dates range from around 8000 BC

Metallography: Studying the composition and structure of metals

Micro-contour survey: A detailed survey using accurate sensitive equipment to reveal subtle variations in the ground surface to reveal the plan of buried sites.

Microliths: Tiny stone or flint blades. Associated with the Mesolithic period

Middens: A rubbish tip. In some periods may have had other functions including a source of fertiliser and a ritual site

MNI: Minimum number of individuals. The smallest number of animals that could have produced the bones in an assemblage

Moiety: Organisation of society based on the idea of two different subgroups

Monotheistic: Belief in one god

Mortuary practice: Ritual activity and preparation involving the disposal of a corpse

Neolithic: This label used to describe the period of the first farmers, before the use of metal tools. Increasingly it is used to describe the process of domestication including changing ideas about the world (▶see p. 207). British dates range from around 4500 BC

Neutron activation analysis (NAA): Highly sensitive analysis of trace elements undertaken within a reactor

NISP: Number of identified specimens. A count of all the bones of each species in an assemblage.

NMR: National Monuments Record

Obsidian: Volcanic glass that can be worked to produce hard, sharp edges

Organic residue analysis: Using chemicals to extract and identify traces of plant and animal materials from pottery

Ossuary: A place in which the bones of the dead are stored, for example a charnel house

Palaeolithic: The first archaeological period. Before 8000 BC but subdivided into Lower, Middle and Upper on the basis of stone technology

Palimpsest: A collection of archaeological artefacts, ecofacts and material that may not be related. For example, they are together through accident or natural forces rather than human activity. Also used for a site with a mass of inter-cut features of different periods

Palynology: Studying pollen for dating and environmental reconstruction

Pastoralists: People who subsist largely from the animals they herd. May be mobile

Petrology: Studying the minerals in archaeological material to identify their source of origin

Phosphate analysis: Analysing soil samples to detect high phosphate which can indicate human or animal habitation

Pollen dating: Using local pollen sequences to provide a relative date for a site

Polytheistic: Belief in many gods

Prestige goods chain: Where valuable items are exchanged between high status individuals, often over a considerable area

Primary products: The material gained by killing an animal, for example meat, skin

Probing: Using metal rods to detect walls and other buried features close to the surface

Propitiation: Offerings to gods, for example offerings in pits or deposited in water

Radiocarbon dating (RC): Absolute dating technique based on the known rate of decay of Carbon 14

Reciprocity: Exchange between social equals. Balanced reciprocity implies things of equal value are exchanged

Redistribution: A form of exchange where goods are collected by a central authority and then given to other people or places

Regression: Using clues from the earliest known maps and documents from an area and projecting them back in time to produce a picture of an earlier period

Relative dating: Determining where a site or artefact sits in a sequence in relation to other sites or artefacts

Remote sensing: Detecting archaeological remains from above the surface of the earth, usually from a satellite

Resistivity: Detecting buried remains through differences between them and the surrounding soil in their ability to carry an electrical current

Rites of intensification: Ritual to mark times of change or danger

Rites of passage: Ritual to mark events in the lives of individuals

Sampling: The careful selection of areas to investigate or materials to analyse. Usually based on mathematical probability to ensure that what is selected is representative of wider evidence (▶see p. 11)

Secondary products: Materials gained from animals without killing them, for example milk, wool

Sedentary: Where a group is settled, that is staying in one place. Semi-sedentary groups stay for considerable periods, perhaps moving between sites on a seasonal basis

Segmentary society: Small, relatively self-contained social groups who may sometimes combine with similar groups to form wider alliances

SEM: Scanning electron microscope

Shadow sites: Sites that survive as low earthworks and are seen from the air in conditions of low sunlight

Shaman: Individual who can communicate with, and often interact with, spirits

Shovel pit testing: An alternative to fieldwalking for woods, pasture and gardens. Samples of soil from carefully selected test pits are sieved for artefacts

Signature: Traces in the archaeological record that can be linked to particular patterns of activity

Site: A place where human activity has taken place

Site catchment analysis: Reconstructing the available natural resources within easy reach of an archaeological site to help construct a model of its economy and the diet of its people

SMR: Sites and Monuments Record (p. 6)

Social storage: When an individual gives something of value to another individual, creating an obligation on the part of the second person to return something at a later date. What is exchanged can vary enormously from an exotic gift to a meal, from military service to a bride.

Soil marks: Variations in the tone or colour of ploughed soil due to the destruction of buried features

Sonar: Form of underwater detection based on sound waves

Specialisation: This term can be used in several ways. Economic specialisation can be used to describe a group who rely on one primary means of supporting themselves, for example pastoralists. It can also mean a division of labour where different individuals perform particular tasks rather than working in similar ways, for example miners, iron smelters and smiths in the production of iron tools

State: Society with a territory, central authority and permanent institutions

Stelae: Carved stone pillars or statues

Stratification: A series of layers, strata or deposits laid down over time. Stratigraphy is the analysis of stratification or its use in relative dating

Structured deposition: Material entering the archaeological record through specific (possibly ritual) activities or behaviour patterns (not random). For example, particular animal bones being placed in ditches

Superposition: The principle that in undisturbed stratification, the oldest layer in the sequence is at the bottom

Surface collection: American version of fieldwalking. It can usefully be applied to the systematic recovery of artefacts from places other than fields

Surface survey: Examining the landscape for evidence of underlying archaeological remains

Surveying: Precisely measuring the dimensions, position and orientation of archaeological sites and features

Taphonomy: 'The law of burial'. The processes which transform organic archaeological material in the ground

TAQ: Terminus ante quem. The latest possible date for a site or layer

Tell: A large mound created by successive settlement layers on a site over thousands of years

Temper: Material added to clay to give it strength and prevent it cracking during firing

Thiessen polygons: Shapes created by joining the mid-point between economic centres to provide models for exploring territories

Thin sections: Samples of rock taken for petrological analysis

TL: Thermoluminescence dating

Totemism: A natural object is adopted by a group as their emblem and as an object of worship

TPQ: Terminus post quem. The earliest possible date for a site or layer

Trace elements: Tiny amounts of rare elements within stone and metal. The balance of trace elements varies according to the geological source of the material

Transect: Walking or taking a sample across a landscape

Trend surface analysis: A way of illustrating the distribution of artefacts by using mathematical formulae to create a contour map

Tribe: A society that is larger than a band but still linked together by kinship ties. May number between several hundred and a few thousand people. Likely to be farmers or pastoralists. Unlikely to have wide variations in wealth and status

Typology: Organising artefacts into types based on similar attributes

Unit: An archaeological trust or commercial company that bids to do survey and excavation work

Use wear analysis: Using high-powered microscopes to study marks on tools and bones in order to identify the activity that caused them

Votives: Artefacts deposited as offerings to gods or spirits

X-ray fluorescence (XRF): A non-destructive method of analysing the mineral composition of the surface of artefacts

Bibliography

Anderson, S. (1985) 'Tybrind Vig' *Journal of Danish Archaeology* 4 Odense: Odense University Press

Ashmore, W. and Sharer, R. (1995) *Discovering our Past*, Mountain View, Calif.: Mayfield

Aston, M. (1985) *Interpreting the Landscape*, London: Batsford

Bahn, P. and Vertut, J. (1988) *Images of the Ice Age*, Leicester: Windward

Barnett, J. (1998) 'Monuments in the landscape: thoughts from the Peak', Lecture at conference on Prehistoric Ritual, Oxford

Barrett, J. (1994) *Fragments from Antiquity*, Oxford: Blackwell

Barrett, J. and Bradley, R. (eds) (1980) *Settlement and Society in the British Later Bronze Age*, Oxford: BAR 83

Bayliss-Smith, T. (1996) 'People-plant interaction in the New Guinea highlands' in D. Harris, (ed.) *The Origins and Spread of Agriculture and Pastoralism in Eurasia*, London: UCL

Binford, L. (1978) *Nunamuit Ethnoarchaeology*, Orlando: Academic Press

Binford, L. (1983) *In Pursuit of the Past*, New York: Thames and Hudson

Binford, L. (1989) *Debating Archaeology*, San Diego: Academic Press

Bradley, R. (1984) *The Social Foundations of Prehistoric Britain*, London: Longman

Bradley, R. (1998) *The Significance of Monuments*, London: Routledge

Bradley, R. (2000a) *The Good Stones*, Edinburgh: The Society of Antiquaries of Scotland

Bradley, R. (2000b) *An Archaeology of Natural Places*. London: Routledge

Bruck, J. (1995) 'A place for the dead: the role of human remains in late Bronze Age Britain;, *Oxford Journal of Archaeology* 61: 245–77

Buckland, P. (1976) 'The use of insect remains in the interpretation of archaeological environments', in D. Davidson and M. Shackley (eds) *Geoarchaeology*, London: Duckworth

Champion, T. and Collis, J. (eds) (1996) *The Iron Age in Britain and Ireland: Recent trends*, Sheffield: Sheffield Academic Press

Chapman, R., Kinnes, I. and Randsborg, K. (eds) (1981) *The Archaeology of Death*, Cambridge: Cambridge University Press

Clarke, D. (ed.) (1972) *Models in Archaeology*, London: Methuen

Clark, R. (2000) *Mesolithic Hunters of the Trentino*. Oxford: BAR 832

Coles, B. and Coles, J. (1976) *Sweet Track to Glastonbury*, London: Thames and Hudson

Coles, J. (1979) *Experimental Archaeology*, London: Academic Press

Coles, J. and Lawson, A. (eds) (1987) *European Wetlands in Prehistory*, Oxford: Clarendon Press

Collis, J. (1984) *The European Iron Age*, London: Batsford

Collis, J. (1996) 'Hillforts, enclosures and boundaries' in T. Champion and J. Collis (eds) *The Iron Age in Britain and Ireland: Recent trends*, Sheffield: Sheffield Academic Press

Cooper, N. (2000) *The Archaeology of Rutland Water: Excavations at Empingham 1967–73 and 1990*, Leicester: Leicester University Press

Cornwell, B. (1999) *Stonehenge*, London: HarperCollins

Crossley, D. (1994) *Post Medieval Archaeology in Britain*, Leicester: Leicester University Press

Cunliffe, B. (1992) 'Pits, preconceptions and propitiation in the British Iron Age', *Oxford Journal of Archaeology* 11: 69–83

Cunliffe, B. (1993) *Danebury*, London: English Heritage

Cunliffe, B. (ed.) (1994) *The Oxford Illustrated Prehistory of Europe*, Oxford: Oxford University Press

Cunliffe, B. (1995) *Iron Age Britain*, London: Batsford

Darvill, T. and Fulton, A. (1998) *MARS: The monuments at risk survey of England*, Bournemouth and London: Bournemouth University and English Heritage

Darvill, T. and Thomas, J. (eds) (1996) *Neolithic Houses in North-west Europe and Beyond*, Oxford: Oxbow

Davidson, D. and Shackley, M. (eds) (1976) *Geoarchaeology*, London: Duckworth

Drewett, P. (1982) 'Later Bronze Age downland economy at Black Patch, East Sussex', *Proceedings of the Prehistoric Society* 48: 321–409

Drewett, P. (1999) *Field Archaeology*, London: UCL Press

Ellison, A. (1980) 'Settlements and regional exchange: a case study' in J. Barrett and R. Bradley (eds) *Settlement and Society in the British Later Bronze Age*, Oxford: BAR 83

Fagin, B. (1994) *In the Beginning*, New York: Harper-Collins

Fagin, B. (1995) *Time Detectives*, New York: Simon and Schuster

Fash, W. L. (1991) *Scribes, Warriors and Kings*, New York: Thames and Hudson

Fleming, A. (1988) *The Dartmoor Reaves*, London: Batsford

Fleming, A. (1998) *Swaledale, Valley of the Wild River*, Edinburgh: Edinburgh University Press

Gamble, C. (1986) *The Palaeolithic Settlement of Europe*, Cambridge: Cambridge University Press

Gamble, C. (2000) *Archaeology: The basics*. London: Routledge

Giddens, A. (1989) *Sociology*. London: Polity

Gilchrist, R. (1995) *Contemplation and Action: The other monasticism*, London: Leicester University Press

Gimbutas, M. (1991) *The Civilization of the Goddess*, New York: Harper Collins

Graslund, B. (1994) 'Prehistoric soul beliefs in Northern Europe', *Proceedings of the Prehistoric Society* 60: 15–26

Green, M. (2000) *A Landscape Revealed*, Stroud: Tempus

Greene, K. (1995) *Archaeology: An introduction*, London: Routledge

Grogan, E. (1999) 'Hilltop Settlement in South West Ireland', Lecture at conference on Late Bronze Age Landscapes, Oxford

Harke, H. (1990) 'Warrior graves? The background of the Anglo-Saxon burial rite', *Past and Present* 126: 22–43

Harris, D. (ed.) (1996) *The Origins and Spread of Agriculture and Pastoralism in Eurasia*. London: UCL

Havilland, W. (1994) *Anthropolgy*, New York: Harcourt Brace

Hawkes, C. (1954) 'Archaeological theory and method: some suggestions for the Old World', *American Anthropologist* 56: 155–68

Hill, J. D. (1996) 'Hillforts and the Iron Age of Wessex' in T. Champion and J. Collis (eds) *The Iron Age in Britain and Ireland: Recent trends*, Sheffield, Sheffield Academic Press

Hunter, J. and Ralston, I. (eds) (1999) *The Archaeology of Britain*, London: Routledge

Jackson, P. (1995) 'Footloose in archaeology', *Current Archaeology* 144: 466–70

Kemp, B. J (1993) *Ancient Egypt*, New York: Routledge

Kent, S. (1989) *Farmers as Hunters*, Cambridge: Cambridge University Press

Knecht, L. (1994) 'Late Ice Age hunting technology', *Scientific American* July: 82–7

Lake, M. (1989) *Historic Farm Buildings*, London: Blandford Press

Leroi-Gourhan, A. and Brezillion, M. (1966) 'L'habitation Magdalenienne No. 1 de Pincevent pres Monereau', *Gallia Prehistoire* 9(2): 263–385

Lewis-Williams, J. D. and Dowson, T. A. (1988) 'The signs of all times`: entoptic phenomena in Upper Palaeolithic Cave Art', *Current Anthropology* 29 201–45

Loveday, R. (1998) 'Mother Dunche's Buttocks: a focus for Neolithic interest', Lecture to Neolithics Studies Group, London

Marcus, J. and Flannery, K. (1994) *Zapotec Civilization*, London: Thames and Hudson

Mays, S. (1998) *The Archaeology of Human Bones*. London: Routledge

Mithen, S. (1990) *Thoughtful Foragers: A study of prehistoric decision making*, Cambridge: Cambridge University Press

Moore, A., Hillman, G. and Legge, A. (2000) *Village on the Euphrates*, Oxford: Oxford University Press

Muir, R. (1981) *Reading the Landscape*, London: Michael Joseph

Orme, B. (1981) *Anthropology for Archaeologists*, London: Duckworth

Orton, C. *et al.* (1993) *Pottery in Archaeology*, Cambridge: Cambridge University Press

O'Shea, J. (1981) 'Social configurations and the archaeological study of mortuary practices: a case study' in R. Chapman, I. Kinnes and K. Randsborg (eds) *The Archaeology of Death*, Cambridge: Cambridge University Press

Parker-Pearson, M. (1993) *Bronze Age Britain*, London: Batsford

Parker-Pearson, M. (1999) *The Archaeology of Death and Burial,* Stroud: Sutton

Pitts, M. and Roberts, M. (1997) *Fairweather Eden*, London: Century

Prior, F. (1991) *Flag Fen*, London: Batsford

Rackham, O. (1986) *The History of the Countryside*, London: Phoenix

Rackham, O. (1990) *Trees and Woodland in the British Landscape*. London: Phoenix

Reece, R. (1998) research in progress on the potential of hedges for locating early medieval settlement

Renfrew, C. (1973) *Before Civilization*, London: Jonathan Cape

Renfrew, C. (1984) *Approaches to Social Archaeology*, Edinburgh: Edinburgh University Press

Renfrew, C. and Bahn, P. (1991) *Archaeology: Theories, methods and practice*, London: Thames and Hudson

Reynolds, P. J. (1979) *Iron Age Farm: The Butser Experiment*. London: British Museum Publications

Rue, D. (1989) 'Archaic Middle American agriculture and settlement: recent pollen dating from Honduras', *Journal of Field Archaeology* 10: 177–84

Schele, L. and Matthews, P. (1983) *The Code of Kings*, New York: Thames and Hudson

Schele, L. and Miller, M. (1986), *The Blood of Kings*, Austin: University of Texas Press

Schick, K. and Toth, N. (1993) *Making Silent Stones Speak*, London: Weidenfeld and Nicolson

Service, E. (1971) *Primitive Social Organisation: An evolutionary perspective*, New York: Random House

Shennan, S. (1975) 'The social organisation at Branc', *Antiquity* 49: 279–88

Sherratt, A. (1997) *Economy and Society in Prehistoric Europe*, Edinburgh: Edinburgh University Press

Strudwick, N. and Strudwick, H. (1989) *Thebes in Egypt*, London: BM Press

Taylor, T. (1997) *The Prehistory of Sex*, London: Fourth Estate

Thomas, J. (1991) *Understanding the Neolithic*, London: Routledge

Tilley, C. (1994) *A Phenomenology of Landscapes*, Oxford: Berg

Tilley, C. (1996) *An Ethnography of the Neolithic*, Cambridge: Cambridge University Press

Trigger, B. (1989) *A History of Archaeological Thought*, Cambridge: Cambridge University Press

Van Gennep, A. (1909) *Les rites de passage*, Paris: E. Nourry

Wass, S. (1999) *The Amateur Archaeologist*, second edn, London: Batsford

Welch, M. (1992), *Anglo-Saxon England*, London: Batsford

Wenke, R. (1999) *Patterns in Prehistory*, Oxford: Oxford University Press

Whittle, A. (1996) *Europe in the Neolithic*, Cambridge: Cambridge University Press

Whittle, A. (1998) *Sacred Mound, Holy Rings*. Oxford: Oxbow

Wilkinson, R. (2000) *The Temples of Ancient Egypt*, London: Thames and Hudson

Index